# THE KING'S PROGRESS TO JERUSALEM

*Published under the auspices of the*

CENTER FOR MEDIEVAL AND RENAISSANCE STUDIES

*University of California, Los Angeles*

# Humana Civilitas

*Sources and Studies*
*Relating to the Middle Ages and the Renaissance*

# Volume 2

Published under the auspices of

THE CENTER FOR MEDIEVAL AND RENAISSANCE STUDIES

University of California, Los Angeles

# The King's Progress to Jerusalem:

## Some Interpretations of David during the Reformation Period and Their Patristic and Medieval Background

*by Edward A. Gosselin*

UNDENA PUBLICATIONS

Malibu, 1976

The emblem of
the Center for Medieval and Renaissance Studies
reproduces the imperial eagle of the gold *augustalis*
struck after 1231 by Emperor Frederick II;
Elvira and Vladimir Clain-Stefanelli,
*The Beauty and Lore of Coins: Currency and Medals*
(Croton-on-Hudson, 1974), fig. 130 and p. 106.

Library of Congress Card Number: 76-18603
ISBN: 0-89003-014-6 (hard cover)
0-89003-013-8 (paper cover)

Undena Publications, P.O. Box 97, Malibu, Ca. 90265

©1976 by The Regents of the University of California

By the waters of Babylon, there we
sat down, yea, we wept, when we
remembered Zion.

We hanged our harps upon the willows
in the midst thereof.

For there they that carried us away
captive required of us a song; and they
that wasted us required of us mirth, saying,
Sing us one of the songs of Zion.

How shall we sing the Lord's song in a
strange land?

If I forget thee, O Jerusalem, let
my right hand forget her cunning.

If I do not remember thee, let my
tongue cleave to the roof of my mouth;
if I prefer not Jerusalem above my
chief joy.

(Psalm 137, verses 1-6)

# Foreword

I wish to express my gratitude to those who have given me succour in this labor: to Professors Eugene F. Rice and Paul Oskar Kristeller, who directed my graduate studies and the dissertation from which this book has evolved; to Professors John Mundy, Robert Somerville, and Louis B. Pascoe, S. J., who served on my dissertation defense committee and offered invaluable suggestions; to Professor Charles Garside of Rice University, who, at an encounter at the Annual Meeting of the American Historical Association in December 1967, aroused my interest in pursuing this research; and to Professor Robert M. Kingdon of the University of Wisconsin, who provided me with some valuable bibliographical suggestions.

I wish also to express my gratitude to the Fulbright Commission which awarded me the grant which made it possible to conduct my research in Paris; and to the kind and gentle ladies in the Réserve des imprimés of the Bibliothèque Nationale, who aided me in countless ways and provided me with a continuous flow of texts.

Deep thanks are also due to the Center for Medieval and Renaissance Studies at the University of California, Los Angeles, and to its Director, Professor Fredi Chiappelli for the subsidy and help which have facilitated the publication of this book.

Debts of gratitude are also due to members of the California State University at Long Beach community who advised and comforted me at critical scholarly and mental moments: especially to Professor William R. Svec and to Norman and Nancy Self; to Matthew Brown; and to the typists of various versions of this study: Victoria Johnson and Lois English.

Finally, I wish to dedicate this book to my wife Claudia and to my parents. Without their love and solicitude this work would have been impossible.

# Table of Contents

# Introduction

A statue of David stands today in the Piazza della Signoria in Florence, a witness to the supreme genius of Michelangelo and to the fascination of Western man with that Old Testament king and prophet whose image still draws the attention of passers-by. David's Psalms are recited in Christian churches and Jewish synagogues, also testifying to the perennial and almost universal appeal of his words to men of disparate creeds. Who was this David whose likeness and written words have outlasted centuries of religious and political vicissitudes?

David was born in 1085 B.C. and died in 1015 B.C. The grandson of Boaz and Ruth, he was the youngest of the eight sons of Jesse of the tribe of Judah. In his early years he continued to live in the town of his birth, Bethlehem, tending his father's flock of sheep. Then came the epiphany in which the God of Israel made known to David, through his prophet Samuel, that the shepherd was to be anointed king over Israel, in the place of Saul whom God had rejected for disobedience.

Later, when an evil spirit troubled Saul and cast him into sallow moods, David was summoned before the king, there to comfort and soothe Saul with his songs and lyre. Grateful, Saul retained David in his court as an armor-bearer, whereupon David soon smote down the giant Goliath and routed the army of the Philistines. This remarkable victory gained David both the tender friendship of Saul's son, Jonathan, and a higher position in the court. Popular, and the darling of the court ladies, the travails of David were about to begin, for he had aroused the jealousy of the king.

And so Saul twice attempted to kill David. As the captain of one thousand men, David encountered new dangers in order to win the hand of Merob, Saul's eldest daughter; but, despite the king's promise, she was given to Hadriel. Saul soon discovered, however, that another of his daughters, Michal, loved David, and in the hope that he would be killed Saul stipulated that before he would give his consent to the marriage, David would have to kill one hundred Philistines. Intensifying the king's worst fears, David succeeded in the enterprise and won the hand of Michal. It was only through the intervention of Jonathan that Saul spared David and rescinded his command that he be assassinated. Thereupon, David fled the court.

He wandered throughout the countryside, continuously pursued by Saul's hired killers. Exiled and an outlaw, David fled to Nob where he was harbored by Ahimelech the priest, who was afterwards sorely repaid by Saul for his courageous protection of David. Next, David wandered to the court of Achis, where he escaped death by feigning madness, and he retreated from the new danger into the wilderness of Ziph.

Yet David rejoined Achis and, with a complement of the latter's men added to his own meagre force, he raided Palestine. Since, however, Achis' commander did not trust him, David was not allowed to participate in the battle in which Saul and Jonathan met their deaths. It was at this time that David became king over Judah and warred against Saul's relatives. After seven and one-half years of civil strife David finally became, as he had been promised years before by God, the king of Israel.

As the newly anointed king, David transferred the capital of Israel to Jerusalem, bringing there the Ark of the Covenant in solemn procession, thereby establishing Jerusalem as the holy city of the Jewish peoples. In his regal prosperity, David enjoyed the company of many wives and concubines and he sired several sons.

The wars against his external enemies continued almost incessantly, one of which occasioned David's most heinous sin. He had espied the beautiful Bathsheba who was espoused to one of his commanders, Uriah. In the hope that he might terminate his adulterous relationship with marriage, David ordered his trusting captain to the front where he would die in battle. The adulterer thus committed homicide and acquired a new wife simultaneously. But God was full of wrath at David's sins and He sent the prophet Nathan to reproach David and to advise him of the punishments that would, in God's justice, follow.

The divine anger was carried out when, with the abetment of Achitophel, Absalom raised sedition against his father and drove him out of the kingdom. David, however, quelled the revolt and killed his beloved son. Yet again did David anger God by taking a census of Israel, and God put a pestilence upon the kingdom for three days, killing seventy thousand inhabitants. David's repentance, of course, immediately followed this punishment.

In his final years, David had his son Solomon anointed king by Nathan, and the aging king reorganized the religious services of the kingdom. After he died, Nathan and Bathsheba oversaw Solomon's successful accession to the throne. It was this son, born to David and Bathsheba after David's repentance for his homicide and adultery, who would build the temple in Jerusalem, as God had promised David.

Thus, David's biography, as it is told in the biblical books of Samuel and in the Chronicles. Indeed, the biblical accounts of the life and deeds of David are all that have come down through the ages, except for the autobiographical prayers of David found in the Book of Psalms.[1] Together, the Old Testament histories and Psalms have provided ample material for the creation of a Christian biography of David.

The Psalms have always played a dual role as one of the poetic books of the Old Testament and as songs and prayers for use in Christian liturgy. Christian scholars have therefore always found it necessary to come to grips with David and to explain him to other Christians.

While our main interest in this study is to explore the sixteenth-century Protestant understanding of David, as it was expressed in Protestant Psalm commentaries, it seemed to us that some investigation of Prereformation concepts of David would provide a useful historical background and setting for the Protestant images of the prophet. The staggering number of patristic, medieval, and Renaissance commentaries on the Psalms[2] and our own limitations of time and ability have forced us to restrict our examination of the Prereformation exegetes to Saint Augustine, Nicolaus of Lyra, and Lefèvre d'Etaples.

Hermeneutic and historical considerations have dictated the selection of these three commentators. Each represents a different exegetical mode of scriptural analysis. Augustine's method of interpreting the Psalms was usually to employ allegory in order to fathom the meanings of the Psalms and of David. Lyra's hermeneutic tool, on the other hand, was the careful study of the literal/ historical sense of the Psalms, from which he derived a "double literal sense"; the first applies to Old Testament times, the second to New Testament times. Lefèvre abandoned Lyra's concern for the Old Testament meaning of the Psalms, in favor of the New Testament meaning, which he called the "prophetic sense." According to this method of interpretation, it is really the Holy Spirit Who speaks through the mouth of the psalmist. Lefèvre thus felt that he could avoid the need to allegorize the Psalms as well as the need to dwell upon what he termed the base Old Testament meaning and intention of the words.

Not only do we feel that the selection of these three commentators exhibits three distinct hermeneutic techniques from the Prereformation period but we also recognize that these writers are historically important when considering the Protestant interpretations of David.[3] Augustine's great authority made him an obvious choice. He exerted a continuing, formative influence upon Christian theology and morality throughout the Middle Ages, the Renaissance, and the Reformation. Although overshadowed as a philosopher by the authority of Aristotle in the universities during and after the thirteenth century, Augustine was never abandoned as a source for Christian doctrine and ethics. Indeed, in the Renaissance the rise of Platonism, counter-balancing the dominance of Aristotelianism, contributed to an increase in the importance of and interest in the platonizing Augustine.[4] The Reformation, of course, found in Augustine's theological writings a doctrinal compatibility that few other teachers of the Church offered. In addition, recent studies investigating the history of Old Testament interpretation from patristic times to the Reformation have clearly shown that any scholarly study which involves aspects of Old Testament exegesis in the Latin West must take Augustine into consideration.[5]

We have selected Nicolaus of Lyra and Lefèvre d'Etaples for equally compelling reasons. Lyra has long been regarded as one of the most important medieval commentators, and a religious historian has recently called him the "best-equipped biblical scholar of the Middle Ages."[6] Like Augustine, Lyra was read and studied by many of the Protestant commentators, and he exerted considerable influence upon them.[7] Lefèvre, while not ranking among the greatest of the Psalm commentators, belonged to the generation of biblical scholars just prior to the Protestant Reformation. Protestant exegetes also used his expositions of the Psalms.[8] Thus, the divergencies between his interpretations of David and those of the reformers will be of considerable interest to us.

Our selection of Protestant commentators on the Psalms was likewise not arbitrary. We have begun, as all studies of the Reformation must, with a rather brief discussion of Martin Luther and his interpretations of David. Our comments on Luther are mostly derivative, although they were substantiated by our own selective reading of his commentaries. Indeed, the extensive and valuable work that has already been done on his Old Testament and Psalm hermeneutics made it unnecessary to dwell on Luther more than briefly.

This is especially true since we found that Luther's successors carried the logic and the implications of his exegesis of the Psalms still further. Thus, our last chapters are devoted to the commentaries on the Psalms by Philip Melanchthon, John Calvin, and Theodore Beza. Melanchthon and Calvin were chosen because of their adherence to different, if similar, confessions; and Beza, because of the interesting prospects held out by his involvement as the "high priest" of the Huguenot cause in the French Wars of Religion. Yet, we submit, Melanchthon, Calvin, and Beza are representative of the possibilities for the interpretations of David in the period between the fifteen-forties and the fifteen-eighties, at least for the "right wing" of the Reformation (which has absorbed our interest). Although we also studied Martin Bucer's Commentary on the Psalms,[9] we have used it only as a control against which to assess our evaluation of the other Protestant commentators. His exclusion from this study resulted from the lack of any but the most imperceptible and insignificant differences between his concepts of David and the range of concepts already available for study in the other commentaries we chose. Second, we found it easier to control our material by limiting ourselves to Melanchthon and Calvin, who, by their membership in separate churches, served to illustrate the general tenor of the theological interpretation of David among the sixteenth-century Protestants.

A comparison of the concepts of David found in our selected Prereformation commentaries with those in the Protestant commentaries yields some striking general contrasts. Let us now summarize these contrasts.

Augustine wrote his commentaries on the Psalms after the conclusion of an important and lively debate among Christian biblical scholars over the merits and appropriate uses of the Old Testament. Although Augustine's response to this exegetical debate was more complex than we are suggesting at this point, his interpretations of David were usually allegorical. In order to provide David and his Psalms with theological significance, Augustine tended to pull them out of their Old Testament milieu and to place them in a New Testament setting. The employment of this allegorical method caused David and his Old Testament faith to be almost entirely lost. His value could only be perceived by Christians who realized that David's presence in the Old Testament served to teach Christian lessons and to adumbrate Christ and His Church. Without the New Testament and Christ, Augustine's David had no theological significance, or wholeness, in and of himself.

Nicolaus of Lyra's interpretations of David were also applied to Christian times. However, beneath Lyra's typologies lay a firm respect for the historical David and the literal, Old Testament meaning of his words. This greater appreciation of the Old Testament ambiance made it possible for Lyra to view David as a man of real, if not of Christian faith. We conclude, therefore, that Lyra's David was a *viator* who, by living morally, had set an ethical example for various types of Christian conduct.

Lefèvre d'Etaples offers us still another image of David. Refusing either to follow Augustine's allegorical path or to emphasize the Old Testament literal meaning of the Psalms, Lefèvre "spiritualized" the Psalms and understood their literal meaning to be the *"sensus propheticus."* His David thus became a prophet of New Testament truths, whose words applied not to Old Testament times but to Christian times. In fact, Lefèvre's David became simply a mouthpiece through whom the Holy Spirit spoke. As we shall see, there is a considerable difference between this conception of David as an instrument through whom the Holy Spirit spoke prophetically and the general Protestant image of David as a man sanctified by the Holy Spirit.

In contrast with these images of David found in Augustine, Lyra, and Lefèvre, the Protestant commentators, whom we study in Part II, completely rehabilitated David. We believe that this achievement was possible because they attentively considered both David's words (which they found to be messianic and expressive of the hope and trust that God would fulfill His promises) and the actual circumstances and travails to which David's prayers related. In brief, the Protestants found expressed in the Psalms a faith very like their own and a historical situation which paralleled theirs.

Discovering in David a theological identity with Protestant beliefs and perceiving that he had also suffered persecutions for his faith, the sixteenth-century Protestant commentators welcomed David as a member of the True Church, which was in David's time, and always would be, a remnant Church assailed by the forces of evil. As a result of this perception of David, the Protestant exegetes did not need to harbor David under a cloak of allegory, tropology, or Christological prophecy. Precisely because they perceived David as an Old Testament member of the True Church, the Protestants could invoke him and use him instructionally as an Old Testament saint. In the Protestant commentaries, then, we find a David of complete theological significance, a David come to life as a colleague of the Reformation faithful.

Having explained the bases upon which we selected our commentators and having summarized our most general conclusions, we deem it incumbent upon us to offer some caveats to the reader. Although we have chosen our Prereformation exegetes with reason and care, the mere fact of selection leads to oversimplification of and gross lacunae in the history of patristic and medieval exegesis. We therefore have intentionally eschewed as much as possible speaking of "the exegetical tradition," for such remarks would have overreached the limits of our evidence and the purpose of our study of the Prereformation exegetes. This purpose has been to offer certain aperçus into major types of patristic and medieval interpretations of David which would establish a comparative background to our demonstration of how David was understood and used during the Reformation period.

While we know of no study which offers a continuous or comprehensive analysis of the treatment of David by Prereformation commentators, studies do exist which illuminate the modes of Old Testament exegesis.[10] We would like now to proffer some general comments concerning two aspects of this Prereformation exegesis. The first concerns the revolution in scriptural interpretation that occurred in the twelfth and thirteenth centuries; the second involves the political understanding of King David.

Our selection of Nicolaus of Lyra as the sole representative of medieval exegesis is not intended to suggest that Lyra was the first or the only medieval exegete to place great importance on the literal/historical meaning of the Bible. Indeed, Lyra derived from a tradition that went back to Hugh of St. Victor. A more immediate source of Lyra's approach, aside from the rabbis, may be found in St. Thomas Aquinas' discussion of the meanings of Scripture. Thomas admits that confusion is caused by allowing words to have multiple meanings. Therefore, he argues that words mean only one thing and that the spiritual senses derive from the things signified by the words rather than from the words themselves.[11] While the exegete no longer has to seek Christian doctrine from the Old Testament words and the *sensus historicus* themselves, Thomas is left with the problem that the Old Testament thereby loses theological value (since when the allegorical sense is applied to the Old Testament, it refers to things done in the New Testament; thus only the New Testament can bestow value on the Old Testament). To alleviate this problem, Thomas adds an "ultimate theological definition" to his definition of the literal sense (wherein he accounted for the human intention of the words): "According to this definition, the *sensus litteralis* is that which the divine author intended."[12] In this way, Aquinas opened the door both to the *sensus litteralis* of Lyra and to the *sensus propheticus* (wherein the New Testament becomes the Old Testament's literal sense) of Lefèvre.

While we are cognizant, then, of the importance of Aquinas in the ongoing Christian exegetical debate, it is clear that the separate study of Lyra and of Lefèvre best enables us to demonstrate the ramifications of Thomas' definitions.

Second, we wish to call attention to the rich Prereformation discussion of Davidic kingship. It might seem that we have neglected this topic, especially since we devote Chapter VI to the Protestants' "political David." However, we hasten to note that the concept of Davidic kingship did not significantly appear in the Prereformation commentaries we have studied; this topic, then, was a casualty of the process of selection. We would like to suggest, however, that one of the earliest antecedents of the Protestant discussion of King David might be a Carolingian Psalm commentary (perhaps Alcuin's). The political ideology of the Carolingian era placed great emphasis on the *regnum Davidicum,* comparing the Frankish kingdom and its ruler (whether Pepin or Charlemagne) to Israel and David. The most startling results of this Frankish adoption of the Old Testament model were the definition of the king as the *novus David* (the priestly king, the *rex et sacerdos*) and the consecration of the king with holy oil (the new *David christus Domini*).[13] However, while the concept of the *regnum Davidicum* survived the Carolingian era and, grafted onto fragments of the Roman Imperial ideology, became the basis for medieval divine right and *Dei gratia* kingship,[14] we believe that the naturalness of the Protestants' (and especially Beza's) discussions of the political David was primarily the result of the theological rehabilitation of David by the Protestant exegetes.

We also warn the reader that the literal and favorable treatment of King David may not reflect the attitudes of all Protestants. Henry VIII, for example, though he compared himself with Charlemagne (who had styled himself the *novus David*), warned James V of Scotland not to be like a "Scottish David who lives by raising and fleecing sheep."[15] We must remember that Protestant lay rulers were free to read the Psalms differently from their ecclesiastical mentors and also that biblical literalism can be a two-edged sword.

Finally, a word about bias. We have used in the title of this study the image of a medieval king, journeying throughout his kingdom until, laden with gifts from his subjects, he returns to his royal city. We have also quoted at the beginning the first six verses of Psalm 137 (which was not written by David). The title represents our most general conclusion from the selected commentaries that we have studied; the psalm, on the other hand, represents our bias or, better, our emotional response to our investigations.

After observing the welcome extended to the Jewish king and prophet by each of our Prereformation commentators, we experienced some relief when, at least metaphorically, the Protestant exegetes (especially Theodore Beza) escorted the ancient king into his holy city. We have applied the words of Psalm 137 to David for two purposes: to conjure up what we feel might have been the reaction of David's spirit to his treatment at the hands of some of the commentators studied in the following pages; and to celebrate (albeit in a bittersweet manner) David's return from his "Babylonian captivity," so ironically juxtaposed, as we shall see, to the entrance of Henry IV into Paris.

# NOTES

[1]Nowhere in the Hebrew Bible is there any indication of the Davidic authorship of the Psalms. Seventy-three of the one hundred fifty psalms are designated by *"le-Dāwîd";* however, the precise meaning of this term is uncertain, though very early the Davidic authorship of these psalms was assumed (cf. II Maccabees 2:13). The Greek version extended the Davidic heading to the psalms that had not been so marked in the received Hebrew text (viz., Pss. 33, 43, 71, 91, 93-99, 104, 137). David was first explicitly claimed to be the author of the entire Psalter in the rabbinic literature which compares the five books of Davidic Psalms and the Pentateuch of Moses. However, the attribution of seventy-three of the psalms to David is probably too high; although they are pre-exilic and therefore could be by David, it is nearly impossible to determine which they are. Modern Catholic scholarship does attribute the following psalms to David: 2 (modern Jewish scholarship rejects this as being by David), 16 (Vulgate: 15), 18 (17), 32 (31), 69 (68), 110 (109). On the Psalms' composition and authorship, see *Encyclopaedia Judaica,* Vol. 13 (Jerusalem: Keter Publishing House, Ltd., 1971), coll. 1313-1314; *New Catholic Encyclopedia,* Vol. 11 (New York: McGraw-Hill, Co., 1967), p. 935; *The Jerome Biblical Commentary,* Vol. 1 (London: Geoffrey Chapmen, 1968), pp. 570ff.

[2]It would be impossible to hazard a guess as to the number of commentaries on the Psalms that were written between the patristic age and the beginning of the Reformation. The reader may gain some idea of the vastness of the Psalm literature simply by scanning through F. Stegmüller's *Repertorium Biblicum Medii Aevi* (7 vols., Madrid: 1950-1961) and B. Smalley's *The Study of the Bible in the Middle Ages* (Notre Dame, Indiana: University of Notre Dame Press, 1964). Due to the limitations of our linguistic abilities, we were unable to select one of the Greek Fathers (although Theodore Mopsuestia and St. John Chrysostom would seem to be of particular interest). The Latin literature alone is overwhelming. We mention in passing the commentaries or glosses on the Psalter by the following Prereformation and sixteenth-century writers: Ambrose, Jerome, Cassiodorus, Alcuin, Remigius of Auxerre, Anselm of Laon, St. Bruno, Gilbert the Universal, Hugh of St. Victor, Richard of St. Victor, James Perez of Valencia, Pico della Mirandola, Giles of Viterbo, Erasmus, and Agostino Steuco. While not at all comprehensive, this short list is indicative of the Herculean task awaiting the scholar who would fully survey the concepts of David developed during this period. We might add parenthetically that a comprehensive investigation of just the Protestant commentators would also be an enormous undertaking. At the very least, one would have to add to our list of selected Protestant exegetes (see below, pp. 3-4) such names as Zwingli, Bullinger, Bugenhagen, and Oecolampadius.

[3]However, see our caveats to this and other points, pp. 5-6, below.

[4]On Augustine's influence during the Middle Ages and the Renaissance and Reformation, the following studies serve as useful introductions and bibliographical guides: E. Gilson, *L'Esprit de la philosophie médiévale* (Paris: Librairie J. Vrin, 1969); H.-I. Marrou, *St. Augustine and His Influence Through the Ages* (London: Longman's, 1957); and P. O. Kristeller, "Augustine and the Early Renaissance," *Studies in Renaissance Thought and Letters* (Rome: Edizioni di Storia e Letteratura, 1956/1969), pp. 355-372.

[5]Heiko A. Oberman, *Forerunners of the Reformation,* trans. by Paul L. Nyhus (New York: Holt, Rinehart and Winston, 1966), pp. 283-284; James S. Preus, *From Shadow to Promise: Old Testament Interpretation From Augustine to the Young Luther* (Cambridge, Mass.: Harvard University Press, 1969), Chapter I, *passim.*

[6]Oberman, *Forerunners,* p. 286.

[7]See the literature on this subject cited in Edward A. Gosselin, "A Listing of the Printed Editions of Nicolaus de Lyra," *Traditio,* 26 (1970), p. 401, note 7.

[8]For example, Martin Luther wrote some *adnotationes* to Lefèvre's *Quincuplex Psalterium.* We shall briefly discuss them in Chapter IV.

[9]Aretius Felinus (Martin Bucer), *Sacrorum Psalmorum libri quinque, ad ebraicam veritatem genuina versione in Latinum traducti.* . . . (Basel: Johannes Heruagius, 1547).

[10]See, in particular, the following two works: Henri de Lubac, *Exégèse médiévale: les quatre sens de L'Ecriture* (Paris: 1959-1964); and P. C. Spicq, *Esquisse d'une histoire de l'exégèse latine au Moyen Âge* (Paris: 1944).

[11]Preus, *op. cit.,* p. 51. Cf. Thomas Aquinas, *Summa theologiae* 1.1.10: "Illa ergo prima significatio, qua voces significant res, pertinet ad primum sensum, qui est sensus historicus vel litteralis. Illa vero significatio, qua res significatae per voces iterum res alias significant, dicitur sensus spiritualis."

[12]Preus, *op. cit.*, pp. 52-54 (quotation taken from p. 54). See *ibid.*, pp. 46-60 for a detailed discussion of Aquinas' hermeneutic.

[13]Ernst Kantorowicz, *Laudes Regiae: A Study in Liturgical Acclamations and Medieval Ruler Worship* (Berkeley & Los Angeles: University of California Press, 1946), pp. 56-57. After their victory over the Arabs, the Franks had begun to think of themselves as "the new people chosen by God, the new sacred people of the promise."

[14]*Ibid.*, p. 57. For pictorial monuments of David, and a discussion of them, see Hugo Steger, *David Rex et Propheta: König David als vorbildliche Verkörperung des Herrschers und Dichters im Mittelalter, nach Bilddarstellungen des achten bis zwölften Jahrhunderts* (Nürnberg: Hans Carl, 1961).

The anointing of David by Samuel figured as a *topos* of political theories during the medieval struggle of investitures. For example, we have come across the use of David in this context in Ptolemy of Lucca's *Determinatio compendiosa de iurisdictione imperii* (*ca.* 1308; now in *Fontes iuris Germanici antiqui in usum scholarum ex monumentis Germaniae historicis* [Hanover, Germany: Hahn, 1909]). There (cap. iii: Probatur hoc idem ex regibus antiquis, quod sola electio non sufficiat ad administrationem imperii), Ptolemy argues that even though David was elected by God to be king of Israel, he did not assume his regal duties until after he had been anointed. Ptolemy (d. 1326/7) was a papalist, and he defended the papal position that the Holy Roman Emperor could not assume his duties until he had been approved and crowned by the Pope; Ptolemy's argument indicates, moreover, that David could also be used to prove that the Emperor could assume his duties without a coronation performed by the Pope.

As we shall see in Chapter VI, Beza's emphasis is on David's election, not on his coronation. He may indeed have been influenced by the medieval controversy (in which case he would seem to have come down on the side of the medieval anti-papalists), but, more likely, he was driven to emphasize election by *force majeure*: he could not very well stress the physical anointing of the king (David/Henry of Navarre), because he denied the power of the Pope as well as that of the French Catholic clergy. He does discuss David/Henry as the chosen of God (and here comes closer to the Carolingian ideology), but this is an inward form of election.

In any case, we do not wish to mislead the reader and make him think that the title of this book implies that *King David* is the theme; as we explain at the end of the Introduction, "The King's Progress to Jerusalem" is a metaphor.

[15]Cf. Arthur S. Slavin, *Politics and Profit: A Study of Sir Ralph Sadler, 1507-1547* (Cambridge, England: Cambridge University Press, 1966), pp. 85-86: ". . . Sadler was instructed to . . . talk about the reformation of religion under way in England, broadly hinting at its introduction into Scotland. . . . He was to admonish James, in Henry's name, on a very sore point. James V was a Scottish David, that is to say, he raised and fleeced sheep. Sadler was to suggest that such work was unkingly. The raising and fleecing of monasteries was to be praised as a more fitting and profitable occupation for the king of Scots. James, after all, ought 'to easilie establish his estate in such wise as he should be able to lyve like a king, and yet meddle not with sheep'. . . . Sadler was to urge that James be a Scottish Solomon, choosing and dividing wisely, surrendering whatever pastoral impulse led him to emulate king David." (These instructions were given in the winter of 1540.) *Ibid.*, p. 88, gives the summary of Sadler's mission. Among other things, it reports: "Touchyng the shepe, he [James] answered he had none, and wyth abbeyes he wulde not meddle but by waye of reformacyon. . . ." James was obviously displeased with Sadler's remarks on his pastoral activities, though, as Slavin points out (*ibia.*, p. 90, note 4), the king of Scots lied, for he indeed raised sheep and sold their wool.

PART I

DAVID AS SEEN BY
THREE PREREFORMATION PSALM COMMENTATORS

# Chapter I
## Saint Augustine

A rapid reading of Saint Augustine's commentaries on the Psalms reveals a paucity of material on David. Moreover, when Augustine does discuss the Jewish king and prophet the reader is struck by how little attention the Bishop of Hippo gives to the Old Testament meanings of David's words and actions. The dominant image of David in these commentaries is as the figure of Christ. Starting from this identification, Augustine develops various "meanings" of David as the Christ-figure. Even when he applies David's words to the Church and the faithful, this application proceeds from the identification of the Church with the Body of Christ.

Augustine's Christ-directed interpretations of David, often involving the use of allegory and the translation of Hebrew names as the basis for a spiritual explanation of the Psalms, resulted from the difficulties that previous Fathers of the Church had experienced in coping with the Old Testament. Therefore, before we discuss Augustine's interpretations of David, it will contribute to a better understanding of them if we briefly review both the problems that Christian exegetes had encountered with the Old Testament and the Old Testament hermeneutics which Augustine developed in order to resolve these difficulties.

The apostolic writers had experienced no difficulty with the Jewish sacred book. To them the Old Testament was simply "the Scriptures." With the establishment of the New Testament canon, however, what had been "the Scriptures" to the apostolic church became "the Old Testament." Since the Church continued to claim the Old Testament as part of the canon, exegetes faced the task of explaining how it pertained to Christ and the New Covenant.

Several factors complicated the successful achievement of this task. Jewish literalists refused to accept Christ as the promised Messiah because, they claimed, the Old Testament prophecies had not been literally fulfilled. Gnostics and gnosticizing Christians (especially Marcion) repudiated the Old Testament on the grounds that it was unedifying. Its sometimes angry, sometimes laughing, sometimes vacillating, but always anthropomorphized God seemed the exact opposite of the God of the philosophers or of the loving God of the New Testament.[1] Not only did the Marcionites view the Jewish God as the product of the demiurge, but they also found many embarrassing episodes in the Old Testament, stories in which Old Testament characters either had been disobedient to Yahweh's injunctions or had failed to maintain the moral standards which the Christian Church enjoined upon its faithful.

The Old Testament records that its patriarchs and kings were polygamous and that they had concubines. Could knowledge of such facts edify the Christian reader? God had commanded, "Let not the sun go down upon your wrath," but Joshua certainly disobeyed the spirit of this law, if not the letter, by detaining the course of the sun until his wrath went down. Abraham lied. The Israelites robbed the Egyptians. How were these actions to be explained? Lot committed incest with his daughters. Perhaps it was an inadvertent moral lapse, yet how could his repetition of this act be justified? David committed adultery with Bathsheba and he arranged the death of Uriah. Surely these were not deeds which Christians should emulate. Finally, how could Christians recognize the New Testament God in Yahweh, Who neglected the fifth commandment when He bade Abraham to slay his guiltless son Isaac?[2]

These are only a few of the charges that the Marcionites leveled against the Old Testament in order to demonstrate that it had little to offer Christians and that it was undeserving of study. Some exegetes adopted the allegorical method to counter these charges and to prove that the seemingly embarrassing stories in the Old Testament were really allegories of higher and more edifying truths. The chief exponent of this type of exegesis was Origen.[3]

In reply to Marcion's assertion that the Old Testament had little to offer Christians, Origen maintained that Jewish Scripture contained much edifying material as long as it was understood spiritually, that is to say, allegorically.[4] To Origen, the literal intention of the authors of the Old Testament and of the historical events they had described had little import; more than that, the Old Testament, if understood literally and historically, was meaningless. It could only be understood allegorically.[5] As far as Davidic interpretation is concerned, David spoke *in persona Christi*; as a man, as a king, as a Jew living under the Old Covenant, David was ignored by Origen. David, as all Old Testament prophets and patriarchs, had existed only to prefigure Christ.

From his reading of the sermons of St. Ambrose, who had inherited Origen's Old Testament hermeneutic, Augustine learned the value of the application of allegorical exegesis to the Old Testament. However, Augustine's use of this method differed markedly from Origen's. Whereas the latter had been disinclined to credit the literal/historical sense of Jewish Scripture with any worth for Christians, Augustine maintained that the literal/historical meaning had considerable importance:

> Brothers, I warn you in the name of God to believe before all things when you hear the
> Scriptures read that the events really took place. . . . Do not destroy the historic
> foundation of Scripture, for without it you will build in the air.[6]

What Augustine actually meant here is that the historical events recorded in the Old Testament should serve as a check to the more fanciful exegetical improvisations to which Origen had been prone. Accordingly, an understanding of the literal Old Testament meaning would ensure that the higher, allegorical meaning bore a closer relationship to the text.

Moreover, Augustine did not believe that Old Testament passages should always be interpreted allegorically. The criterion which determined which sense, literal or allegorical, was appropriate for the understanding of a particular passage was whether a literal reading of the passage furthered the Christian reader's faith or love. The entire Bible must be edifying, for God wished all of it to teach faith, hope and love. Consequently, insofar as a literal understanding of an Old Testament text achieves this goal, its literal meaning is normative. If, however, the passage does not readily nourish faith, hope and love, then the text must be interpreted figuratively:

> Whatever appears in the divine Word that does not properly pertain to virtuous behavior
> or to the truth of faith, you must take to be figurative.[7]

The subsequent allegorical interpretation thus raises the text to the edifying, normative level of the Bible, which, of course, corresponds to the teachings of the New Testament.

As we shall presently see, Augustine follows these exegetical guidelines in his interpretations of David.[8] On those relatively few occasions when he explicitly discusses David, he usually finds that the historical meaning is unedifying and that an allegorical reading of the passage will instruct the Christian reader in Christian virtue or doctrine. We have discovered only one psalm, Psalm 50, in which Augustine allows that the literal meaning of its words and the events they describe are normative.

Because his exegetical approach to David is most often allegorical, Augustine seldom alludes to David's Old Testament faith as it is reflected in the psalmist's words. Rather, David's words and the events to which they referred become for Augustine prophetic hieroglyphs for New Testament events and teachings. Consequently, the actions of David and of those around him normally form the basis for Augustine's definition of David as a prophet: implicit in Augustine's interpretations of David is the idea that the *gesta Davidis*, not the *verba Davidis*, are, when understood allegorically, prophetic.

In part, Augustine's allegorical method involves the unveiling of the hidden meanings of Old Testament names. By this method, for example, he shows that the story of David's tragic relationship with his son Absalom had an importance not for the Old Testament but for the New Testament. In order to make sense of this Old Testament event, Augustine interprets the true significance of the name "Absalom": *"pax patris."* It signifies David's forbearing attitude towards his son, as well as the peace which Absalom lacked but which David cherished; however, even this identification is without significance until Augustine informs the reader that David prefigures Christ, while Absalom signifies Judas.[9] Two other figures who played a role in the story of David and Absalom elicit parallel meanings. David's friend, Chusi, who approached Absalom in an attempt to counteract the perfidious influence of David's erstwhile friend, Achitophel, on Absalom, also represents Christ, while the name "Achitophel" hides within its veil the definition, "ruin of his brother," in other words, Judas.[10] By these interpretational devices Augustine explains that the story of David and Absalom foreshadowed the deepest mystery of Christ. David exhibited peace towards his son at the same time as he waged war against him because of his sedition. The disciples in the New Testament are called "sons" or "brothers" of Christ; consequently, the disciple who would betray Christ to the Roman authorities is called, under the rubric of Achitophel, the "ruin of his brother." Chusi, whose name means "silence," portends the silence with which Christ would suffer His mysterious Passion, for by His resigned acceptance of Judas' betrayal and of His crucifixion, Christ was to save all men.[11]

Hence, the Old Testament account of David's betrayal by his beloved son, referred to in Psalm 7, becomes significative of the betrayal of Christ and thence of Christ's ultimate redemptive victory. The analysis of the names, applied in a wholeheartedly Christological manner, reduces the historical event in the Old Testament which involved four persons to one involving only two, and deprives the psalm and the event it describes of any contemporary Old Testament value. This one example of Augustine's interpretational subtlety demonstrates how the great Father will proceed throughout his discussions of the Psalms and of David. To Augustine, David is above all a *sacramentum*, a mystery, whose historical individuality and role are subordinated and lost in his attempt to show that the Old and New Testaments are in agreement. Only by pursuing this route can Augustine "rescue" the Old Testament for the use of Christians.

We have seen in Psalm 7 how the Bishop of Hippo manipulated David and his historical situation as an archetype of Christ. Yet Augustine does not limit David's significance solely to the image of Christ, for through his allegorical association with Christ, David can also represent the Church and all mankind.

In explaining Psalms 25 and 26 Augustine states that David is not, in this case, the equivalent of the Mediator Christ in His human form. Instead, he represents the whole Church now perfectly established in Christ.[12]  God had chosen David to be anointed king over Israel, and in ancient Hebraic times, says Augustine, only kings and priests were anointed, because God ordained these two social elites to prefigure Christ in His mission as both King and Priest.  Christians know that "Christ" is "the anointed one" and that the Savior leads and rules them as a king and intercedes for them as does a priest.  Moreover, not only has Christ, the Head of the Church, been anointed, but so have Christians, who form His Body.  Christ's priestly self-sacrifice redeemed Christians and incorporated them into Himself.  In this way, then, the faithful and the Redeemer, Body and Head, are one and the same Christ, the anointed ones.  All Christians thus share in the anointing that had once been the prerogative of the Old Testament kings and priests.  Looking forward to the New Testament Church in Christ, David's kingship again has the significative purpose of foreshadowing and representing that which would only exist and be fulfilled after the Resurrection:  the extension of the role of Jewish kings and priests as the "anointed ones" to the entire body of the Christian faithful.[13]

Furthermore, David's prayer is that of one who longs for the promised life of spiritual perfection.  David composed the prayer "before he was anointed" king, in contrast to the contemporary Christian who receives the holy unction sacramentally, the sacrament being a sign of what the faithful man is yet to be.  Augustine urges his readers to long, as did David, for precisely that ineffable spiritualization of their lives.[14]  David's prayer prior to his anointing is, and thus prefigures, the Church's and its members' prayer while awaiting the sacrament.

It might appear that Augustine deviates from his interpretation of David as merely a shadow, for here both David and the Christian assembly await spiritual edification.  This similarity raises David so that, standing outside the synagogue, he is identified with the New Covenant, not the Old.  Yet we must remember that Augustine has already said that the regal anointing of David was a prefiguration of the installation of Christians as members of Christ in His Church.  Although David strains in Psalm 26 to attain common faith with Christians, he remains incomplete and prefigurative.

If Augustine freely employs David as a type or figure of Christ and, by extension through Christ, of His Church, he also applies a redemptive interpretation to the name of David.  As an appellation, "David" yields two arcane meanings:  "strong-handed" and "desirable" (or "well-beloved").  Neither of these epithets, however, applies to David qua David, but to David qua Christ.  As a result of David's identity with Christ, it is the latter Who is "strong-handed," because Christ conquered death and overcame the terrors which had been the consequences of the loss of eternal life caused by Adam's Fall.  Moreover, Christ-David is called "desirable" because He promised eternal life.  What hand could be stronger, asks Augustine, than that which conquered death from the Cross; and who could be more desirable than Christ, Whose eternal presence and kingdom have been sought by martyrs born long after His Ascension?[15]

These first examples of Augustine's exegesis have shown us that Augustine saw little need to approach the Psalms from more than a superficial historical perspective.  David has functioned only as a shadow; his actions, his words, even his name have been given no Old Testament meaning or value except insofar as they demonstrate to Christians that the Old Testament has been fulfilled by the coming of Christ.  Moreover, it is problematical whether Augustine believed that the Jews could understand the "true" meaning of David, since his allegorical interpretations of David presume on the part of the Old Testament reader a knowledge of the New Testament.

Although the thrust of Augustine's allegorical interpretation of David has been delineated, several more examples of his exegetical method will serve to demonstrate more fully with what subtlety and facility Augustine lifted David from the context of ancient Israel and the Old Covenant and used him to prefigure the doctrinal and moral teachings of Christianity.

Augustine's distaste for a literal understanding of the Psalms and David, which could only be detrimental to the worth of the Old Testament, manifests itself most clearly in his commentary on Psalm 131. Augustine recognizes, of course, that some kind of literal or historical understanding of David could have been attempted, but he quickly refutes the appropriateness of such an approach.  Instead, he uses the literal or historical events to shed light upon the hidden mystery.  The psalm commends the humility and resignation of David, attributes with which David conquered his enemies.  These qualities and victories, however, are only shadowy figures of the Passion of Christ, by which He conquered Satan and, through Him, the Church conquers its enemies.  In addition, David's humility prefigures the submission of Christians to Christ and His Church.[16]

This kind of allegory is the result of Augustine's attitude towards the Old Testament in its entirety.  He himself explains why the subject of David's Psalms must be Christ and the Church.  Though his remarks are general, they aid in understanding his lack of interest in what the Psalms actually might have meant to David.  In Old Testament times the New Testament lay concealed within the Old Testament, just as the fruit is concealed potentially within the root.  The Old Testament Jews descended carnally from the wife of Abraham, while the people of the New Testament proceed spiritually from the seed of Abraham; and, since the Jews were carnal, the prophets proclaimed God's wishes in prophecy, speaking to a future age and people.[17]  The implications of these statements are clear enough.  The importance of the Old Testament lies in its "emblematic" nature as the veiled repository of Christian truths and of the mystery of Christ.  Thus, even the most "historical" events found in the Psalms offer material for the employment of Augustine's philological and allegorical expertise.  It is to such psalms that we wish to turn now.

Since Augustine insisted that there are no "neutral" passages in the Bible and that God's Word must always nurture Christian readers, we find that he allegorized the simple historical event recorded in Psalm 55.  From David's account of his flight from Saul into the city of Gath, Augustine constructed one of his most intricate allegories.

The basis of his interpretation is once again the hidden meanings of words, and the allegories that can be elicited from these meanings.  Augustine explains that "Gath" means a wine cellar.  Moreover, the city of Gath was inhabited by a foreign people who were hostile to David; these "foreigners" signify men who were not holy.  Finally, David is the figure of Christ.

These initial identifications prepare the way for Augustine's allegory.  David's presence among his enemies in Gath represents Christ surrounded by the Jews who, not having accepted Him as their king, contrived His Crucifixion.  In addition, since there is always a winepress in a wine cellar, "Gath" signifies the Passion of Christ.  When grapes are crushed in the press the injury done to them is not sterile, for only by being crushed can the grapes yield their essence, that is, wine.  So too did Christ's Crucifixion in the "winery" of His enemies bear fruit; it accomplished the Redemption of mankind, while, moreover, His Resurrection presaged "our" resurrection.

Since the Church is the Body of Christ, its faithful are also in "Gath."  Gath now signifies the world and those of its inhabitants who are the latter-day enemies of Christ.  The allegory therefore instructs Christians that they must endure suffering and persecution because the world is also their enemy.  Yet Christians should not shrink from these inevitable trials, for Psalm 55 teaches Christians that just as David's eventual escape from Gath foreshadows Christ's Resurrection, so too it foreshadows their own eternal deliverance from the travails of this life.[18]

If we may be excused a metaphor that is overly precious (but is not intended ironically), David's experience in Gath, when squeezed in Augustine's exegetical press, has yielded wholesome wine.  He has taken an historical fact and made of it a prophetic message.  The Old Testament event allegorically refers to the doctrines of Redemption and of the Resurrection, as well as to the doctrine of the Calling, wherein Christians are taught to bear with Christ the Cross of suffering.  Finally, the psalm teaches the theological virtue of hope.

While David can thus be used allegorically to portray doctrinal teachings, the vagaries of David's character are available to instruct the Christian faithful morally.  Augustine skirts through the Scylla and Charybdis of David's adultery and homicide in such a way that it will present an edifying lesson, although he does this not without a noticeable wince.  He admits that the story of David, Bathsheba, and Uriah makes hard reading for pious eyes:  "I say not what I wish, but what I am forced to.  I speak of it not to exhort imitation, but to teach [men] to fear."[19]  Christians, then, must regard this episode as an example of flagrant wickedness, a fact which also had not been overlooked in David's own time, as David's censure by the prophet Nathan attests.

Augustine, moreover, does not need to seek the allegorical meaning of David's adultery and homicide.  The literal/historical meaning is normative because David's actions and attitude after having committed these sins teach Christians the danger of falling into sin as well as the need for sinful men to rise up and to look to God again.  The psalm is thus admonitory in two ways:  may they who have not yet fallen into such serious sin hear this psalm lest they sin; and let them who have so transgressed also hear this psalm so that they may look to God.

Indeed, the Christian is more fortunate than David who had no similar example to teach him the heinous nature of adultery.  David fell because of concupiscence and was immediately reproached by God's prophet.  The Christian, on the other hand, has not David's excuse of ignorance since the book of God makes it so plain that such a sin displeases Him.  Beware, then, of this weakness of the flesh:  David saw Bathsheba from afar, but for him and all men, "a woman afar off is a desire near."  Sin is always present, but we must not allow it to reign over the body:  "Sin is present when one delights, but it reigns if the Christian consents."[20]

Augustine shows, then, that the desire of the flesh is exceedingly strong in man.  He cites David, the man chosen to be the ancestor of Christ, as an example to Christians that they must be on their guard against this sin, an example which is a warning to prevent the similar fall of Christians.

Furthermore, David's temporal status when he gave himself to this sin is instructive.  His fall came not while he endured Saul's enmity, but later, after he had become king.  Since David had not lusted after another's wife when he fled from the persecution of Saul, Christians are informed that tribulation, like the iron knife of a doctor, is useful.  The temptation and sin were coincidental with David's period of regal prosperity and security.  This sequence of events should stir Christians to fear and distrust their security and prosperity and to call upon God for strength.  Even though Christians should learn from David's example to be cautious, yet if they have fallen they should not despair; for the psalm bears a consolation even to the sinner.  Just as David, having heard Nathan's reproach and not disdaining it, prayed God for mercy, so should Christians turn to God for the strength not to persist in sin and to escape the morass of fleshly desire.[21]

Here, as we have seen, is an exposition in which, for once, the historical David has not been obliterated by an allegory.  Augustine, in fact, comes very close to the Reformation perception of David.  He emphasizes David, who was shown mercy, rather than Nathan, who delivered the divine censure; in this way, David operates, as do Christians, under the Covenant of Mercy.  But is the resemblance to the Protestant conception of David, as it has been briefly described in the Introduction, as close as we might think?

David's words, "For behold, I was born in iniquity," describe the condition of all men, that of being born with original sin.  Assuming here the *persona* of humanity, David considers the fetter by which all are born under sin; and, by reflecting upon the source and cause of mortality, he instructs the faithful about the origin of man's inherent iniquity, the fall of Adam.[22]  Moreover, even though he is shown mercy, David patiently endures the just punishment of God, which takes the form of Absalom's revolt against his father.  Indeed, when one of David's captains proposes to slay the rebellious son, David deters him, saying, "God sent him so that he might curse me."  Thus realizing his sin, David blesses God at all times.  Augustine's lesson is clear.  By sinning, David had wronged himself and the majesty of God, and he awaited the divine punishment even though his sin had been forgiven him.  The righteous Christian, the man who loves God, also willingly bears the affliction meted out to him by God's justice.[23]

Thus, the handling of David in Psalm 50 derives from the historical fact of David's sin and his reflections upon the nature and cause of human iniquity.  His adultery and homicide are warnings to Christians of the nefarious strength of fleshly desire, and David stands before Christians as an example of the sinner who was forgiven by the merciful God of the New Testament.  He reminds them that they must accept their tribulations which are the results of their sins, and, with a joyous heart, praise God.  While the lesson of the psalm is firmly rooted in its literal meaning, there exist important differences between Augustine's exegesis of this psalm and what will be the Protestants' exposition of this same theme.  Augustine offers David as an exemplary model not for his own faith as much as for the Old Testament agreement with the New Testament on the doctrine of repentance and the doctrine of gratuitous mercy which will be revealed fully only under the New Covenant.  Since the vision of the psalm therefore looks forward to what will be fulfilled by Christ, the subject of the psalm is New Testament teaching rather than David's faith.  This fleeting and rare concern for the historical David is thus supportive in nature; it results from the fact that Augustine found a clear correlation between the literal sense of the psalm and the normative (i.e., New Testament) meaning of Sacred Scripture.  This means, in effect, that David's is a hollow faith, without real substance.

David's Psalms present many opportunities for an exegete to discuss the nature and quality of David's Old Testament faith.  David's words, expressing his trust in God's continuing aid, are suggestive of a vibrant faith and reliance on the goodness and kindness of God.  These are precisely the attitudes which the Protestants will stress in their discussions of David.  Yet this is the only psalm commentary in which Augustine actually dealt with David's faith.  Since this image of David as a man of faith is unique, we conclude that Augustine did credit David's faith with having some depth or reality; nevertheless, it had a largely figurative quality, displayed in the Old Testament both to foreshadow Christian faith and to demonstrate that both testaments teach the same lessons.

Had Augustine's concern for the historical and existential situation of David really been grounded upon the premise that Old Testament faith was identical to that of the New Covenant, he might have made something other than a Christological allegory in his explication of Psalm 56:  the flight of David from Saul into the cave.  But David's gentleness, his restraint in not killing Saul, has not, for Augustine, the significance it will have for the reformers.  Rather than displaying the perpetual persecution of the "faithful remnant" by men of the Flesh, Augustine finds in the psalm another allegory for a New Testament event.  Saul pursues not David, but Christ, and David's restraint in not killing Saul signifies Christ's long-suffering humility which did not reproach or injure those who crucified Him.  Furthermore, it is Christ's forbearance towards his persecutors, not David's, which should be emulated by Christians.

The importance, then, of David's flight into the cave is its relevance to Christ and the New Testament. As Augustine states, "Since everything which then occurred were figures of future things, we discover here Christ."  The first words of the psalm, "*Ne corrumpas*," also do not pertain to David, but to the inscription, "King of the Jews," carved on the Cross at the time of the crucifixion, which was intended to reproach the impudence of those who disdained their king, Christ.  Since David is the progenitor of Christ in the flesh, Saul, who persecuted David, also persecuted Christ.  The carnal lineage of Christ from David is also seen in the inscription on the Cross.  In this way, then, Saul's hostility to David represents the Jews who sought Christ's death and who were indignant that Pilate ordered the epithet, "King of the Jews," inscribed on the Cross, because it testified that they were crucifying their king.

Augustine does not find David in this psalm, for the historical event portrayed in the psalm portends what will occur during the Passion of Christ.  Besides the historically-based allegory, Augustine finds even a deeper meaning in David's flight from Saul into the cave.  Why, asks Augustine, does David flee into the cave?  In order to be concealed and to remain undiscovered.  The cave is covered by earth, which symbolizes the flesh within which Christ cloaked His identity lest He be discovered by the Jews.  After all, if they had known that Christ was the Messiah and the Lord of Glory, they would never have crucified Him.  So it was necessary for Christ to conceal His divinity with the infirmity of the flesh in order that man's redemption might be achieved.[24]

Augustine's explication of Psalm 143 offers us another example in which an Old Testament event alludes not to the faith of David but to a lesson that is of far greater significance to Augustine.  He sacrifices a consideration of the significance of David's words in the psalm for an allegorical explanation of the event which occasioned its composition:  the story of David and Goliath.

Although Psalm 143 is brief, Augustine insists that it contains a profound meaning,[25] for the historical event to which the psalm refers is a *sacramentum* containing deeper layers of meanings:  the opposition of piety and impiety, pride and humility, Satan and Christ, and, ultimately, the Law and Grace.  While admitting that David's piety contrasted with Goliath's impiety, this historical and existential condition serves only as the foundation upon which Augustine builds his allegorical interpretation of the event.

David armed himself with five stones taken from a riverbed.  He then went forth against Goliath and conquered him.  David is Christ in Head and Body:  therefore it is Christ and the Church who arm themselves with five stones to combat Satan.  The remainder of Augustine's interpretation revolves around the Pauline concept of the fulfillment of the Law by Christ and faith.[26]  The Grace of the New Testament was veiled in the Old Testament Law and is revealed in the Gospels.  Just as the curtain of the Temple was torn away at Christ's Crucifixion, Augustine uses the light of the New Testament to reveal what is behind the shadows of David and Goliath.

David's five stones signify the five books of Moses, and the riverbed from which David gathered the stones represents the Jews, who knew only the Pentateuch.  Aided by God, David's stones-Pentateuch, formerly empty, useless, producing nothing, were made more useful.  So too the Law without Grace bears no fruit, for "The fullness of the Law is Charity,"[27] which comes only through Grace.  Demonstrating that the Law is useless without Grace, David put the five stones into the vessel in which he collected sheep's milk.  Thus armed with the sweet nectar of Grace, David struck Goliath on the forehead and cast him down with only one stone, that is, with the New Testament.  Just as the five books of the Law are read but only Grace saves, so David used only one stone, one book of the Law of Moses made efficacious because it was transformed by Grace into the New Testament.  David then drew Goliath's sword and, with it, he severed the giant's head.  This sword also symbolizes the Law.  Since David and Goliath are, in reality, Christ and Satan, the Old Testament victory of David is an allegory of Christ's victory over Satan.  By fulfilling the Law, Christ conquered Satan.  Thus, the "good news" of the New Testament is that the Savior's love for mankind has, by conjoining the Law and Grace, turned for all time the Devil's own weapon (the Law which, before the Mediator came, could only condemn men) against him.[28]

Implicit in this discussion of the battle between David and Goliath is a judgment on the faith of Old Testament Jews.  The river perfectly symbolizes them, says Augustine, because just as the river current flows over the stones on the riverbed, so did the Jews, who had received the Law, pass it by.[29]  On the other hand, Augustine describes David as having been armed spiritually for battle by the Grace of God.

We have therefore seen in two instances (in Psalms 50 and 143) that Augustine spoke of David as a man imbued with faith and grace.  Yet, he also described David's fellow Jews in a less complimentary fashion; they did not know that Grace fulfills the Law.  We can only conclude from this contrast between David and the other Jews that David's spiritual qualities were, to Augustine, prefigurative.  These qualities made of David a prophet whose actions had not been properly understood by the Jews and whose faith and divinely-given strength were eccentric.  Else why would Augustine have deemed it necessary to allegorize so many of the *gesta Davidis*?  Obviously, only Christians could understand the hidden, New Testament meaning of David's actions.

We have examined a number of Augustine's images of David.  We have found that, for the most part, these images were drawn allegorically and that they subordinated David to Christ.  Let us, then, in concluding our investigation of Augustine's interpretations of David, follow the exegete as he fully develops the allegorical meaning of the title of Psalm 33:  "A Psalm of David, when he changed his countenance before Abimelech, and he dismissed him, and he went his way."

Augustine begins by insisting that "this really happened . . . and because it really happened, it was recorded."  However, he admits that he has not been able to find this particular incident recorded in the Books of Kingdoms,[30] "and yet we do find one from which this would seem to be derived."  He discovers this source in I Kings 21:12-14:  "He [David] feared him [Achis, King of Gath], and he changed his countenance before them, and affected, and drummed against the doors of the city, and was carried in his own hands, [31] and he fell down at the doors of the gate, and his spittle ran down upon his beard."

Augustine asserts that the title of the psalm conceals something mysterious. The first mystery is the discrepancy between the names given in the two texts; this alteration spurs him on to search out the hidden meaning of the two passages:

> We are free to think that the incident I have just related to you from the Books of Kingdoms concerning David signifies nothing. . . . I say then that not for nothing was the name altered, not for nothing does it say "before Abimelech."

Augustine explains that "Abimelech" means "the kingdom of my Father," while "Achis" means "How can that be?" Since David's name is again interpreted as "strong of hand," the Old Testament event refers to Christ.

These identifications allow Augustine to unravel the hidden meaning both of the psalm's title and of the passage in the Books of Kingdoms to which the title refers. Christ, not David, "changed his countenance." Christ, the eternal food which the angels eat, had to change into a food appropriate for children—fallen man—to eat; Christ had to be converted into milk:

> But now how does food become milk? Food is transformed into milk by passing through flesh. This is what a mother does. What she eats, the baby eats; but since the infant is unfit to eat bread, the mother makes the bread flesh. Thus, by the lowly act of suckling and the flow of her milk, she feeds her child on that very bread. How then did the Wisdom of God nourish us on His bread? "Because the Word of God was made flesh and dwelt among us."

Through the Incarnation, then, Christ assumed a human form "before Abimelech," that is, before the kingdom of His Father (the Jewish kingdom).

Since "Achis" and "Abimelech" refer to the same person, according to Augustine, the title of the psalm can read, "he changed his countenance before Achis, and he dismissed him, and he went his way." Augustine recalls Christ's words to His disciples:

> Except a man eat my flesh and drink my blood, he shall not have life in him. For my flesh is meat indeed, and my blood is drink indeed [John 6:54,56].

Hearing His words, the disciples recoiled in horror, "exclaiming in so many words: 'How can that be?' "[32] They were under the reign of King Achis and, therefore, of the kingdom of ignorance and error.

In order to further explain the mystery of the title of Psalm 33, Augustine now returns to a consideration of I Kings 21:12-14. David "affected," that is, Christ took compassion on man's infirmities, became man, and suffered death on the Cross. He "drummed": His skin was stretched across wood and He was crucified. David-Christ drummed "against the doors of the city," in other words, against the gates of the kingdom of ignorance and error which had hitherto been opened only to Satan. Thus, Christ opened the hearts of mortal men so that they might behold the Word of God, as do the angels, and gain eternal life.

Augustine asserts that the psalm's title and the passage from Kings are, because of the words "and was carried in his own hands," clearly applicable only to Christ. For, as Augustine asks,

> Who can be carried in his own hands? A man can be carried in the hands of others, but in his own, never. . . . [But] Christ was literally carried in His own hands when He set before us His own body with the words, "This is my body." He was obviously carrying that body in His own hands. Such is the humility of our Lord Jesus Christ. . . . He urges us to live according to it, that is, to imitate His humility . . . [and] to conquer pride.

Therefore, men must imitate Christ when He "fell down at the doors of the gate," when He abased Himself to the depth of humility. By thus imitating Christ, men humble themselves at the entrance of faith. Indeed, such humility is a sign of the beginning of faith, whereby they are saved.

Augustine next explicates the meaning of the words, "his spittle ran down upon his beard." It was at this point that Christ "changed his countenance before Abimelech, or Achis, and he dismissed him, and he went his way." This means that Christ dismissed the Jews who did not understand and He turned to the Gentiles. Christ turned from the Jews because they could not grasp His seemingly foolish words, "Eat my flesh and drink my blood." To the Jews these words were spittle, the slobbering which occurs when an infant babbles. The Jews interpreted Christ's words as a sign of weakness, for they did not realize that

> Such childish babbling cloaked His strength. The beard symbolizes strength. Therefore, in the spittle that ran down upon his beard, what are we to understand if not that words of weakness served to cloak His strength?[33]

With these words, Augustine ended his exposition in this, his first discourse on Psalm 33. On the following day he delivered a second discourse to his congregation. After briefly summarizing his previous interpretation of the title of the psalm, Augustine began an explanation of the meaning of the words of the psalm.

We can, without having to follow Augustine as he explains each of the psalm's twenty-two verses, appreciate the tenor of his exposition by reproducing his remarks on the second verse:

> Now let us listen to His very words as He affects and drums upon the gate of the city. "I will bless the Lord at all times; His praise shall always be in my mouth." Christ says this. Let the Christian repeat it, because the Christian is incorporated into Christ, and Christ became man for this purpose, that the Christian might become an angel who cries: "I will bless the Lord." When shall I "bless the Lord?" When He confers benefits upon you? When earthly possessions abound? When you have plenty of corn, oil, wine, gold, silver, servants and cattle, when you enjoy good health and freedom from disease, . . . when everything is thriving? Is it only then that you should bless the Lord? No. You must bless Him at all times, both when He bestows these gifts and when He takes them away. For it is He Who gives and it is He Who takes away. But Himself He never takes away from those who bless Him.

Augustine continues by explaining that only the humble of heart bless the Lord at all times. Only those bless Him who have become Christ's Body and imitate His humility when He gave them His body and blood, His "spittle" which "ran down upon His beard."[34]

Augustine's exposition of Psalm 33 underlines several points that we have made in this chapter: the importance for Augustine of the allegorical interpretation of the event which occasioned the writing of each psalm; his application of the allegory in order to arrive at an edifying or Christian understanding of the psalm; and his subordination of the historical David to Christ and the New Testament.

Both in his explication of Psalm 33 and in his discourses on the other psalms, we have seen that Augustine looked backward and forward; that is, he sought out the Old Testament event as well as the New Testament meaning. Since, as Augustine said, the Old Testament event "signifies nothing," he allegorized it so that it became a New Testament event.[35] Having thus raised the Old Testament event to the normative meaning of the Word of God, Augustine began, as we have seen in Psalm 33, an allegorical, that is, a Christological interpretation of the psalm itself. In this way, the speaker in the psalm became Christ or, through Him, the Church or the faithful Christian.

This latter fact is true not only of Psalm 33 and of the other psalms we have examined but also of Augustine's entire commentary. Even in those psalms (and they are by far the greater number) where Augustine does not interpret David allegorically, we find that they are described variously as the "voice of Christ," "the voice of Paul," or that of the Church or even of the martyrs. In himself, then, David stands almost mute, hidden behind the Christian allegory or the Christian "voice." Thus, David remains throughout Augustine's expositions a shadow whose Old Testament existence and words, when taken out of their Old Testament context, bear witness to the teachings of the New Testament.[36] As Augustine himself said: "The Old Testament is nothing but the New covered with a veil, and the New Testament is nothing but the Old unveiled."[37] So, too, David is merely Christ and the Church veiled, and they are David unveiled.

## NOTES

[1] Heiko A. Oberman, *Forerunners of the Reformation*, trans. by Paul L. Nyhus (New York: Holt, Rinehart and Winston, 1966), p. 281.

[2] Roland H. Bainton, "The Immoralities of the Old Testament Patriarchs According to the Exegesis of the Late Middle Ages and of the Reformation," *Harvard Theological Review*, 23, 1 (1930), pp. 39-40.

[3] There were several precedents for using the allegorical method of interpretation. Among them were the use of this method both by Greek philosophers in their investigations of Homer and by rabbis in their exegesis of the Scriptures. St. Paul seemed to have permitted the Christian use of allegory in Galatians 4:24 ("These things contain an allegory."). Influenced also by Philo, the Alexandrian School of Clement and Origen further developed allegorical interpretation in order to search out the hidden meanings of the Old Testament. The School of Antioch, on the other hand, used this method very sparingly. Its adherents, such as St. John Chrysostom, preferred the historical/literal sense of Scripture. The fifth ecumenical Council of Constantinople in 553 declared both the extremes of Origenistic allegory and Antiochian literalism heretical. Cf. Oberman, *Forerunners*, pp. 282-283; cf. also H. A. Wolfson, *The Philosophy of the Church Fathers*, Vol. I (Cambridge, Mass.: Harvard University Press, 1964), pp. 24-72; R. M. Grant, *The Letter and the Spirit* (London: 1957), pp. 121ff; and R. P. C. Hanson, *Allegory and Event* (London: 1959), *passim*.

[4] However, even Origen was forced to admit that allegory could not resolve every exegetical problem encountered in the Old Testament. Speaking of the incest of Lot, Origen said, "This is a mystery not understood by us." (Cf. Bainton, *art. cit.*, p. 39.)

[5] For Origen's use of typology in interpreting the Bible, see Jean Daniélou, *Origen*, trans. by Walter Mitchell (New York: Sheed and Ward, 1955), pp. 139-173; in particular, see pp. 139-143 for a succinct discussion of the conflicting attitudes towards the Old Testament in Origen's time.

[6] *Sermo II* (PL, Vol. 38, col. 30), quoted by Emile Mâle, *The Gothic Image: Religious Art in France in the Thirteenth Century*, trans. by Dora Nussey (New York: Harper Torchbook, 1958), pp. 135-136.

[7] *De doctrina christiana*, III. 10.14 (PL, Vol. 34, col. 71), quoted by Preus, *op. cit.*, p. 13.

[8] Augustine's interpretations of David are of course found in his expositions of the Psalms (written between 392 and 418 A.D.). Many of them were originally sermons. They bear the generic title of *Enarrationes in Psalmos*. They are found both in the *Corpus Christianorum: Series Latina*, Vols. 38-40, and in J.-P. Migne, ed., *Patrologiae latinae cursus completus omnium ss. patrum, doctorum, scriptorumque ecclesiasticorum*, Vols. 36-37. We give citations from both editions. References to Augustine's commentaries will hereafter be given as "CC 38/39/40, Ps.__, p(p).__" and PL 36/37, Ps.__, col(l).__."

[9] CC 38, Ps. 7, p. 35; PL 36, Ps. 7, col. 97.

[10] CC 38, Ps. 7, pp. 35-36; PL 36, Ps. 7, coll. 97-98.

[11] CC 38, Ps. 7, p. 36; PL 36, Ps. 7, col. 98.

[12] CC 38, Ps. 25, p. 140; PL 36, Ps. 25, col. 187.

[13] CC 38, Ps. 26, pp. 154-155; PL 36, Ps. 26, coll. 199-200.

[14] CC 38, Ps. 26, p. 155; PL 36, Ps. 26, col. 200.

[15] CC 38, Ps. 34, p. 300; PL 36, Ps. 34, col. 323. David is called "fortis manu" and "desiderabilis."

[16] CC 40, Ps. 131, pp. 1912-1913; PL 37, Ps. 131, coll. 1716-1717.

[17] CC 39, Ps. 72, p. 986; PL 36, Ps. 72, col. 914.

[18] CC 39, Ps. 55, pp. 678-680; PL 36, Ps. 55, coll. 648-649.

[19] CC 38, Ps. 50, p. 600; PL 36, Ps. 50, col. 586: "Dicam ergo non quod volo, sed quod cogor; dicam non exhortans ad imitationem, sed instruens ad timorem."

[20] CC 38, Ps. 50, p. 601; PL 36, Ps. 50, col. 587: "De longe enim vidit David illam, in qua captus est. Mulier longe, libido prope . . . . Inest peccatum, cum delectaris; regnat, si consenseris."

[21] CC 38, Ps. 50, pp. 600-602; PL 36, Ps. 50, coll. 586-587.

[22] CC 38, Ps. 50, p. 606; PL 36, Ps. 50, col. 591.

[23] CC 38, Ps. 50, p. 611; PL 36, Ps. 50, col. 595.

[24] CC 39, Ps. 56, pp. 695-696; PL 36, Ps. 56, coll. 662-663.

[25] CC 40, Ps. 143, p. 2072; PL 37, Ps. 143, col. 1855.

[26] Galatians 3:21-22: "Is the law then contrary to the promise of God? By no means. For if a law had been given that could give life, justice would truly be from the law. But the Scripture shut up all things under sin, that by the faith of Jesus Christ the promise might be given to those who believe."

[27] Romans 13:10.

[28] CC 40, Ps. 143, pp. 2072-2074; PL 37, Ps. 143, coll. 1856-1857. Mâle, *op. cit.*, pp. 136-137, describes an almost identical rendering of the story of David and Goliath in another work by St. Augustine (*Sermo, XXXII*, cap. V & VI).

[29] CC 40, Ps. 143, pp. 2073-2074; PL, Ps. 143, col. 1857.

[30] The Books of Kingdoms (*Regnorum libri*) is the Septuagint title of the Books of Kings.

[31] Because he used the *Vetus latina*, Augustine here differs from the Vulgate. Where Augustine gives "he was carried in his own hands," the Vulgate reads "he slipped down between their hands."

[32] The disciples actually said, "How can this man give us His flesh to eat?" (John 6:53).

[33] CC 38, Ps. 33, pp. 273-281; PL 36, Ps. 33, coll. 300-307.

[34] CC 38, Ps. 33, pp. 283-284; PL 36, Ps. 33, coll. 308-309.

[35] The one exception that we have seen to the type of allegorical exegesis which we have examined rather fully in Psalm 33 was, of course, Psalm 50.

[36] That Augustine's allegorical and Christological treatment of the Psalms was part of a dominant strain of early Christian exegesis is attested to by Dom Pierre Salmon, *Les "Tituli Psalmorum" des manuscrits latins* (Paris: Les Editions du Cerf, 1959), pp. 38-39: "Il y a, dans l'antiquité, trois manières possibles d'aborder les psaumes et d'en tirer profit: rechercher leur sens littéral et historique, en traitant les psaumes comme des prophéties qui se rapportent à l'histoire du peuple juif; ainsi fait Théodore de Mopsueste; donner des explications allégoriques et des explications morales à partir de leur texte, méthode de Saint Jean Chrysostome et d'un petit nombre d'auteurs anciens; enfin proposer une explication franchement et pleinement chrétienne, qui fasse rentrer la prière des psaumes dans le grand mystère chrétien, ainsi que firent Tertullien, Origène, Eusèbe, Athanase, Hilaire, Ambroise, Jérôme, Augustin, Théodoret, Cassiodore. Ces derniers exemples, les plus nombreux, les plus autorisés, devraient nous indiquer la voie." See also Maurice Pontet, *L'Exégèse de St. Augustin prédicateur* (Paris: Aubier, [1946]), pp. 387-418, for a discussion of the background to and contours of Augustine's exegesis of the Psalms.

[37] *De civitate Dei*, lib. XVI, cap. XXVI: "Quid enim quod dicitur Testamentum Vetus, nisi occultatio Novi? Et quod est aliud quod dicitur Novum nisi Veteris revelatio?" (Quoted in Mâle, *op. cit.*, p. 136.)

# Chapter II
# Nicolaus of Lyra

Augustine's David was the figure of Christ. As such, Augustine did not study David as a man of faith, as a king, or as a prophet prophesying to his own people. While we can derive no conclusions from the evidence that we have presented about the images of David developed by other patristic or medieval commentators who followed Augustine's allegorical hermeneutic, we do believe that his interpretations of David are indicative of the type of interpretation to which the allegorical method led.

We wish now to turn to another method of Old Testament and Psalm interpretation, that which gave careful attention to the literal and historical meaning of Jewish Scripture. Of the many patristic and medieval exegetes who strove to understand the Psalms *historice et literaliter,*[1] we have chosen Nicolaus of Lyra. It is to him that we now turn our attention.

The major role of this fourteenth-century Franciscan biblical commentator has long been recognized, although it has only been in this century that there has been a revival of interest in Lyra.[2] His importance for the development of biblical studies is attested to by the one hundred seventy-seven editions of the works by or attributed to him, most of them published in the fifteenth and sixteenth centuries. Indeed, Nicolaus of Lyra's *Postillae super bibliam* were the first Bible commentaries to be printed.[3] In addition, more than eight hundred manuscripts of his works are extant in the libraries of Europe,[4] offering further evidence of the widespread interest in his works. His merits have been stressed at least from the time of Richard Simon to our own century.[5]

In fact, a rather pedestrian limerick from the sixteenth century provides, if not the most authoritative, at least the most popular evaluation of Lyra as a biblical exegete:

> Si Lyra non lyrasset,
> Totus mundus delirasset,
> Lutherus non saltasset.[6]

Needless to say, the generalization expressed in this rhyme is overly facile. The verse and its variant do contain an element of truth in that they express the decisive role of Nicolaus of Lyra, the extent of his fame, and his influence on Luther and perhaps on the whole of Reformation biblical scholarship.[7] As we shall see from Lyra's interpretations of David, he may indeed have had an influence on certain Protestant writers.

Nicolaus of Lyra therefore plays a central role in our study. There are, as we have noted, two general modes by which to interpret David. There is, first of all, the path indicated by St. Augustine by which David is seen as the figure of Christ Himself;[8] second, there is the path sketched out in Lyra's interpretations of David, through which David comes alive as a man of faith in the context of his own time and whose character is worthy of devout imitation by the faithful under the New Covenant. It is our belief that it is Nicolaus of Lyra who first broke the ground that several reformers would build upon, by which David would become—and along with him the Old Testament—a bearer of theological and spiritual relevance in his own right.

Nicolaus of Lyra's major contribution to biblical exegesis is his *Postilla litteralis et moralis super totam bibliam.*[9]  Lyra intended to restore the state of biblical studies with his *Postillae* by using Rashi (Solomon ben Isaac, 1040-1105) and other rabbinical sources.  Following Augustine's *dictum,* Lyra states in his second prologue to the *Postilla litteralis* that the literal sense of Scripture must be the *fundamentum* of all mystical interpretations.  In true scholarly fashion, he complains that the literal sense has been obfuscated by the inability of some commentators, by the heedless errors of copyists, and by the frequent departure of the Vulgate from the Hebrew.  He then agrees with St. Jerome that one must correct the errors that have crept into the Vulgate by referring to the Hebrew codices and to the rabbinical commentators.  Finally, he adds that previous Catholic commentators have choked Holy Scripture with mystical interpretations.[10]

Lyra's interest in the literal or historical sense of the Bible does not prevent him, however, from interpreting the Old Testament *mystice.*  He devotes meticulous attention to the historical situations in which David found himself.  Whereas Augustine had stressed the fundamental importance of the literal meaning as the basis for arriving at and understanding the edifying meaning of the Old Testament, but had really spent little time in discussing the Psalms *litteraliter,* Lyra devotes his *Postilla litteralis* just to that purpose.[11]  In his *Postilla moralis* he resumes his comments on the literal sense of the passages, and then proceeds to offer mystical interpretations which, he believes, will not belie the intention of the literal message.

Given the foregoing remarks as *prima facie* evidence, what might the reader expect of singular importance from Lyra's interpretations?  First of all, one should *not* expect the abandonment of all Christological interpretations of David.  This would be too radical a deviation from exegetical tradition and practice.  However, one might justifiably expect a shift away from the all-encompassing Christological approach found in Augustine's *Enarrationes in psalmos.*  This is exactly what the student of Lyra's psalms does discover.  David is often treated as a man operating very well under the Old Dispensation and, as such, he emerges not as a "type" of the Christian man, but rather as a man of faith who is worthy of emulation by those operating under the New Dispensation.  This attitude toward David, although not rigorously and only sometimes tentatively developed by Nicolaus of Lyra, presages important developments in the attitude toward the Old Testament as a whole, an attitude that will only fully emerge among the writings of the reformed  theologians of the sixteenth century.

In his prologue to the *Postilla super psalterium,* Nicolaus of Lyra runs counter to the Augustinian tradition concerning the authorship of the Psalms.  Augustine had argued that David was *the* psalmist.  This in itself was one concept of David:  David as the sole author of all the Psalms.  Lyra, however, sides with the authority of St. Jerome (and the rabbinical commentators).  Nicolaus denies Augustine's claim and argues that David, not at all *the* psalmist, was merely *a* psalmist, one among several:

> Instrumentalis autem est ipse David cui secundum Augustinum omnia contenta in hoc
> libro fuerunt *revelata* et ab eo descripta.  Secundum vero Hieronymum et omnes doctores
> hebraicos David non fecit omnes psalmos, sed maiorem partem.  Plures autem alii aliquos
> psalmos scripserunt, ut Salomon et aliqui alii ut magis patebit infra prosequendo per
> titulos psalmos.[12]

Furthermore, arguing on grammatical and stylistic grounds, Lyra agrees with Rashi that the psalms by David are scattered throughout the Psalter and that, therefore, the psalms were not written in the order in which they were discovered (for example, Lyra claims that Ps. 144 was one of the first to be composed).[13]  Lyra's attention to historical and grammatical problems, as well as his choice of authorities, allowed him to offer substantive proof for his vision of David as a psalmist.

Lyra's emphasis on the importance of the literal and historical sense of the psalm passages actually involves a second literal sense; together, they form what Lyra calls the *duplex sensus litteralis*. The first literal meaning applies to the prophet's time, portraying the actual Old Testament event, mood, or situation which elicited the composition of each psalm. Lyra maintains, moreover, that the prophet consciously intended another literal meaning; this second literal sense applies to the time of Christ or, as we shall see, to the Christian era from the Resurrection to Lyra's own day.

We may gain an insight into the nature of this double literal sense, though not into its unique exegetical possibilities (these we shall examine below), from the following two examples. Commenting upon Isaiah 11:1 ("And there shall come forth a rod out of the stem of Jesse, and a branch shall grow out of his roots:"), Lyra remarks that the prophet proclaims a two-fold prophecy, one pertaining to Old Testament times, the other to New Testament times, wherein "the prophet turns again to a description of the mystery of Christ, his main intention."[14] In the second example, Lyra comments upon I Chronicles 17, where God says of Solomon, "I will be a father to him, and he will be like a son to me." Lyra writes:

> [T]his is understood as speaking of Solomon literally. . . . The aforesaid authority
> [I Chron. 17], then, was fulfilled literally in Solomon, yet less perfectly because he
> was a son of God by grace only; but in Christ [it is fulfilled] more perfectly, because
> he is a son of God by nature. Now, although each exposition is literal simply speaking,
> still the second one, which concerns Christ, is [also] spiritual and mystical in a derived
> sense, in that Solomon was a figure of Christ.[15]

Both of these examples show that the hermeneutical divide between the Old and New Testaments is inconsiderable. The double literal sense is found within the Old Testament itself. The double intention of the Old Testament speaker obviates the allegorization of the Old Testament words and history.

Taken to the extreme, however, this idea of the double literal sense could work to lessen, even destroy, the worth of the primary, Old Testament meaning in favor of the second literal sense.[16] This denigration of the actual Davidic meaning of the psalms does not occur in Nicolaus of Lyra's commentaries, as it will occur radically in the work of Lefèvre d'Etaples. Certainly, moral, mystical, or allegorical methods are at work in Lyra, but in such a way that the parallel literal and Christian meaning of the psalms is not seemingly as forced in Lyra as in Augustine, and in such a way that the concepts of David in Lyra are more original and universally applicable. Finally, the heavily Christological interpretations of David in Augustine's commentary, which seem to have more of a theological and doctrinal bent, give way in Nicolaus of Lyra's *Postilla super psalmos* to Davidic interpretations of a more *pastoral, devotional* emphasis, the more so as Lyra breaks away from a purely Christological approach.

The variety of Lyra's images of David made possible by his literal/historical approach to the Old Testament are inherent in the differences between his vision of David as prophet and the view of St. Thomas Aquinas. Aquinas considered that David was inferior to Moses as a prophet. Following the Jewish commentator Maimonides,[17] St. Thomas establishes Moses as the superior prophet on three grounds: that Moses was allowed to see God, the 'divine essence,' during his lifetime (here he is referring to the Burning Bush on Mt. Sinai), indicating that Moses' vision was the clearest, and that the object of that vision was the most distant and the highest; second that, coming down from the mountain, Moses announced his prophecy to the whole people, *ex persona Dei;* and, last, that Moses performed greater miracles than those performed by David or any other prophet.[18]

It is Lyra's very interest in the niceties of literal exposition that allows him to demolish this Thomistic position and, in so doing, to enhance the role of David as prophet *vis-à-vis* Moses.  Lyra advises the reader that Deuteronomy 34:10 is written in the phraseology of Joshua and that it means not that Moses was unsurpassed as a prophet, but rather that Moses had not been superseded as a prophet up until the time of Joshua.  This leaves open the possibility for a greater prophet to arise.[19]  Since Moses prefigured and made ready the path for "the far greater prophet and legislator" (David), and since the end is more noble than those things leading to it, David acquires more prestige than Moses.[20]

While St. Thomas Aquinas had defended the prophetic superiority of Moses because he had immediately perceived the vision of God and had heard God speak, Lyra sees this type of prophetic experience as being a step lower than the prophetic inspiration received by David.  The revelations made to David came without the sense perception of any figures or signs; instead the suprasensual truths were comprehended by David through divine revelation.[21]  Thomas' conception of the prophet was of one who received the prophetic light in the manner of a passing impression.  Such had been the Mosaic experience on Mt. Sinai.  Lyra, on the other hand, gives the highest accolade not to this type of inspirational phenomenon but to the prophetic light which comes in a perpetual and unceasing stream.  Such was the type of inspiration given to David, who becomes, for Lyra, the greatest of the Old Testament prophets.[22]

Because of his stand on prophetic inspiration, Nicolaus of Lyra is able to transcend the conceptual boundaries of David as found in St. Augustine.  Whereas Augustine's main, almost sole, idea of David was as the figure of Christ and, *through* Christ, of the Church, Nicolaus of Lyra is able to achieve a rather remarkable spectrum of concepts of David.  Seeing David as a prophet who received inspiration "in a perpetual and unceasing stream of light," Lyra can imagine or interpret David in a more vital way than could Augustine.  Augustine's David is fulfilled makes sense—only through the figure of Christ.  Lyra's David is fulfilled through a kind of historical parallelism.  Certainly the passage of centuries from Augustine's to Lyra's times aided this development.  More events had passed; whereas Augustine could (probably) rightly see David and the Old Testament having their fulfillment and their theological fruition achieved *via* the Savior, Lyra had over a millennium of Christian history to choose from in order to see the ongoing fulfillment of Davidic (and Old Testament) events.  This author feels, however, that something more important, even if still tacit, is at work in Lyra's Psalm commentary.  Since David was the recipient of constant inspiration and since David's psalms are given a much greater historical and literal importance, David himself comes to be, in Lyra, a man of faith under the Old Covenant.  As such he is a figure and an *exemplum* of Christian types living under the New Covenant.  The emphasis, then, has changed from Augustine to Nicolaus of Lyra.  Where St. Augustine sees David as a figure of Christ, both in head and members, Lyra sees David as an historical and religious character whose deeds and feelings are applicable to the Christian historical and religious character.  Thus, David affords an example to be emulated precisely because of his historical role, his righteousness, and his sinfulness and subsequent repentance.  He becomes, finally, a figure of pastoral and devotional importance as well as of theological import.  This type of role for David has its consummation, to be seen later, in the commentaries of the reformed theologians.[23]

There are four major categories of David as prophet that can be inferred and discerned in Nicolaus of Lyra.  First, there is David as the prophet and figure of Christ.  This type or concept has already been seen in St. Augustine's *Enarrationes in psalmos,* although even on this point there appears a difference between the allegorical references found in Augustine and Lyra.  Second, is the concept of David as the spokesman of the Christian Church.  This concept has also been found in the commentaries of Augustine, though here, too, there is a difference:  David is the prophet of the Church through himself, not through the mediator-ship of Christ; and the application of David's words to the Church is more historically relevant than in

Augustine.  The third category is that of David as the parallel type, in a devotional sense, of popes, prelates, and kings, referring to them as general figures and, occasionally, to specific historical characters; the alliance between David and general and specific popes, prelates, and kings is found not so much in that he prefigured them, but in that his devotion and the performance of his duties offer parallel experiences to theirs.  Finally, we find the category in which David is referred to as the individual Christian man.  Here the parallel approach is perhaps most clearly seen, as David exhibits attitudes toward God and faith under the Old Covenant that are equally applicable to men of Christian faith.  The latter two categories are newly found in Nicolaus of Lyra; they had not appeared at all in St. Augustine.

David is the prophet and prototype of Christ mainly because of the similarity of circumstances in which the greatest of prophets and the God-Savior found themselves.  The confidence of David is often extolled as being an allegory for the confidence of Christ.  In Psalm 10, for example, Lyra informs the reader that literally the psalm refers to David's confidence, as told in I Samuel 22, when he was warned by the prophet Agab, as he was about to settle in Israel, not to enter the Kingdom.  Nonetheless, having been warned, David trusted that God would protect him from Saul and all his enemies.  Similarly, says Lyra, the man Jesus was told he should leave Israel on account of the persecution of Herod.  David gave no assent to the warning, nor did Jesus.[24]  Here we find that in viewing David as the figure of Christ in his trust in the Father, the lesson taught by Lyra is less theological than pastoral.  The concept of David as Christ serves to teach the Christian reader the necessity of imitating Christ and David, by placing his hope in the Father Who will deliver the Christian from dangerous adversity, as He once delivered both David and Christ.[25]

A further example of David as the figure of Christ, beyond the similarity of their confidence in the efficacy of the Father's help, is seen in the parallelism that Lyra sketches between the persecutions endured by David and by Christ.  Psalm 35, which David begins by saying, "Contend, O Lord, with those who contend with me," literally refers to David's pleadings that God come to his assistance when he was suffering persecution at the hands of Saul.  Mystically, the psalm can be expounded concerning Christ who endured— both in Himself and His members—the tyrannies of the Jews and Gentiles.  Just as David sought aid in punishing his persecutor, Christ implored the Father to avenge His and His Church's sufferings.[26]

Even the unused opportunity presented to David to kill his persecutor, Saul, appears as a Christological analogy to Lyra.  For Christ is the allegorical subject of Psalm 58, which was written by David after he had gazed at Saul sleeping next to his sword and had had the power to murder his enemy.  Christ, His miracles repudiated and scoffed at by the Jews, might have destroyed His detractors, but chose the path of clemency instead.[27]

We have, then, three psalm expositions wherein Christ is the allegorical subject of the psalms through His figure, David.  While the concept of David in each case is applied to the Lord Christ, the purposes of each Christological application differ.  In Psalm 10, David—and through him Christ—teaches the rightness of full trust and confidence in God.  In Psalm 35 we are told of the similarity between Christ and David in the sufferance of persecution.  And, finally, in Psalm 58, the power or ability of Christ and His figure David to demolish their enemies is set forth.  Just as the three uses of David as the Christ-figure differ in their explanations, so do their applications.  Psalm 35 is more theological and it applies to Christ alone.  It teaches us only, through David, of the animosities Christ encountered from His own people; in a sense, it promulgates a historical lesson that was prophesied by David's life and fulfilled in the harassment of Christ.  Psalm 58 teaches much the same lesson in that just as David could have rid himself of an obstinate enemy, Christ might have used His power to humble the Jews who were ignorant of His messianic qualities.  Besides serving as a Gospel prophecy, David's choice not to harm Saul is also a moral lesson to all faithful Christians of the virtue of forbearance toward their enemies.  Psalm 10 finds David and Christ in the role of pastoral teachers.  They both teach trust in God.  Here, instead of David merely foreseeing by his actions an event that will "come to life" historically in the Gospels, David and Christ point out a virtuous attitude applicable until the Last Judgment.  Thus, David as the prototype of Christ teaches a pastoral lesson, instructing the man of faith's attitude *vis-à-vis* his Creator.

We may also remark on a difference here between Augustine and Lyra.  Whereas Augustine made reference to the literal sense of the psalms, there was little intimate connection between what occurred literally/historically and the conception of David he employed.  It is worthy of note that in Lyra there is, even in these three psalms, a closer relationship between David's attitude or action literally/historically described and the higher meaning given the passage.

The persecution of David at the hands of Saul and his other enemies becomes a historically parallel prefiguration not only of the sufferings of Christ but also of the Church, pristine and medieval.  Surely it was not impossible for St. Augustine to see David as the figure of the early Church of the Apostles.  Lyra, writing in the early fourteenth century, enjoys a longer view and consequently he sees David's persecution as being parallel to the harassment of both the early Church and the medieval Church.  This implies, moreover, that David as a prophet is not fully delineated, for once and all, by the events of the time of Christ.  Rather, his is an ongoing relevance, applicable to later times as well.[28]

David's prayer in Psalm 55 was written when he fled from the persecution of Saul and the Kai'lites, both of whom sought his death.[29]  Mystically, David's prayer in this historical situation, adds Lyra, is that of the Church which endured persecution at the hands of the Jews, as is told in the Acts of the Apostles.[30]  The application of David's suffering to the early Church is further mentioned in Psalm 122, which David wrote as a prayer beseeching deliverance for himself and his army from the Philistines.[31]  Again, the Philistine animosity has its parallel in the suffering of the early Church, and Lyra refers the reader once more to Acts.  The first verse of the psalm, "If the Lord had not been on our side when men rose up against us," refers, morally, to the Jews molesting the Christians.  The psalm continues by offering thanks to God for His beneficence.  Mystically, this divine assistance took the form of the Roman army, which, as we have seen, Lyra holds to have been a divine instrument in subduing and punishing the Jews.[32]

If David's prayers for release from the persecutions of Saul and the Philistines could be seen mystically as the prayers of the early Church enduring harassment from the Jews, Lyra employed the same image of David prophetically acting as spokesman for the Church seeking deliverance from the tyrannies of Rome, that very Rome whose army had been, an instant before, the *deus ex machina* which had liberated the Christians from the Jewish malevolence.  Lyra refers particularly to the cruelties of emperors such as Diocletian and Maximianus.[33]  Speaking always for the Church in joyous thanksgiving, the same Davidic *mise-en-scène* can be applied to two different Christian historical events.

But this is not the end of Lyra's exegetical treatment of the story of the attacks on David by Saul and his other enemies.  For the years fly by and the tribulations of David become, for Nicolaus of Lyra, the trials of medieval Christians faced with the shameful occupation of the Holy Land by the Infidel.  Psalm 5, says Lyra, ought to be recited devoutly and intently by the priests, since in it David states allegorically that it is not fitting that the Muslims live next to Christ's tomb, nor that they remain in the land upon which the Savior's eyes gazed.  These Saracens must be destroyed:  Mohammed was a villainous false prophet, and his followers, having seized the Holy Places by the sword, will die by that very instrument.[34]

It would be well to note here parenthetically that the application of Psalm 5 delineates rather neatly the difference in approach between Augustine and Nicolaus of Lyra. If St. Augustine had (as he did not) begun his comments as did Lyra—"David wrote this psalm to be sung by the priests for the conservation of the kingdom of Israel . . ." —he might well have explained David's intention allegorically as referring to the Church militant in this world and the Church triumphant in the heavenly kingdom. This kind of manipulation would, at least, have been consistent with what we have previously noted of Augustine's Davidic interpretations.[35]   Nicolaus of Lyra turns to an allegorical interpretation of this prayer of David, yet he, unlike even his contemporaries,[36] fails to turn what he sees as being literally a petition for the preservation of the Chosen People's kingdom into a prophetic prayer for the heavenly city.   This remarkably "missed" opportunity may, we believe, be an example in miniature of what was meant when we stated that Lyra's use of David is more heavily pastoral than theological.   If, as for Augustine, Lyra's David were a *persona* primarily related to the New Testament itself (i.e., by seeing David primarily as the prefigurer of events to be fulfilled Christologically) then almost certainly Lyra would have chosen the normative allegorical reading, rendering the literal content into the doctrinal teaching about the kingdom of God.   We feel, however, that Lyra's manifest interest in searching out the literal/historical sense of the psalms influenced him also to keep his allegorical renderings of the psalms—and his concepts of David—on an equivalent, often even worldly, higher level.   The historical kingdom of Israel led him to look historically and geographically for the analogous sense of the passage.   Hence, the allegory stays within the temporal confines of this world, and Lyra sees David's prayer as the Church's crusading prayer.   It is this type of approach that will be deliberately carried even further in the Psalm commentaries of the reformed exegetes.

This same technique informs Nicolaus of Lyra's exposition of Psalm 19, which begins, "May the Lord answer you in the day of trouble."   This time David and his army are about to fight against David's rebellious son Absalom.   This prayer for David is mystically that of the Church on behalf of those Christians who were about to lock arms with the Muslims.   When the name of Jacob is invoked for David's protection, the power of the name of God is mystically meant in order to crush the Infidel.   The divine aid comes from the merit of Christ through the Church.   Trusting in divine power, the Christians will defeat their enemy who merely trusts in human force.[37]   We have seen in previous psalms that David is the type of man who relies utterly on God for his safekeeping.   Thus he would correspond to what Lyra terms the "*dux bonae dispositionis.*"   The circle is completed and David's prayer becomes the prayer by the leader of good character for the success of his army against Absalom and, mystically, of the Church for the victory of the crusading armies against the Infidel.

We find in Lyra's *Postilla* one final way in which David acts as the figure of Christ.   Lyra's exegetical maneuvering in this case is most unusual, for he makes David the figure of Christ through the agency of a second Old Testament prophet.   Literally, David wrote Psalm 64 in the person of Daniel who was about to be sent into the lions' pit, thence to be divinely liberated.   Allegorically, Daniel, desiring release from his impending ordeal in the lions' den, signifies Christ.   Christ, like Daniel, was delivered up to be killed by invidious men and underwent the Passion.   And, just as Daniel did, Christ prayed to the Father for deliverance.   David's psalm is Daniel's and Christ's prayer, and thus it is spoken in the person of Christ.[38]

The citation of Daniel gives us once again, as in Psalm 5, a miniaturized example of Nicolaus of Lyra's innovative approach in interpreting David.   He read Psalm 64 and he saw in it the agony expressed by Daniel's prayer.   Daniel in the lions' den being the figure of the Passion of Christ, the prayer becomes, for Lyra, allegorically the prayer of Christ.   Nothing like this has been found in the expositions of

St. Augustine.  The crux of the difference between Lyra and Augustine seems once again to be the greater emphasis on the literal sense in Nicolaus of Lyra and the consequent seeking out of parallel meanings rather than Augustine's "layered" meanings.[39]  Thus, David's words are the prayer of Christ only indirectly and incidentally, because of the parallelism between the imminent passion of Daniel and Christ. It is first of all the parallel historical connection, seen in the words, between David and Daniel that Nicolaus of Lyra cites.  We may further conclude that Lyra's method of exegesis, by leading first to Daniel and then to Christ, shows that the fulfillment of the Old Testament David is not only discerned in the New Testament, but also occasionally in the Old Testament.

The third broad conceptual category for Lyra's interpretation of David relates the great prophet to prelates and kings.  Here too, though the references are at times general, at times specific, Lyra's exegetical method remains identical to what has gone before.

There are several psalms in which David appears as the type of the good prelate and good king.  When David wrote, "The Lord is my light and my salvation," he was prayerfully preparing to assume his role as king over all Israel.  David praying is not a prefiguration of a type but, instead, his prayer is one worthy of repetition by anyone readying himself for pontifical[40] or regal unction, for the qualities enumerated in the prayer by David are sought also by the latter-day speaker.[41]  David's constancy in opposing malign insults, his diligent efforts on behalf of religion, and his seriousness in performing good acts all insure that his reign will be prosperous.  Apparently Lyra has construed David as priest-king, for his regal prayer is equally applicable in both the sacerdotal and lay spheres.  Or, perhaps more accurately, Nicolaus of Lyra sees no difference between the duties and purposes of prelates and monarchs.[42]

The theme of David as the model for the good prelate continues in Lyra's interpretation of Psalm 60. Here Lyra finds David lamenting the destruction of Israel prior to his reign, when God had been displeased with His chosen people, and beseeching the Lord for its reformation. David, the shepherd become king, signifies again the good ruler, either secular or religious.[43]  David's petition for the shoring up of the kingdom is the prelate's prayer for the release of Christians from servitude to sin.  David as prelate further speaks of dividing the burden placed on the shoulders of the bishop by arranging that the duties of preaching and hearing confessions be committed to suitably capable people.[44]  The parallel between the literal and moral levels of David's prayer is beyond question.  David, ever the "pastor"(as king his charge became greater and more burdensome), prays for *"reformatio"* of his kingdom, brought low by God's just dealings with an abusive people.  It is in the same spirit that the bishop seeks to have his people become unblemished by sins so they will be *"coram Deo."*

The devout concern of David's prayer, then, ought to be inherent in the good prelate who seeks the better ordering of his spiritual realm by assigning pastoral duties to various capable subalterns, just as David oversaw the practice of the divine cult in ancient Israel.

The prosperous religious state of a people is thus insured by the well-ordering of the rites of the Church. The personal qualities of the prelates are equally vital for the success of the faith.  Just as David typified the leader of "good disposition" in the struggle against the Infidel, so too his character is remarked in Psalm 100 as being worthy of imitation by the prelates of state and Church.  David says, "misericordiam et iudicium cantabo tibi Domine, / . . . perambulabam in innocentia cordis mei, / . . . non proponebam ante oculos meos  rem iniustam," three verses which ought to be studied by prelates.  The prelate reciting the first phrase sings, "in prosperous times of God's love, in adverse times by trusting in His justice."

When David speaks the second phrase, the prelate adds, "I will walk perfectly in innocence of heart," that is, without faults. The third phrase the prelate meditates upon, and recites: "I will not set before my eyes anything that is base by doing it knowingly." Furthermore, the prelate extrapolates on the remainder of the psalm, vowing his hatred of those who fall away by sin; he will not approve them, but will condemn them. Those who are faithful to God shall be his counsellors and judges. The prelate's official family must be pure and honest. Finally, he vows to cast down sinners, the lay prelate with the sword, the ecclesiastic with spiritual weapons, lest "the community of good men be destroyed by evil men."[45]

There appears to be more, then, to the onerous task of supervising society through state and Church than merely being of good disposition and disposing well the ecclesiastical functions. The prelate must also be zealous in defending the faith against degeneracy, and he must maintain himself and his *curia* in their integrity. The noteworthy point about Lyra's explanation of this psalm is not only that David is the figure of the prelate who will fulfill the prophecy by perfecting himself and his entourage but also that Lyra suggests that David himself exhibited fully those qualities. David's prayer is not one wherein he ardently desires that these qualities be fulfilled in the age following the coming of the Messiah, but rather it is a prayer wherein he himself vows that he will be the good prelate in all respects. That David speaks in the first person indicates that it was a personal vow and that the vow demands imitation rather than fulfillment. Parallel to David's prelacy is the prelacy of kings, bishops and abbots in Lyra's time. The Old Covenant was a living faith, David its chief exemplar. The concerns expressed by Nicolaus of Lyra are pastoral, having to do with the care of the flock (a concept buttressed by David's earlier characterization as the good shepherd, the good king). Once again we find Lyra showing that David and the Old Testament are manifestations of pastoral integrity, complete unto themselves, needing imitation in Christian times, not fulfillment. Lyra's David may have operated as the prophet (foreteller) of Christ; he may, in other words, not have been a figure of theological validity; but as the prelate he was complete, and so he must be studied by future aspirants to his role. By extension, the Old Testament needed the Christ and the New Testament to be fulfilled, but in its pastoral efficacy and its ability to demonstrate a pastoral, though not theological, parallelism it was a living Covenant for Lyra.

The prelate's concern for the well-being of the spiritual and temporal kingdom (for Lyra, they are one on earth) means yet more beyond the overseeing of the various rituals so that they are performed carefully, and it entails more than selecting good advisers and stamping out turpitude. All these things have to do with the present, whether in the time of David or in the time of Nicolaus of Lyra. The truly good *pastor* will devote his thoughts to the future, to his successors. Since men are unable to effect much for the future, as they cannot guarantee the quality of those who follow, such things should rightly be left to divine agency. The good prelate, then, will pray to God for a good succession.

Psalm 130 ("O Lord, remember David and all the hardships he endured") literally expresses David's desire for the construction of the Temple and for the succession to his kingdom. David, morally, is the good prelate whose desire is for the building of the Church in morals and in faith, and to have worthy successors. "The Lord swore an oath to David," reads the psalm. This oath established that the sons of David would succeed to the throne, signifying that God had provided that the Apostles would have good successors from among their disciples; as, for example, St. Peter was succeeded by St. Clement. The Lord chose Sion and He watched over the succession to the Israelite kingdom. The Christians are His new chosen people and He will do as much for them. The succession means also that God has promised David and His Christian people that the good services of the Church—through the Eucharist and the Holy Spirit—will continue.[46] The problems of the Church are the same for the Old and New Dispensations.

Finally, we see David as the good prelate acting to fire his people with holy zeal. One supposes that the portrait is that of the preaching bishop, at least of one whose actions and words reach down to the lowest levels of his diocese. Lyra explains that in Psalm 143 David arouses himself and others to the praise of God. David speaks as the good prelate, stimulating first his own faith ("I will exalt You my God-king"), and then the others' ("Generation to generation shall praise Your works").[47] David is not a complacent, hypocritical prelate. He feeds the zealous fires of his parishioners out of the flames of his own holy passion. His religious zeal and his joy in God serve as an instructive and contagious example to his flock. They may be one among the qualities of the *"dux bonae dispositionis."* Lyra says that "bonus prelatus per David figuratus." *"Figuratus."* David is the figure of the good prelate, but, as we have seen in the foregoing discussion, his role as a figure is unique and non-Augustinian. Augustine might have made some of David's words prefigure a New Testament or Christian truth that would be brought to fruition in the episcopal vocation. But Nicolaus of Lyra's David is a much more vital figure. He is able to be the good prelate in all his nuances, all his roles. Why? We believe because Lyra was able to see David's psalms—and perhaps the Old Testament as a whole—as primarily a book of pastoral truth, or so it appears from his commentary. Interested in the literal sense of the psalms, Lyra applies David literally and vocationally; thus he can serve as a model, as the first of a type (the good prelate) who is not superseded in his role under the New Covenant. David, as the good prelate, teaches Christian prelates what they must do. His characterization as good prelate is ethical rather than theological. Lyra preaches the *imitatio Davidis.*

We come now to the final broad category which Nicolaus of Lyra constructs around David: David as everyman or, more accurately, David as the just man. We find that the prophet not only acts as the figure of the man Christ, not only represents the Church, not only offers consoling pastoral lessons to the prelacy of Church and state, but also that he becomes the figure of the man of the Christian faith. We believe this last figure, moreover, does not operate solely as an archetype, but that the just man, David, is painted in such a manner that he is a model for the just man of the Christian faith; a model because he operates under the Covenant, the promise in a living faith, Judaism.

We discover him fully delineated as the virtuous man (*homo virtuosus*) in Psalm 88. Here Lyra extolls David as the servant of the Lord; the Lord's anointed, who is "strong of hand."[48] The virtuous man "walks in the ways of the Lord" (Psalm 1–*Beatus vir*), he is as steadfast as is humanly possible. There is, however, a *caveat* built into the humanness of the *vir virtuosus*. Humans can be tempted and they may stray from the righteous path. David, then, is not only the example of the virtuous believer, but he is also the example of the believer who falls into sin. Lusting after Bathsheba, he arranges for her husband Uriah, a captain in his army, to be placed in the front ranks so that he may be killed in battle. Thus David is a homicide.[49] David, the righteous man, has free will; God has "permitted him to be threatened in his goods, as it is said about the unsteady man who loses his goods in his youth," like the Prodigal Son. The man of faith, however, recognizes his sin and he abhors it, as did David, and he seeks God's love and mercy. The psalmist cries to the Lord, "How long?" My life is short, it is all too easy for frail men to sin; have mercy lest all men be sinners. David the murderer is accorded mercy. The enormity of sin does not cause God to renege His Promise to David and other virtuous men. It is right that the mercy of God shine on good men fallen into sin, for otherwise the example of their failing would be used to upbraid and taunt other virtuous men. These taunters mock the anointed of the Lord; the guilty sinner accepts these taunts patiently, awaiting God's beneficence.[50]

Such is the message of Lyra's commentary on this psalm, which is a dialogue between the psalmist and God about the virtuous man, David. He remains human, liable to sin; having sinned, he sincerely regrets his failing and seeks reinstatement as one of God's friends, patiently bearing malicious taunts, concerned only for those other faithful ones to whom he will be a scandal. His repentance and his concern for scandal are the qualities which perhaps most clearly mark David as the *vir virtuosus.* David offers hope, too, to feeble men, hope of reacceptance, based on God's Promise.

This latter point is important. God's covenant has been made with David, who still sins. This puts him into the position of being a *viator,*[51] standing between the beatified and the damned. Clearly from Lyra's words, David fell into mortal sin through homicide. Though having God's Promise on his side, David might have lost his salvation but for his penitence. The virtuous man must certainly fall into error. His actions and attitudes after he has sinned determine his fate. The tenor of Lyra's exposition of the psalm shows explicitly that David's eternal fate was undetermined, able to go either way. He repented and God's promise of salvation became operative again.[52] This is no figurative story. It is the tale of a man of living faith, living under constraints known also to Christians. The *vir virtuosus christianus* must respond to his own sins in the same manner as did the *vir virtuosus judaicus,* David. We have once more discovered the *imitatio Davidis* to be at the root of Lyra's commentary.

Being a virtuous man does not at all exclude the suffering of dire temptations, nor does it exclude sometimes giving way to the snares of the Devil.[53] Temptation is an integral part of virtue, one supposes, for without the former the latter remains untested and unproven.[54] To face the certainty of trial, there are, according to Nicolaus of Lyra, certain psalms of David which are prayers in which David, the just man, seeks God's aid.

Beginning, "Incline Thine ear, O Lord, and answer me," David wrote Psalm 85 asking to be liberated from the persecution of Saul, who is the figure of Satan.[55] Moving from this literal/historical ambiance, Nicolaus of Lyra informs the reader that it can be interpreted as the prayer of any faithful man whose spirit is afflicted by the Devil or whose body is tormented by an evil man, the demon's instrument. He proclaims his indigence, need, and innocence (purity of heart), throwing himself utterly upon God's clemency. "Have mercy on me, Lord, save Thy servant who trusts in Thee."[56]

In his explanation of Psalm 16, Nicolaus of Lyra expands this theme in three ways: in terms of the innocence of the suffering one, in terms of God's justice, and in terms of the evil quality of the pursuer (Saul-demon). As to the first, Lyra says that the just man proclaims the justice of his cause, his innocence. Second, he prays God to vindicate him, to come to him in the "dark night of the soul" as doctors visit the sick in order medicinally to restore them to health. Since there is no iniquity to be found in him, though there is danger that it might be inflicted upon him, the virtuous man seeks deliverance from evil through His mercy—for without God's help none could survive temptation. Third, protect me, he says; protect the just man from the demon-pursuer lest his iniquities defeat the unaided man of virtue. Evil temptations and machinations surround the just man to destroy his honor. He has need of God.[57]

That this struggle between the just man and the demonic temptations afflicting him can best be described as a kind of warfare is demonstrated by Nicolaus of Lyra in his *postilla* on Psalm 142. In this psalm David remains the just man, but Goliath has replaced Saul as the figure of the evil tempter. David again reflects upon the needed divine assistance, for, just as in earthly war the combatants fight with their own hands, so against acts of sin the war must be waged by God Himself.[58] David is again the *viator* and, thus, a fitting example of how the Christian should act in time of tribulation.[59]

Lyra's David offers an edifying example of the *viator* in another generalized instance. In Psalm 26, the historical parallelism that we have noted in various parts of the above discussion is absent. Instead, we find that Nicolaus of Lyra practices the kind of allegorizing that was so prominent a feature of Augustine's interpretations. The result, however, is not the same as it was so often in St. Augustine — a Christological explanation. Rather, Lyra allegorizes in order to represent David as the man of faith in the midst of his earthly pilgrimage. Literally, the psalm concerns the situation of David when, after the death of Saul at Ebron, he commenced his reign over the tribe of Judah. The first years of David's rule were fraught with dangers since his enemies still flourished. The little kingdom over which David was to reign represents, morally, his own spiritual state; the enemies betoken the threats to the health of his soul. The literal condition of the psalm is matched by the fact that Nicolaus of Lyra interprets it in such a way that it is analogous to the entering of the faithful man into adulthood. David, the man who would be pious, must begin his majority by always regulating the agitations (*motus*) of his soul. He invokes God's assistance in controlling his passions.[60]

The passage from adolescence to the moral responsibilities of adulthood is not the only biographical moment signalled by David. The death of the faithful man is perhaps the most important event in a man's life, for it is at that instant that the final decision will be made by God as to whether the *viator* finds his final abode among the blessed or the damned. The psalm David wrote when filled with anxiety in the cave is the prayer at the approach of death. This is the prayer that St. Francis of Assisi is said to have recited faithfully as he approached his end.[61]

The sum of all the foregoing discussion is that Nicolaus of Lyra finds an equivalency between the just or virtuous men of the Old and New Testaments. Lyra discovers a correspondence in the spiritual turmoils encountered by the *viator* operating under both the Old and the New Dispensations. This means that Lyra was less scornful of the religion of the Old Testament than, for example, Origen, Ambrose, and Augustine. The parity between the spiritual experiences in the Old and New Testaments is thus established by Nicolaus of Lyra. Secondly, because David emerges as the *viator*, Lyra is able to use him devotionally and pastorally. David's example is edifying to all men who would be virtuous, and so David's example is worthy of study and of being preached to the faithful. The only thing that separates David from Christians is Christ, though perhaps since he knew of and prophesied the Messiah, even this difference is minimal. In short, the pious Christian would do well to read the Psalms, not only to find the Christological mysteries explained, but in order to grow in faith. David's viability as a perfect man of faith under the Mosaic law may be due to the fact that, as Lyra stated (see above, page 28), David enjoyed the constant infusion of the Holy Spirit; it is this divine animation which is sought by and necessary for the virtuous man to keep him from faltering, both in the Judaic and the Christian eras.

Nicolaus of Lyra creates still another type of image of David, linking him with specific Christians. We hesitate to stipulate this as another broad category, for it fits well into the existing spectrum which we have delineated. This type of exegetical technique, however, is significant enough for us to have not included it within the four categories.

Nicolaus of Lyra's scholarly fascination with the literal sense of the psalms, which allowed him to find parallels between the events of the Church, the attitudes of prelates, and the pilgrim's progress of the individual man and the story of David, also led him to establish more specific parallel relationships between David and the Christian era. We have already seen how David's prayer at the coming of death finds its equivalent in the thoughts on final things by the father of the Franciscans. Moreover, we have noted the equivalency within the context of the Old Testament itself between David and the prophet Daniel.[62]

The prayer of David the just man is taken up again in Psalm 59, wherein David begins, "Deliver me from my enemies, O my God." The historical context is that Saul had sent his men to kill David in his house, from which danger David won salvation through Michal's warning. Here David foreshadows any just man who escapes the danger of death by divine assistance. But the moral sense of the psalm especially refers to one particular just man of the New Covenant who found himself in a roughly parallel danger: St. Peter, who was incarcerated, faced capital punishment, and escaped imminent death with the aid of an angel (Acts 12:6-11). The prayer, then, is more than the offering of any just man, but is the prayer of St. Peter and his Church. Like David, Peter suffered not for any sin of his own; he suffered for God's justice.[63] Thus, Psalm 59 forms a kind of prophecy that has its fulfillment in the New Testament. Christ, however, is not the one who fulfills the literal event, but, rather, it is St. Peter.

In two psalms which have as their subject the good prelate, Nicolaus of Lyra turns the interpretations of the psalms to a specific person. Psalms 70 and 116 refer to the martyred "good prelate" of the twelfth century, Thomas à Becket, Archbishop of Canterbury. In the former of these psalms, David and the martyred saint pray for deliverance and for the welfare of their spiritual flocks. David's persecution by his son Absalom finds its allegorical-historical counterpart in the untoward treatment of Becket by his spiritual son, King Henry II. David's deliverance from this evil occurred during his own lifetime. The good bishop's liberation came through martyrdom and his reception into the kingdom of God. The latter psalm (116) is morally a thanksgiving for the coming of Christ. It continues as the prelate's incitement of his fold to reflect upon the advantage of trusting in God's steadfast Promise rather than hoping in princes whose motives are self-seeking. Every good prelate must endure the harshness of persecution, a point made manifestly obvious in the case of St. Thomas à Becket, in whose person David says, "The nations all encompassed me, for, living in the manner of their country they sought to kill me, and in the Lord's name I crushed them." Cut off by the Lord, they died terribly, and Thomas of Canterbury was borne to the glory of Paradise.[64] The man, even the king, who would bring low the Lord's anointed, whether he be David or the good bishop, must needs be defeated in his purpose. David, the good prelate, rejoices and looks to the coming of Christ; Becket, the good prelate, accepts his fate at the hands of Henry, knowing that the justice of God will avenge him, concerned only with the spiritual welfare of his faithful.

The final historical link that Nicolaus of Lyra finds between David and the Christian era involves both two particular individuals and the type they represent. Psalm 63 recalls David's flight into the desert from the persecution of Saul; there David experiences divine consolation in visions. Here Saul, on the moral plane, represents the world, from which David, representing the Christian hermits, seeks to escape in order to taste the undiluted goodness of God. Lyra mentions St. Hilarion and St. Francis as two such anchorites who, by lonely habitation, were able to achieve the ascension of the mind to God; indeed, Lyra reports that St. Francis's body levitated.[65] David, then, is the figure of St. Hilarion and Francis of Assisi and of all religious zealots who feel that in order to commune directly with God they must search out the wasted areas of the earth. David thus becomes for Nicolaus of Lyra a mystic, a world abnegator, attempting (successfully) to discover the essential religious experience.

It should be clear by now that Nicolaus of Lyra's expositions of the psalms of David transcend the chronological limits which he established when describing the purpose of his double literal sense of Scripture in his comment on Isaiah 11:1: "Here the prophet turns again to a description of the mystery of Christ, his main intention"; the double literal sense implied here applies first to the time of Isaiah or the Old Testament, the other to the time of Christ or the New Testament.[66] Certainly, his interpretations of David *in persona Christi* follow the lines set down by St. Augustine, although Lyra's remarks often apply to the suffering of the man Christ rather than to theological constructs (as in Augustine). Indeed, this concern with equating David, as a figure, with the suffering Jesus is no more than had been demanded by the founder of the order to which Nicolaus of Lyra belonged, and of which he was a prominent member. "Throughout his life the goal of Francis' endeavor was not only an outward imitation of Christ . . . but also a personal closeness to Jesus, the Son of Man, in his joys and sorrows, in which the soul of man can in some way share."[67]  Nicolaus of Lyra's concept of David as the *persona* of Jesus echoes St. Francis' sentiment almost exactly. On one level, the study of David, by the reader of the *Postilla super psalmos,* becomes a method of learning how to imitate Christ, the Son of Man.

If Nicolaus of Lyra had confined his Davidic interpretations to the prophet's fulfillment in and by Christ, he would have remained within the limits of Augustine's work on David, as well as within the limits of his own gloss on Isaiah 11:1. But he did not. Instead, Nicolaus of Lyra pushed the *intentio authoris,* David, beyond the limits of the New Testament era. His exegesis of David reached beyond Christ Himself to embrace the apostolic period by equating David with St. Peter, and even extended to the Middle Ages. From St. Hilarion to St. Francis of Assisi, David is, for Lyra, the model for the anchorite whose mystical yearnings find fulfillment through God's gracious response. David is the good prelate of the Middle Ages, the king who is, or is almost, a priest,[68] or the good prelate who attends to the well-being of the Church in his charge.[69]  David as the *vir virtuosus* is a figure who transcends New Testament times, for the parallel is drawn not only between David and St. Peter but also between David and *any* pious faithful. The main lesson Lyra teaches in this category is the need for the *imitatio Davidis* in order to be a just man, or a sinner who repents and rests his hope upon God. Here Lyra goes beyond the above-mentioned imitative and sympathetic goal of St. Francis, but he is still playing a variation on the same theme: the need for a conscious involvement and empathy on the part of the Christian not only with Christ but also with David, the sterling example of God's beloved who goes astray and yet can, with God's help, find his way back to the path of salvation.

This very emphasis on the need for reliance on God's mercy and aid, seen again and again in the equating of David with "any just man" naturally capable of sin, formed an integral part of the programme of the Friars Minor. Their appeal in the towns and villages of Europe rested in large part on the hope they gave to people whose lives included vast amounts of suffering and despair.[70]  For them, after his teachings filtered down from the cloister and university milieu to the mendicant preacher, Lyra's David would offer a readily recognizable example of the good man, fallible to be sure, who, relying on God, had transcended his miserable lot of persecution and had remained the beloved of God.

Nicolaus of Lyra's concern for the cultivation of the perfect Christian prelate, as seen in those psalm expositions in which David becomes the model for this type, must, of course, be partly attributed to the great reforming zeal found in the Franciscan movement, though somewhat broadened from the rather individualistic mystical intentions of the order's guiding spirit, St. Francis of Assisi. Nicolaus of Lyra's preaching of the good–shepherd bishop has, as its ultimate goal, the heightened religious fervor of the laymen who fall under the bishop's supervision. The distribution of duties to capable priests, the need for ethical impeccability, the enthusiasm of the prelate in the love of and reliance on God, all these qualities contribute, as Lyra says, to the spiritual welfare of Christendom. One may surmise still another motivating factor behind Lyra's advocacy of the good prelate. Although the psalm commentaries of Lyra do not allude to this motive, we are justified in presenting it. St. Francis himself probably never imagined that a Friar Minor would be a bishop. Indeed, his concept of his brothers as *minores* or underlings would have made the very idea of a Franciscan episcopacy repugnant to him. Historical circumstances, however, had involved the Friars in the administration of the Church. Friars had been brought into the service of the Church as members of the pope's household, as diplomatic emissaries, in the Inquisition and the Crusades. Finally, Franciscans had become bishops.

The first Franciscan bishop for whom clear evidence exists was Leone Valvassori, appointed Bishop of Milan in 1244 by Innocent IV. Thereafter, we find that many Friars Minor were seated on episcopal thrones: in 1274, just after Nicolaus of Lyra's birth, there were thirty-two Franciscan bishops, and in 1311 there were fifty-six.[71] Aside from his broader goal in equating David with the good bishop, Nicolaus of Lyra may have intended moral instruction for the propagation of proper actions and attitudes among those of the Franciscan Community who had been or were to be appointed bishops.

Nicolaus of Lyra's association of David with the crusading ideal would also prick the consciences of those who still responded to it in the first half of the fourteenth century. The preaching of the crusade was, moreover, another element added to the Franciscan programme to meet the exigencies of the papacy. In 1227, Pope Gregory IX requested the Friars Minor to preach the crusade and to accompany the Christian army to the battlefront. Again in 1245, when the Patriarch of Jerusalem appealed to Innocent IV, the pontiff turned to the Franciscans as an ally in the endeavor. Since King Louis IX was to lead the Christian host, naturally the French mendicants, in their sermons, urged men to volunteer or to contribute monetary aid. Though the results were disappointing, the attempt was made once more to raise the needed force for the same leader, Louis IX. By this time, however, the eastern Christian kingdom had been lost.[72] It is rather obvious that Lyra's equation of David with the Church militant and the *dux bonae dispositionis* is the continuation, if somewhat belated, of this Franciscan duty of preaching the crusade. David, then, would be the symbol of the Church persecuted in the Holy Land as well as the symbol of the pious and righteous leader of such a venture. This teaching, drawn from the example of David and the Psalms themselves, would carry the moral weight of Scripture and righteousness.

The foregoing remarks thus delineate the probable influences working upon the Davidic interpretations offered by Nicolaus of Lyra. David as the man Christ, as the figure for the crusade, as the good prelate, and as the just man who must needs suffer persecution and spiritual tribulation, all these themes are found in the literature and operations of the Franciscan movement up to the time of Lyra. They help to explain the specific purposes to which the concepts of David were put. They do not, however, fully elucidate the uniqueness of Lyra's concepts of David when compared to the Davidic exegesis of men like St. Augustine. The complete explanation follows, we believe, from two factors which conjoin in Nicolaus of Lyra's Psalm commentary to make David the *viator* comparable to the Christian *viator,* whether he be the Church militant on the road to becoming the Church triumphant, the prelate constantly striving for perfection, or the layman working his way spiritually through the "dark woods" of this life to the glory of the next. These two factors are Lyra's concentration on the literal sense of the psalm passages as the foundation upon which the higher exegesis is built, and the imitation that Nicolaus of Lyra seemingly preaches, which is a corollary to the normal Franciscan emphasis of fostering conformity with Christ.

Nicolaus of Lyra's real concern for the double literal sense, whereby the intention of David applies both to his own special circumstances and, in a parallel manner, to the theme of the just man, the prelate, etc., is a perilous road. It might have been possible for Lyra to go from the literal situation to higher Christological truths, as did Augustine and as some exegetes would do in the Renaissance.[73] However, the parallels that Nicolaus of Lyra draws between David in the psalms and the higher lessons contained in them are pastoral ones.

We might note, first of all, that Nicolaus of Lyra eschews discussing the controversies that plagued theologians during his lifetime.  The forces of strict adherence to the Franciscan rule and the advocates of relaxation produced a not insignificant number of tracts by Franciscans in the late thirteenth and the early fourteenth century.  The controversy concerning the poverty of Christ (and consequently whether the Church should be wealthy) intensified during the reign of Pope John XXII (1316-1334).[74]  Finally, the nascent doctrine of the Immaculate Conception fostered attacks and counter-attacks from the pens of the maculists and the immaculists.  This *querelle* had its inception with Duns Scotus' critique of Thomas Aquinas.  Scotus' influence spread rapidly through Franciscan thought at Oxford and Paris (and was generally accepted among Franciscans by the second half of the fourteenth century).[75]  Surely Lyra knew of the debate on the Immaculate Conception, for Scotus had died in 1308 and in that year Nicolaus of Lyra's figure was sculpted on Scotus' tomb where Lyra is called one of the "most famous doctors of the Church."[76]

We might expect that Nicolaus of Lyra, writing his *Postilla super psalmos* in the heyday of these controversies, would not only make reference to them but also would use the psalms and David to present his views on these issues.  It would not be too far-fetched to imagine Psalm 63 (see page 37 above) on the flight of David into the desert—which Lyra refers to the anchorites—eliciting from Nicolaus of Lyra some comment on hermits forsaking worldly goods and on the need for apostolic poverty and also the hard Franciscan rule; the very fact that he mentions St. Francis, a strict observant of the rule of poverty, would have offered Lyra the perfect opportunity for such comments.  Instead, Nicolaus of Lyra gives the reader no indication of the moral-theological struggles which rent his Order or the Church in the early fourteenth century.  He refuses to utilize David for polemical purposes; he preaches no theological doctrine through David as had Augustine.

Although he could have done otherwise, Nicolaus of Lyra puts his concepts of David to work, as we have said, pastorally.  He teaches through David the *vita religiosa*.  By looking at the literal sense of the Psalms,[77] Nicolaus of Lyra finds in David a man of faith both in his official duties and in his private person.  The literal/historical situations in which David finds himself bear, for Lyra, all the marks of the career of the Christian man of faith, be he prelate or layman.  Because of this equivalency or parallel, David, like the Christian, becomes a *viator*.  There is no moment at which David's salvation appears certain or settled.  He is the Lord's anointed, of course, but by this Lyra means the good man of faith who receives God's grace as an aid to salvation.  He is forever capable of failing, of losing his salvation: Bathsheba, Uriah, the demonic temptations and persecutions of Saul, they all offer opportunity to sin.  And sin David does.  Lyra emphasizes David's repentance after which God's promise of help is restored.  How like this is to the Christian:  he is in *The* Church, yet he sins; but with repentance comes the renewal of the covenant.  Salvation is assured neither to David nor to the Christian *viator*, but if they try, if they grieve over their faults, they may gain the ultimate reward.

Lyra has no need to plunge into the heady Davidic interpretations of Augustine.  It is easy enough for Lyra to proceed from the literal events in the era of the Old Covenant to the parallel events in the period of the New Dispensation.  Whether the analogy concerns the Church, the prelate, the anchorite, Becket, or the faithful Christian, the lines of comparison are drawn clearly without subtle maneuverings.  This is possible because David lived in the ambiance of a religion founded on God's Promise, as does the Christian.  By relying on trust in the Lord, and doing his best, the Jewish David differs only theologically from the Christian.  As far as living the faith and living spiritually in the faith are concerned, David offers an *exemplum* for the Christian.  Lyra's *Postilla* is part of the literature of *exempla* that so intrigued the

Franciscans.[78] Finding edifying examples of *viatores* in the Bible, and in Nicolaus of Lyra's *Postilla,* the Franciscan preachers could more handily preach spiritual reformation. The example of David was one method of teaching the spiritual life. In Lyra we find not the *imitatio Christi,* but the *imitatio Davidis* which instructs the faithful and the officials of the Church how to find their salvation and contribute to the good of the Church.

And, finally, since David is the example for Christians because they both live in the knowledge of God's Promise and therefore rely on Him, the Old Testament and its religion are salvaged in a way impossible with the allegorizing of Origen or St. Augustine. Lyra shows that the Old Testament is worthy of study and David is worthy of emulation on the spiritual and pastoral level, if not on the theological-doctrinal level where Christ is still needed for its fulfillment. Christian commentators no longer have to be embarrassed by the Old Testament patriarchs.[79]

## NOTES

[1]Smalley, *op. cit.,* pp. 14-19, discusses the Antiochian school. See also Chapter I, note 3, above. Some of the greatest exponents of the literal/historical method of interpretation in the Middle Ages were the Victorines. They studied the rabbinic commentaries on the Old Testament and, as legend has it, Hugh of St. Victor actually conversed with Rashbam (the grandson of Rashi) in the Abbey of St. Victor's gardens (Smalley, *op. cit.,* p. 104). For a discussion of the Victorines, see *ibid.,* pp. 83-111 and Preus, *op. cit.,* pp. 24-37.

[2]Two books deserve special mention for their analyses of the exegetical work of Nicolaus of Lyra: Herman Hailperin, *Rashi and the Christian Scholars* (Pittsburgh: University of Pittsburgh Press, 1963) and Preus, *op. cit.* Also see Gosselin, *art. cit.,* pp. 399-403 for a bio-bibliographical summary on Lyra. Nicolaus of Lyra (ca. 1270-1349) entered the Franciscan Order about 1300 and he became a Master of Theology in 1308. Until 1330, Lyra served in various administrative posts; at that time he resigned as the Provincial of Burgundy and returned to purely scholarly activities, resulting in the completion of his most important exegetical work (see below, note 9). He died in Paris and was buried in the convent of the Cordeliers (where the Ecole de Médicine now stands).

[3]Gosselin, *art. cit.,* pp. 401 and 406.

[4]*Ibid.,* p. 402.

[5]Hailperin, *op. cit.,* p. 252; John Moorman, *A History of the Franciscan Order from Its Origins to the Year 1517* (Oxford: Oxford University Press, 1968), pp. 395-396; Preus, *op. cit.,* pp. 61-62. Hailperin claims Nicolaus of Lyra "may be called the greatest early Bible Scholar after Jerome"; Moorman says that he is the "most notable commentator of the 14th century"; and Preus remarks that Lyra is to be considered "perhaps the greatest Christian commentator of Scripture in the Middle Ages."

[6]Quoted in H. Labrosse, "Biographie de Nicholas de Lyre," *Etudes Franciscaines,* 16 (1906), p. 383. There is a variant which reads: "Si Lyra non lyrasset/ Ecclesia Dei non saltasset."

[7]For a tentative evaluation of Lyra's influence on other Protestant reformers besides Luther, see Gosselin, *art. cit.,* p. 401.

[8]The latter concept will be dealt with again in Chapter III when we treat Lefèvre d'Etaples.

[9]The *Postilla litteralis* was written in the years between 1322 and 1331; the *Postilla moralis* was composed in 1339. They were variously printed separately and together. See Gosselin, *art. cit.,* pp. 406-411 for a listing of these editions. The *editio princeps* of the *Postilla litteralis et moralis super totam bibliam* appeared in five volumes in 1471-1472 (Rome: Sweynheym and Pannartz). It was the first biblical commentary to issue from the printing press.

[10]See Gosselin, *art. cit.,* p. 400; Hailperin, *op. cit., passim;* and T. Plassmann, "Nicolaus de Lyra," *The Catholic Encyclopedia,* 11 (New York: Robert Appleton, Co., 1911), p. 63.

[11]Lyra's concern for the literal/historical sense can be clearly seen by merely perusing through his literal expositions of the first several psalms in the *Postilla litteralis super psalterium* (Mantua: Paulus Johannis de Putsbach, 1477). (HR 10376; Gosselin, *art. cit.,* no. 83.)

[12]Nicolaus of Lyra, *Postilla litteralis in Vetus et Novum Testamentum* (Venice: Octavianus Scotus, 1488), Vol. II, fol. aa recto. (Cf. Hailperin, *op, cit.,* pp. 232-234, and Gosselin, *art. cit.,* no. 36). Lyra here relies on the authority of Jerome (PL 22, col. 1169) and Rashi rather than on Jerome and "omnes doctores hebraicos." Origen (PG 12, col. 1066) had defended the plurality of authorship, but Ambrose (PL 14, col. 923) and Augustine (PL 41, col. 547) believed David was the only author. Jerome and Rashi listed ten known psalmists. In siding with these two, Lyra went against the authority not only of Ambrose and Augustine but also of the Talmud and Midrash. The Protestants would also follow Lyra and Rashi. (Hereafter, the above-cited 1488 edition will be referred to as: "N of L, PL, 1488, Vol. I/II, fol. —— ".)

[13]N of L, PL, 1488, II, fol. ff8 recto. (Cf. Hailperin, *op. cit.,* pp. 232-233, 350-351, n. 734.)

[14]N of L, PL, 1488, II, fol. BB6 recto: "Hic propheta revertitur ad describendum Christi mysterium: quod erat suum principale intentum."

[15]N of L, PL, 1488, I, fol. l₃ verso. The full text reads: "Potest etiam aliter exponi: ut referatur ad sensum litteralem tantum sicut et aliae. Circa quod considerandum, quod eadem littera habet aliquando duplicem sensum litteralem. verbi gratia: I Paral. 17 [:13] dicit dominus de Salomone: 'Ego ero illi in patrem et ipse erit mihi in filium.' Et intelligitur de Salomone ad litteram. . . . Predicta enim auctoritas impleta fuit ad litteram in Salomone, minus tamen perfecte, quia fuit Dei filius solum per gratiam. In Christo autem perfectius, qui est Dei filius per naturam. Licet tamen utraque expositio sit litteralis simpliciter, secunda tamen, que est de Christo, spiritualis et mystica est secundum quid, inquantum Salomon fuit figura Christi." (This is from the "Prologus secundus de intentione auctoris"; see also Preus, *op. cit.,* p. 68.)

[16]Oberman, *Forerunners,* pp. 286-289; see also Chapter III, below, for a discussion of the dominance of the second literal sense, the *sensus propheticus,* in Lefèvre d'Etaples.

[17]We are indebted to Hailperin, *op. cit.,* for the following section on prophecy. In the Talmudic literature, the Pentateuch, written by Moses, was considered of higher value than the later books of the prophets. Indeed, to the rabbis, the later prophetic books (including the Psalms) were merely commentaries on the Torah. (Cf. Hailperin, *op. cit.,* pp. 223 and 345, n. 659.)

[18]The Roman Catholic Church apparently later adopted Aquinas' position on Moses as normative. See the article by Jean Calès entitled "Prophecy" in *The Catholic Encyclopedia* 12 (New York: Robert Appleton, Co., 1911), p. 477: "Moses, . . . holding a degree of authority unequalled till the coming of Jesus Christ." The criteria for this judgment are the same as for Aquinas' (Deut. 34:10 ff., Num. 12:7, and the fact that God manifested Himself only to Moses in audible speech, not in dreams and visions).

[19]N of L, PL, 1488, II, fol. aa2 verso (prologue to the Psalms): ". . . quod illud est verbum Josue [scribentis de Moyse, et tempore Josue] non surrexerat propheta maior Moyse. Tamen non est contra illud dictum quod postea maior surrexerit. Et oportet hoc dicere saltem de prophetis novi Testamenti." (Cf. Hailperin, *op. cit.,* p. 347, n. 669; Hailperin erroneously cites Vol. III rather than Vol. II.)

[20]N of L, PL, 1488, II, fol. aa2 verso: "Et ideo cum finis sit nobilior his quae sunt ad finem, prophetia David videtur sortiri quandam excellentiam." (Cf. Hailperin, *op. cit.,* p. 347, n. 672.)

[21]N of L, PL, 1488, II, fol. aa2 verso: "Quartus autem gradus prophetiae proprie dictae est quando sine apparitione alicuius figurae vel signi sensibilis capitur veritas intelligibilis de occultis per Divinam revelationem. Et hoc modo factae sunt revelationes ipsi David, ut dicitur in principio Glossae super [librum Psalmorum]. (Cf. Hailperin, *op. cit.,* p. 348, n. 698.)

[22]N of L, PL, 1488, II, fol. aa recto: "Alii prophetae per quasdam rerum imagines atque verborum tegumenta prophetaverunt, David autem solus Spiritus sancti instinctu sine omni exteriori adminiculo suam edidit prophetiam." (Cf. Hailperin, *op. cit.,* p. 350, n. 722.)

[23]We shall discuss the elaboration of these themes by the Protestants in Chapters V and VI.

[24]Nicolaus of Lyra, *Postilla moralis super psalterium,* in *Postilla moralis super totam bibliam* (Cologne: Johannes Koelhof de Lübeck, 1478). (Gosselin, *art. cit.,* no. 60.) Lyra's commentary on the Psalms runs from fol. p7 recto to fol. v8

verso. Hereafter, this edition will be cited as: "N of L, PM, Ps. —— , fol(l). —— ." The present reference is to Ps. 10, foll. q1 verso - q2 recto: "Psalmum istum litteraliter exposui de confidentia David qui monitus [ab] Agad propheta venit ad manendum in terra Israhel ut habetur I. Reg. xxii, Confidens quod dominus eum protegeret a Saul et aliis eius inimicis, licet monitus fuisset a viris suis extra terram Israhel habitare.  Allegorice vero exponi potest de Christo per David figurato.  Nam et ipsi Christo similiter persuasum fuit quod exiret de terra propter persecutionem Herodis. . . . Et sicut David non assensit viris suis, sic nec Christus talibus verbis. . . . Sic ergo in persona Christi hominis dicatur 'In domino confido'."

[25]One might well question the legitimacy of suggesting that Lyra is advising the Christian reader to place his trust in the Father, and that the lesson seeks to instruct the Christian public.  Certainly, no such explanation of his purpose is explicitly proffered by Lyra.  It would make little sense, however, for Lyra to urge Christian confidence if this advice were not to be directed at a larger audience than that of the scholarly clerical world.  Since, as we shall see below, Franciscan teaching was ultimately aimed at the edification of a lay audience, and since his *postillae* were often published separately as sermons, one can only surmise that their purpose was inherently to reach and instruct laymen *via* preaching friars; indeed, they often relied on stock books of sermons and lessons.

[26]N of L, PM, Ps. 35, fol. r2 verso.  Lyra does not discuss what form this divine retribution took in the case of David. He does, however, make it utterly clear who was the avenging angel for the mystical level of the psalm: " 'Judica domine' . . . puniendo eos secundum ordinem iustitiae tuae . . . quod factum fuit per exercitum romanorum qui debellavit Iudeos in ultionem mortis Christi et discipulorum suorum:  et in hoc Romanus exercitus fuit divinum instrumentum."

[27]N of L, PM, Ps. 58, fol. s2 verso:  "Psalmum istum fecit David quando dormiente Saul cum exercitu tulit hastam qui ad caput eius erat, et per hoc ostendit quod potuerat eum iugulasse si voluisset, et per hoc arguit falsitatem illorum qui dicebant ipsum quaerere Saulis mortem.  Allegorice vero potest exponi de Christo qui solum verbo quaerentes eum ad mortem prostravit et hic suam potentiam declaravit. . . ."

[28]Perhaps this tendency to see David offering parallel examples to medieval times influenced the Protestant theologians to apply Davidic events to their own time.

[29]The events are described in 1 Samuel 23.

[30]N of L, PM, Ps. 55, fol. s1 recto.  Lyra's reference to Acts is erroneous:  " . . . ut habetur act. viii et viiii."

[31]See 2 Samuel 5:17.

[32]N of L, PM, Ps. 122, fol. v4 recto:  "Psalmum istum fecit David pro liberatione sua et sui exercitus a Philisteis eum quaerentibus occidere cum audissent eum unctum esse regem super Israel. . . . Mistice vero potest exponi de Christo et eius fidelibus quorum nomen quaesierunt extinguere Iudei post eius assumptionem a dextris Dei . . .; et sic in persona ecclesiae dicitur 'Nisi quia Dominus erat in nobis etc.,' scilicet per custodiam specialem. . . ."

[33]N of L, PM, Ps. 61, fol. s3 verso:  "Psalmum istum fecit David pro sua evasione de manu Saulis et eius exercitus qui cingebant David . . . ut habetur 1 Regum xxii.  Allegorice vero potest exponi de evasione ecclesiae a persecutione crudeli romani emperii maxime tempore dyocletiani et maximiani. . . ."

[34]N of L, PM, Ps. 5, foll. p8 recto & verso:  "David fecit . . . ad cantandum per sacerdotes . . . pro conservatione regni Israel in quo erant xii tribuum haereditates.  Sic ergo allegorice iste psalmus est oratio ecclesiae contra infideles terram sanctam occupantes. . . . Iste psalmus dici debet ab ecclesiae ministris cum mentis attentione et debita pronunciatione et magna devotione. . . . 'Neque habitabit iuxta te malignus,' q.d. non est dignum ut Saracenus vel alius infidelis habitet iuxta sepulcrum tuum; 'neque permanebunt iniusti ante oculos tuos,' id est, non decet quod increduli maneant in terra super quam sunt oculi tui. . . . 'Perdas omnes qui loquuntur mendacium,' id est perdas Saracenos qui falso dicunt Machometum vilissimum fuisse prophetam domini magnum. . . . Ergo hi viri sanguinum dicuntur machometus et tenentes legem eius quae gladio cepit et per gladium tenetur.  Et, ut dicunt aliqui doctores, per gladium terminabitur. . . ."

[35]That is, Augustine's method of referring David to Christ and the Church.

[36]On the universality of this practice, see, for example, Augustin Renaudet, *Préréforme et humanisme à Paris pendant les premières guerres d'Italie (1494-1517)* (Paris: Librairie d'Argence, 1953), p. 55.

[37]N of L, PM, Ps. 19, fol. q5 verso:  ". . . mistice vero est oratio ecclesiae pro Christianis contra infideles pugnaturis, ut dicatur 'exaudiat te domine' catholice exercitus 'in die tribulationis,' id est belli mortalis, 'protegat te nomen dei Jacob' quod interpretatur supplantator ut sit sensus:  virtus divini nominis ponat inimicos tuos sub pedibus tuis. 'Mittat tibi auxilium de sancto,' id est ex merito Christi qui est sanctus sanctorum, 'et de Syon tueatur te,' per meritum ecclesiae per Syon significatae. . . . Hic describitur pugnandi modus cum dicitur 'hi in corribus,' id est infideles

confidunt in virtute humana; nos autem in divina. Ipsi obligati sunt, id est peccatorum funibus ligati. 'Et ceciderunt' iam spiritualiter et utinam cadant corporaliter. 'Nos autem surreximus,' scilicet a peccatis. Procedentes enim ad bellum etiam iustum debent esse vere contriti et confessi ut sic pro defensione fidei vel iusticiae audeant mori. 'Et erecti sumus,' scilicet in spe obtinendae victoriae a Deo . . . , 'Domini salvum me fac regem,' id est exercitus ducem qui dici potest rex a regendo licet non sit rex ex statu vel officio etc. . . ."

[38]N of L, PM, Ps. 64, foll. s4 recto & verso: "Psalmum istum dicitur fecisse David loquens in persona Danielis, quem praevidit mittendum in locum leonum et inde divinitus liberandum. Allegorice vero per Danielem qui dicitur vir desideriorum significatur Christus . . . . Ipse vero per invidiam fuit morti traditus et in agonia passionis imminentis positus oravit patrem. Et de eius oratione potest exponi Psalmus iste ut in eius persona dicatur."

[39]By "layered" we mean that Augustine's allegorical interpretations of David do not exhibit a close, parallel relationship between the actions or attitudes of David and those of Christ. Instead, Augustine's interpretations usually proceed from the interpretation of names (e.g., Architophel means "the ruin of his brother") or from the symbolic meanings of Old Testament scenes (e.g., in the battle between David and Goliath, the five stones symbolize the Pentateuch and the riverbed symbolizes the ancient Jews). Thus, the *gesta et verba Davidis* are overlaid by New Testament meanings which bear little resemblance to the Old Testament events.

[40]Lyra's words (see footnote 41, below), "unctio pontificalis," certainly refer to popes. Lewis and Short's *Latin Dictionary* states that "pontifex" means a bishop, in the Christian era. Perhaps Lyra intends also the episcopal coronation. The text does not make this point clear, so we shall give the word the narrower meaning of "pope" with the understanding that it can also apply to bishops.

[41]N of L, PM, Ps. 27, fol. q8 recto: "Hunc psalmum fecit David quando debuit inungi rex super Israhel universum, ii Reg. II. Moraliter autem potest esse oratio preparantis se ad suscipiendum unctionem pontificalem vel regiam devote in qua tria petuntur sine quibus neutrum regnum potest bene procedere; scilicet constantia contra malignos insultus, diligentia divini cultus ibi 'unam petii etc.,' perseverantia in bonis actibus. . . ."

[42]This point is borne out in Lyra's exposition of Psalm 100 which, he says, David wrote when he found himself confirmed as king over Israel. Comparing King David to the good prelate, Lyra writes: "Moraliter autem potest exponi de quolibet rege bono vel prelato quia rex est in spiritualibus." He continues by citing 1 Peter 2:9, "Vos estis genus electum regale sacerdotium, etc." (N of L, PM, Ps. 100, fol. T7 recto.)

[43]Since Lyra occasionally gives a restrictive meaning to "prelatus" (see note 45, below, where it means "bishop"), there is some ambiguity in the words "bonus prelatus secularis vel religiosus." It could mean "a good and religious king" or "a good prelate (ruler), lay or ecclesiastical, king or bishop." We believe that Lyra intends the latter meaning. This interpretation is substantiated by his later comments on Psalm 27, where he clearly speaks both of secular and ecclesiastical rulers. For example, in commenting on verse 3 ("Ne tradideris in animas tribulantium me"), Lyra writes: ". . . id est, in voluntates demonum qui sunt testes iniqui et mendaces contra homines, et maxime contra pontifices et reges quos magis nituntur subvertere propter altitudinis statum. . . ." Moreover, Lyra cites 1 Peter 2, referring to verses 5 and 9: "Be you yourselves as living stones, built thereon into spiritual houses, a holy priesthood to offer sacrifices acceptable to God through Jesus Christ. . . ."; and, "You, however, are a chosen people, a royal priesthood, a holy nation, a purchased people. . . ." Lyra clearly does not suggest that these lines restrict the meaning of "prelatus" to ecclesiastics, for he says (PM, Ps. 27, fol. q8 verso), ". . . id est, eucaristiam que offeretur cum laudibus divinis quem offerunt pontifices per seipsos, et principes per alios . . . ." Historically, after the Carolingian era, certain sacerdotal attributes were claimed by and accorded to kings and emperors. Cf. the elaborate discussions of sacerdotal kingship in Ernst Kantorowicz, *The King's Two Bodies: A Study in Mediaeval Political Theology* (Princeton: Princeton University Press, 1957) and in Marc Bloch, *Les Rois thaumaturges: études sur le charactère surnaturel attribué à la puissance royale particulièrement en France et Angleterre* (Paris: Armand Colin, 1961.)

[44]Lyra may be alluding to that commingling of duties among secular and mendicant clergy which wreaked so much havoc during and after Lyra's time. Cf. Renaudet, *op. cit.,* pp. 10-21, who touches upon this rivalry between the secular and regular clergy in and around Paris, and the consequent confusion of duties. Cf. Y.M.-J. Congar, "Aspects ecclésiologiques de la querelle entre mendiants et séculiers dans la seconde moitié du XIIIè siècle et le début du XIVè siècle," *Archives d'Histoire Doctrinale et Littéraire du Moyen Age,* 36 (1961), pp. 35-151. Cf. also Erasmus' colloquy, *The Funeral,* for a satirical portrayal of this same problem in the sixteenth century. N of L, PM, Ps. 60, foll. s3 recto & verso: "Psalmum istum fecit David lamentans destructionem terrae Israel antequam veniret ad regnum et deprecans devote Dominum pro eius reformatione. Moraliter autem per David qui fuit pastor ovium, postea rex, significatur bonus prelatus secularis vel religiosus secundum illud pe. ii, 'Vos estis genus, etcetera'. . . . qui peccata populi sui plorat, et pro eius reformatione Deum orat. . . . Ideo per ipsam onus impositum episcopis significatur, quod

bene dividitur quando officium praedicandi et confessiones audiendi personis ydoneis committitur. . . ."
Apparently David was successful in recalling his people to the ways of the Lord. Psalm 106 is the expression of David's joy over this turn of events. Mystically, it is the prayer of the good prelate for his people's adherence to the Ten Commandments and for their faith in the Trinity: "Psalmus iste secundum litteralem sensum est exultatio in Deo pro statu regni sui meliorato. Et mistice potest exponi de bono prelato seculari vel religioso in Domino gaudente de subditorum suorum melioratione . . . ." (N of L, PM, Ps. 106, fol. vl verso.)

[45]N of L, PM, Ps. 100, foll. t7 recto & verso: ". . . intendente [sic] ad tria dicta studere et quantum ad primum dicit, 'Misericordiam et iudicium cantabo tibi Domine,' in prosperis tuam misericordiam laudando et in adversis tuam iusticiam confitendo. . . . Quantum ad secundum dicit, 'perambulabam' id est perfecte ambulabam, 'in innocentia cordis mei,' id est, sine falsa fictione exteriore. . . . Quantum ad tertium dicit, 'non proponebam ante oculos meos rem iniustam' ad faciendum eam scienter. 'Facientes praevaricationes odivi,' quantum ad culpam sed non quantum ad naturam. 'Non adhesit mihi etcetera,' id est non approbabam sed condemnabam . . . 'Oculi mei ad fideles terrae,' ad ipsos promovendum 'ut sedeant mecum' in consiliis et iudiciis. 'Ambulans in via immaculata hic mihi ministrabat,' nam familia principis et prelati debet esse munda et honesta. . . . 'In matutino etcetera,' celeriter ad precanendum de infectione aliorum. 'Interficiebam omnes peccatores terrae,' materiali gladio quantum ad principes et spirituali quantum ad prelatos, 'ut disperderem de ciuitate domini etc.,' id est, de communitate bonorum ne per malos interficiantur."

[46]N of L, PM, Ps. 130, fol. v5 verso: " . . . Moraliter autem per David intelligetur bonus prelatus qui desiderat edificationem ecclesiae in moribus et fide et bonum successorem habere . . . . 'Juravit dominus,' hic agitur de secundo, scilicet de bono successore in ecclesiae regimine, . . . per iuramentum enim Domini factum David quod filii sui succederent sibi significatum fuit quod Deus paratus est providere pastoribus bonis de successoribus in discipulis suis, sicut beato Petro providit de sancto Clemente . . . et sic de aliis pluribus. Ideo subditur 'de fructu etc.,' id est de filiis tuis spiritualibus nutritis tua doctrina."

[47]N of L, PM, Ps. 143, fol. v8 recto: ". . . David se et alios excitat ad Dei laudem. Sensus moralis est ut bonus prelatus per David figuratus ad laudem Domini excitet se primo et consequenter populum Christianum. Quantum ad primum in eius persona dicitur, 'exaltabo te Deus . . .,' id est, quantum potero te laudabo. . . . Hic consequenter ponitur aliorum excitatio ad laudandum cum dicitur, 'generatio et generatio laudabunt opera tua,' id est, omnes homines presentes et futuri. . . ." Indeed, there is a kind of circuit established by Lyra from David to his people, and, analogously, from the good prelate to the Christian fold. The transference of holy enthusiasm from David-prelate to Jews-Christians can be understood as a specific instance of the virtue of the religious leader and its influence upon the general public, as outlined briefly in N of L, PM, Ps. 129, foll. v4 verso and v5 recto: "Iste psalmus declarat ipsius David humilitatem in bonum populi redundantem, per hoc autem moraliter ostenditur quod bonitas prelati cedit ad bonum populi sibi subiecti. . . . 'Si non humiliter sentiebam etcetera,' id est si non fui humilis corde puniar supple modo, qui sequitur, 'sicut ablactatus super matrem etcetera,' a quo subtrahitur matris mammilla sic a me subtrahatur consolatio divina et quia meritum prelati cedit in bonum populi subditur 'speret Israel in Domino.' "

[48]The implication here is not that of David the anointed king, but rather of David as having been anointed with the covenant, that is, the Promise. Augustine had interpreted David as the "strong-handed" but in such a way that he intended Christ. Lyra's emphasis is on constancy and on the unction of infused grace: ". . . 'Inveni David servum meum,' constantem virum quia David manu fortis interpretatur. 'Oleo sancto meo unxi eum,' scilicet gratiae tanquam pugilem contra dyabolum. Sed quia cum habituali gratia requiritur mocio divina sicut instrumentum perfectum per formam artis agere non potest sine motione artificiis. . . . [V]irtuoso non mentiar," (N of L, PM, Ps. 88, foll. t4 verso - t5 recto.)

[49]Remembering that in Dante's *Inferno* Murderers are placed in circle seven, round one, we might suspect in our further discussion of Psalm 88 that David's readmittance *coram Deo* was made possible because homicide was less of an affront to God than, say, the betrayal of Christ. Yet Lyra, assuming that he roughly accepts the scheme of sins found in Dante, parenthetically adds that David's homicide can be compared with the sin of another just man: Peter's denial of Christ: " . . . licet autem homo sit perfectus in virtute cadere tamen potest Deo permittente et dyabolo procurante, sicut patet de David in facto Urie et de Petro in Christi negatione." (*Ibid.*, fol. t5 recto). The answer, then, is that the man of virtue may fall into any sin; his penitence determines whether God forgives him.

[50]N of L, PM, Ps. 88, foll. t4 verso - t5 verso: Continuing with his comments on Psalm 88 (note 49, above), Lyra writes: "Ideo de tali dicitur, 'Tu vero repulisti etcetera,' post eius casum nam de se cadit in peccatum. . . . 'Prophanasti in terra sanctuarium,' id est prophanari permisisti in terrenis desideriis cor eius quod erat templum spiritus sancti prius. 'Destruxisti omnes saepes eius,' id est, permisisti destrui in eo clausuras virtutum. . . . 'Factus est opprobrium vicinis

suis,' id est, fidelibus aliis . . . . Sed quia . . . penitet et petit misericordiam, ideo dicitur in persona eius . . ., id est quantum fragilis est ad peccatum. 'Numquid vane constituisti omnes filios hominum,' quasi diceret, non quod tamen esset, si non misereris peccatorum cum omnes sint peccatores. 'Ubi sunt misericordiae antiquae Domine' quibus David homicidam et adulterum ad misericordiam recepisti et sic iuramentum propter enormitatem peccatorum suorum non retractasti. 'Memor esto opprobrii servorum tuorum,' quasi diceret, et si non pro me mihi misereris miserere pro servis tuis quibus improperatur peccatum meum, nam peccatum unius personae notabilis improperatur aliis de statu suo . . . . 'Quod exprobraverunt inimici tui,' communicationem meam de bono in malum qui tamen fueram crismate consecratus tibi; et quoniam talia opprobria pacienter sunt tolleranda maxime ab eo que est culpa [sic; read: culpabilis], subditur 'Benedictus Domine etcetera.' "

[51] For the concept of the *viator* during the Middle Ages, see Gerhart Ladner, "Homo Viator: Medieval Ideas on Order and Alienation," *Speculum,* 42 (1967), pp. 233-259. Cf. Heiko A. Oberman, *The Harvest of Medieval Theology: Gabriel Biel and Late Medieval Nominalism* (Cambridge, Mass.: Harvard University Press, 1963), pp. 476 ("*viator*"), 39, and *passim.* Aspects of the Nominalist definition of *viator* could still apply to Lyra's David.
Although we have not discovered such a precise use of the term "*viator*" by Lyra, the special sense of this word is present, as we show, in other, indirect ways. Certainly Lyra's use of the word "*fideles*" implies as much. For Lyra, "*fideles*" connotes both those who belong to the Church only *numero* and those who belong *numero et merito.* This usage of course encompasses those who move from grace to sin and vice versa. Cf. Scott H. Hendrix, *Ecclesia in Via* (Leiden: E. J. Brill, 1974), pp. 59-62.

[52] According to Lyra, Psalm 50 is the prayer of repentance which David wrote after he had arranged Uriah's death and after his adultery with Bathsheba. As such it may be the prayer of any contrite sinner: ". . . fecit David penitens de adulterio cum Bersabee et homocidio Urie, petens a Deo remissionem humiliter et devote. Moraliter autem est oratio cuiuslibet vere penitentis et devote veniam postulantis. . . . Hic allegatur ratio ad propositum ex parte peccatoris que est humilis recognitio peccati, cum dicitur 'quoniam iniquitatem meam ego cognosco,' id est, recognosco 'et peccatum meum contra me est semper,' id est ante oculos cordis mei per recordationem amaram. . . ." (N of L, PM, Ps. 50, fol. r8 recto.) Lyra stresses the *viator*'s sense of guilt and penitence; he does not mention the need for performing penance.

[53] David's free will is implicitly sh~~vn in the above quotation (note 49, above), since David is allowed to be tempted by Satan. As the definition of the *viator* suggests (note 51, above), faith determines David's eternal fate.

[54] This brings to mind Milton's *Comus* which is the tale of virtue tried and proven. Milton's message is that virtue must meet and conquer agreeable temptation; otherwise, virtue would be an empty ideal rather than a living reality.

[55] In this context, Saul represents the Devil. However, as we conclude from Lyra's words quoted immediately (as well as from those quoted in notes 56 and 57, below), he sees Saul not merely as an empty figure of Satan but as his instrument at a certain moment on earth; in this way, then, David is no sterile or hollow shadow, but a real man who once had to contend with the machinations of the Prince of Evil on earth. Thus, Lyra's conception of David as a *viator* approximates the later Protestant conception of David. In his comment on Psalm 25 (PM, fol. q7 verso), Lyra also says: ". . . Saul autem interpretatur abutens et ideo significat dyabolum qui bonis naturalibus abutitur ad malum. . . ."

[56] N of L, PM, Ps. 85, fol. t4 recto: "Psalmum istum fecit David orans a Deo liberari de Saulis persecutione. Moraliter autem potest exponi ut sit oratio cuiuslibet fidelis in afflictione spiritus per demonem excitata vel corporis per hominem malum qui est demonis instrumentum. Et primo allegat exauditionis decenciam ex parte sui propter suam indigenciam, . . . et [alligat] suam innocentiam ex parte Dei scilicet propter suam clementiam, . . . et etiam suam in Deo confidentiam. . . ."

[57] N of L, PM, Ps. 16, foll. q3 verso - q4 recto: ". . . Moraliter enim est oratio viri iusti in persecutione demonis vel hominis mali . . . . Circa quod talis oratio est exaudibilis propter tria, scilicet propter pacientis innocentiam, et propter Dei iusticiam, et propter persequentis maliciam. Quantum ad primum dicitur . . ., quasi diceret innocens sum in hoc casu. . . . Quantum ad secundum dicitur . . ., quasi diceret ab eo non potest procedere nisi iustum. . . . 'Et visitasti nocte,' id est persecutionis tempore, sicut medicus visitat egrum propinando ei medicinam ad consequendum sanitatem. . . . '[M]irifica misericordias tuas,' id est fac eas mirabiles in me quia non possum liberari sine te. Circa tertium . . . dicitur 'a resistentibus dexterae tuae' cuiusmodi sunt demones et iniqui homines. 'Custodi me' ne possint mihi finaliter prevalere, 'sub umbra alarum tuarum,' scilicet tuae misericordiae et iusticiae. . . ."

[58] N of L, PM, Ps. 142, fol. v7 verso: "Secundum Ieronimum David fecit hunc psalmum de pugna contra Goliad. Moraliter autem potest exponi de bello viri iusti contra dyabolum, et sic in eius persona dicitur, considerando auxilium divinum,

'Benedictus Deus etcetera.' Circa quod sciendum quia sicut in bello corporali . . . pugnatur de prope manu ad manum,. . . sic in bello spirituali fit bellum de Deo prope cum pugnatur contra actum peccati. . . ."

[59] Needless to say, the virtuous man should also imitate David in thanking God for preserving him and giving him the divine aid to overcome the demonic temptations which afflict him. Lyra's comments on Psalms 31 and 113 (PM, foll. r1 verso & v2 verso) provide the Christian *viator* with a proper formulation for thanksgiving.

[60] N of L, PM, Ps. 26, fol. q8 recto: "Psalmum istum literaliter exponi de statu David quando, post mortem Saul in Ebron, ascendit et cepit regnare super tribum Juda quamvis eius adversarii adhuc essent in multitudine magna. Moraliter autem exponi potest de quolibet fideli ad etatem adultam veniente, tunc enim debet regnum suum incipere bene regendo motus animae. Et quoniam in hoc difficultatem patitur, rogare debet Dominum ut ab eo dirigatur. . . ."

[61] N of L, PM, Ps. 140, fol. v7 recto: "Psalmum istum fecit David anxius in spelunca. Moraliter esse potest oratio propinquantis ad mortem, sicut fecisse legitur beatus Franciscus. Dicat ergo 'voce mea etcetera' et dicitur hic bis, 'voce mea,' ad significandum mentis orationem et oris. 'Effundo in conspectu eius orationem meam,' id est, toto conatu oro, 'et tribulationem meam etcetera' propter mortem imminantem. . . ."

[62] See above, pp. 31-32.

[63] N of L, PM, Ps. 59, fol. s3 recto: ". . . Moraliter autem potest exponi de quolibet iusto evadente mortis periculum ex Dei beneficio. Specialiter autem de beato Petro in carcere recluso ut occidatur, sed per angelum fuit liberatus, ut habetur Act. xii [:6-11]. . . ."

[64] N of L, PM, Ps. 70, fol. s6 recto: ". . . Moraliter autem possunt exponi de bono pastore ab apostolico filio suo spirituali, tamen iniquo persecutionem paciente, sicut de sancto Thoma cantuariensi et rege angliae legitur esse factum a qua persecutione petit divinitus liberari. . . ." Also N of L, PM, Ps. 116, foll. v2 verso & v3 recto: "Hunc psalmum fecit David invitans populum suum ad gratias agendum Domino pro bono statu Christi spirituali et adventu Christi futuro. Moraliter potest exponi de bono prelato ad Dei laudem suum populum invitante pro bono statu Christi spirituali. . . .'Omnes gentes,' hic describitur acerbitas persecutionis quae contingit aliquibus bonis prelatis ut patet de sancto Thoma cantuariensi in cuius persona dici potest, 'omnes gentes circumierunt me,' id est gentiliter viventes quaesierunt mihi nocere. 'Et in nomine Domini quia ultus sum in eos' nam ultione divina fuerunt terribiliter mortui et ipse translatur ad gloriam paradisi. . . ."

[65] N of L, PM, Ps. 63, fol. s4 recto: ". . . Fecit David quando, fugiens persecutionem Saulis, habitabat in desertis iudeae sterilibus et asperis. Propter quod Deus faciens cum tentatione proventum consolabatur eum illuminationibus suis. Moraliter autem potest exponi de quolibet anchorita qui mundum fugiens petit deserta ut sentiat beneficia divina. . . .Exemplum de sancto Hilarione qui heremum ingressus est . . . per magnum desiderium consolationis tuae. . . . Et de beato Francisco legitur quod aliquando in oratione quae est ascensus mentis in Deum, corpus eius a terra sublevabatur. . . ."

[66] Quoted in Oberman, *Forerunners,* p. 286.

[67] Moorman, *op. cit.,* p. 256.

[68] See Kantorowicz, *Bodies,* pp. 77, 81, and 83 for suggestions about the medieval concept of David as a priest-king and its importance for the theory of kingship. As the English scholar Cathwulf wrote to Charlemagne, setting forth the Carolingian notion of Davidic kingship: "Thou art the viceregent of God, and the bishop is in the second place only, the viceregent of Christ." (*Ibid.,* p. 77.) We may recall that Charlemagne was given the appellation "David" by his *"familiares."*

[69] Surely by Lyra's time this was an ideal conception. Using David as the good episcopal prelate, Nicolaus of Lyra seeks a return to the fraternal concern of the early bishops.

[70] Moorman, *op. cit.,* pp. 295-297, 303.

[71] On Leone Valvassori, see P. Sevesi, "B. Leone dei Valvassori da Perego, O. M. Arcivescovo di Milano," *Studi francescani,* XIII-XIV (XIV-XV, 1927-1928). (Cited by Moorman without pagination.) Moorman, *op. cit.,* pp. 295-297, discusses the role of Franciscan bishops.

[72] *Ibid.,* pp. 300-301.

[73] See below, Chapter III, for a discussion of Lefèvre and Erasmus.

[74] Moorman, *op. cit.,* pp. 397-398, 403.

[75] Oberman, *Harvest,* p. 284.

[76] P. Glorieux, "Les Maîtres en théologie de Paris au XIIIè siècle " II, no. 345, in *Etudes de Philosophie Médiévale,* edited by Etienne Gilson, 18 (1933); also, Lucas Wadding, *Annales minorum,* Vol. 6 (Rome: 1733), p. 121.

[77]We hasten to note here that the literal/historical approach to Scripture had its precedents in the Franciscan movement among others besides Lyra. For example, Thomas Docking (fl. 2nd half of the 13th century) wrote a *Commentary* on the Pauline Epistles, wherein he sought out the literal/historical meanings (cf. Smalley, *op. cit.*, pp. 278-280, 307, 323, 325, 327). In the early fourteenth century Francis of Meyronnes and Peter Auriol wrote literal compendiums on the Bible. However, Lyra remains the greatest of the medieval postillers, attested to by the fact that his *postillae* were among the most widely read biblical commentaries in the later Middle Ages. (Cf. Moorman, *op. cit.*, pp. 394-396.)

[78]*Ibid.*, pp. 276-277, remarks that for the Franciscans the Bible was a collection of *exempla;* furthermore, it was their and the other mendicants' use of the Bible as a series of examples that revolutionized the art of preaching.

[79]Bainton, *art. cit.*, pp. 39-49, shows, however, that the sense of awe-struck horror at Old Testament immoralities still continued and remained even in the sixteenth century. Since Lyra and the Protestants whom we shall discuss below emphasized the faith of David (in a somewhat consolational manner) rather than the dread character of his sins, they were able to overcome the embarrassment of David's adultery and homicide and see him as a living man.

# Chapter III
## Lefevre d'Etaples

The investigation of the literal or double literal sense of Scripture continued after the death of Nicolaus of Lyra. Paul of Santa Maria, Bishop of Burgos, criticized some aspects of Lyra's work in his *Additiones ad postillas Nicolai Lyrani,* although he did not abandon the essential attempt to reconcile the literal interpretation of the Old Testament with faith in Christ.[1] James of Valencia continued the process on a path that would lead to the Old Testament hermeneutics found in the young Luther.[2]

The path of the double literal sense of Holy Scripture was, however, fragile. Fragile, too, were the parallel pastoral lessons suggested by Nicolas of Lyra's concepts of David. Adherence to Lyra's so-called double literal approach could cause an exegete to follow a path manifestly different in intent from Lyra's. The student of the interpretation of David finds that it is among at least some of the humanists of the Renaissance that Lyra's achievement of reconciling Old and New Testaments on the pastoral level slackens off, indeed fails. Perhaps the change of view we shall find in Lefèvre d'Etaples[3] has something to do with his and his circle's absorption in resurrecting the biblical commentaries of the Patristic Age. Such humanists rose to the heights of superlatives in describing the commentaries of early exegetes like Origen, Cyprian, Hilary, and Augustine. Each of these Fathers was described as *sapientissimus, potentissimus* and *sanctissimus,* and their doctrines were categorized collectively as *absolutissima.* They discovered true piety and doctrine in the writings of the ancient founders of the Church:

> By extension [the Fathers were] authorities and models for a profound reform of theological writing and teaching on the basis of the cultural program of humanism. For the piety of the Fathers was, in their eyes, of a special and attractive kind: it was eloquent; it was simple affective wisdom . . .; it was, finally, peculiarly authoritative, far closer to the primitive source of Christian illumination than the Scholastics. They found in the Fathers, indeed, precisely what they missed in high and late medieval scholasticism. A principal aim of their enthusiasm was to undermine the authority of the one by magnifying the authority of the other.[4]

If the search of Lefèvre d'Etaples and other humanists vitally concerned with *"reformatio"* was indeed for doctrine as well as piety, they found precious little of the former in Nicolaus of Lyra. As we have seen, he taught Christian piety through the example of David, but, aside from a few psalms in which David was approached Christologically, his *Postilla* was aimed at being more of a "mirror of 'viators' " than at being a doctrinal piece.

Perhaps, also, the humanists found the Old Testament a source of embarrassment. Certainly if they had read much patristic and medieval literature they would have soon learned that the Old Testament offered all too many examples of scandalous behavior.[5] We may recall the opening lines of St. Augustine's exposition of Psalm 50,[6] in which he states that it is with great hesitancy that he takes up discussion of this psalm which deals with David's adultery with Bathsheba. It was perhaps only his confidence that he could pull an appropriate Christological lesson out of the psalm and the heightened embarrassment that would have resulted from leaving a *lacuna* that led him into such muddied waters. Nicolaus of Lyra seems to have experienced and expresses no such scruples in dealing with David's adultery and homicide, for they easily fitted into his pastoral purpose: to show that even the best of men can sin grievously and that true penitence and trust in God's mercy will assuredly restore the fallen state of the *viator*. It was only natural that humanists like Lefèvre d'Etaples, adulating the Church Fathers, would, when carrying on the tradition of the double literal sense of Scripture, achieve something very different from the tone of Nicolaus of Lyra, something closer to the tenor of Augustine's commentary on the Psalms. The method of Augustine and traditional qualms about the Old Testament would be sufficient to cause such a change.

Nor is it only in Lefèvre that we can find this more "traditional" (or Augustinian) approach to the Old Testament and particularly to David. The typological and largely Christological allegorical style of Augustine and Ambrose can also be discerned in the great Erasmus' traditional treatment of the Old Testament. When Erasmus discusses Old Testament figures, he views them as types of the Dispensation that would come— in Christ. Hence, the serpent lifted up in the wilderness by Moses is, for Erasmus, a type of Christ lifted up on the Cross; the crossing of the Red Sea by the Israelites signifies baptism; with Erasmus, the concubines of Solomon become so many virtues, and the Canaanites, who were to be exterminated by the Israelites, so many vices. The continuity discovered by Erasmus between the Old and New Testaments and the types found in the Old Testament both refer to Christ and to the vehicles of grace established by Him in His Church, not to the concept of the pilgrim between life and death or to specific historical parallels.[7]

It appears, then, that Erasmus considers the Old Testament *per se* a dead letter. It has no intrinsic worth except in its types, which all refer to and become meaningful through Christ. Lefèvre, too, approaches the Old Testament David in the same manner.

We may appraise quickly enough the cause of the difference between the Davidic interpretation of Nicolaus of Lyra and that of Lefèvre d'Etaples. Lefèvre's preface to the *Psalterium David*, his "concluding exhortation" to the *Psaultier de David,* and his dedicatory epistle to the *Quincuplex Psalterium* provide us with the hermeneutic framework upon which he will build his "arguments" which precede each psalm.[8]

Although Lefèvre's comments on both the Psalms and David, with which he prefaces the Latin Psalter and concludes the French Psalter, are of a general nature, they are expressive of the conclusions which we shall see him draw in his preface to the *Quincuplex Psalterium.* He describes the reading of Sacred Scripture as a pilgrimage to God, for God Himself speaks in Scripture. The Psalms are a short-cut for the pilgrim, allowing him to reach his destination more quickly, since, Lefèvre adds, "I know no place where God's word . . . is more clearly present than in the Psalms of David."[9]

Yet, in a sense, these Psalms are not by David. Lefèvre says that they are "holy odes" through which the Holy Spirit speaks about the Father and Christ. Even though the Psalms were written "one thousand sixty-nine years before the coming of Christ," the Holy Spirit, speaking through David, predicts Christ's birth, His words and deeds while on earth, His crucifixion, resurrection, ascension, and enthronement at the right hand of the Father. In addition, the Holy Spirit speaks through David about His descent on the Pentecost and about the mission of the Apostles.[10]

In sum, then, the subject of the Psalms is Christ. Lefèvre supports this conclusion by citing the testimony of the Evangelists and St. Paul as well as the witness of both David himself and the rabbinical scholars. If the reader of the Psalms realizes that they are about Christ, he will find it "marvellously easy" to understand them. However, if it is not admitted that Christ is the subject of the Psalms (and, indeed, of the entire Bible), then "Scripture is the letter which killeth."[11]

Lefèvre's dedicatory epistle to the *Quincuplex Psalterium,* written fifteen years before the preface to the *Psalterium David,* offers us a more detailed discussion of his Old Testament and Psalm hermeneutic. He begins by saying that he has visited several monasteries and has found that pious theological studies are no longer being pursued. The sweetness of these studies, and of life itself, comes from the Word (*via* the Holy Spirit) which emanates from the mouth of God. Lefèvre finds the monks no longer in love with this sweetness; consequently,

> Devotion dies out, the flame of religion is extinguished, spiritual things are traded for earthly goods, heaven is given up and earth is accepted—the most disastrous transaction conceivable.[12]

The reason for this degeneration of the religious sensibility is that, according to the monks themselves, when they tried to comprehend the Psalms they pursued them according to the literal sense. Failing thereby to experience the sweetness of the Psalms, they lost heart and became downcast. Apparently the study, by Nicolaus of Lyra and others, of the Old Testament literal meaning of the Psalms failed to meet contemporary religious needs.

Unwilling to throw away as so much ballast the literal sense of Scripture, Lefèvre immediately adds that what had been thought to be the true literal sense was not. Rather, states Lefèvre, there is another sense of Scripture which is "the intention of the prophet and of the Holy Spirit speaking in him. This I call the 'literal' sense, but a literal sense which coincides with the Spirit."[13] The problem is that those interested in the literal meaning have blindly followed the false path of applying the psalms to David himself and the persecutions which afflicted him, making of David a chronicler, not a prophet.[14]

"Spiritus Domini locutus est per me, et sermo eius per linguam meam: here is the proof-text which casts into disrepute all of Nicolaus of Lyra's *Postilla super psalmos,* and the rabbinical sources from which he worked.[15]

Although Lefèvre criticizes the present-day practitioners of literal exegesis, his critique is a thinly-veiled attack upon Lyra's achievement. Lefèvre's implicit critique is that Lyra was wrong to search out the literal/historical meaning of David's psalms, for the higher meanings drawn therefrom display a dangerous servility to the medieval Jewish tradition of Scriptural interpretation; dangerous, because, as Lefèvre says, this "judaicizing" method of exegesis is responsible for the current lack of enthusiasm in the monastic centers of learning. The reader may therefore infer that Lyra's literal sense—and consequently all that is built upon this edifice—is base, of the flesh, an abomination.

What must be done to rectify this unfortunate trend of interpretation? Lefèvre has said already that the "true" literal sense must be sought in the Psalms, the sense which "coincides with the Spirit." The remedy that Lefèvre outlines in his epistle makes use of the "twofold literal sense." The first is the Old Testament historical meaning sought out by Lyra and by those who lack "open eyes," for the primary sense of Scripture is distorted. Only those exegetes "who can see and receive insight" are able to uncover the "true" literal meaning; this insight is possible solely as a gift of God's Spirit.[16] The remainder of Lefèvre's remedy for the exegetical *cul de sac* within which he believes scriptural interpretation was entrapped might be epitomized by the words, *"de Christo."* Look not for David in the psalms; look for Christ, "Who is the key to the understanding of David and about Whom David spoke, commissioned by the Holy Spirit."[17] All the Psalms are about Christ, not David, thus negating Lyra's vision of David as a man of living faith. Lefèvre's is a position that is close to that of St. Augustine. Lefèvre, moreover, approaches Marcionism in that he regards the Psalms as having a base sense—what is written—; and it is only by constantly referring everything to Christ that he is able to salvage the Psalms (and the Old Testament) as well as to restore "sweetness" to monastic scriptural scholarship.

Even in this introduction, Lefèvre provides the reader with examples which demonstrate the repercussions of this twofold literal concept. At the same time, Lefèvre stipulates that his method is essentially the same as the approach of the Apostles to the Psalms. Undoubtedly he meant thus to align his interpretations of the Psalms with the purity and holiness of the primitive Church. Clearly, the implication is that a "Lefèvrian" hermeneutic, if followed by other commentators, too, will effect the *"reformatio"* of the Church and will restore to it the age of glory which preceded its corruption by scholastic scholarship. The reform and purification of exegesis should, therefore, walk hand-in-hand with the reform of morals and practices. A grand and noble scheme—at least from the vantage point of a humanist who gazes reverently at the early Church—but a scheme which, in the field of biblical exegesis, will lead to the evaporation of the Old Testament as a truly existential religious work; in other words, we believe Lefèvre's approach to the Psalms to have been an exegetical *cul de sac*, completely lacking in that vibrancy and applicability breathed into the Psalms by Nicolaus of Lyra.[18]

The example of three psalm interpretations, found in Lefèvre's dedicatory epistle, will clarify just what his method reveals for scriptural interpretation. Psalm 2 ("Why do the nations conspire and the peoples plot in vain? The kings of the earth set themselves up and the rulers take counsel together against the Lord and His Anointed") was interpreted by the rabbinical commentators as literally referring to the inhabitants of Palestine who revolted against David, the Lord's anointed. The Apostles, including St. Paul, saw the literal sense as referring to the Anointed of the Lord, Jesus Christ. The literal interpretation furnished by the rabbis (and again this refers to Christians like Nicolaus of Lyra) of Psalms 1 and 21 deals with the persecution of the Israelites in the time of Artaxerxes. However, Saints Matthew, John, and Paul, "full of God," understood these two psalms to refer, *in a literal sense,* to those things which happened to the Anointed of the Lord in His Passion.[19] Again we find reiterated the point that Lyra's literal meaning is base, is not really the literal sense at all. Finally, says Lefèvre, there is no need to flush out the four senses of Scripture or to find allegory, for we have either the vile literal sense (which has so discomfited the monks) or the true literal sense, that which "the Holy Spirit intends as He speaks through the prophet."[20]

The difference between Lefèvre d'Etaples and Nicolaus of Lyra is clear. Lefèvre has rejected the so-called "base" literal sense that Lyra so labored over in order to go from that meaning to the appropriate higher senses. Gone, too, is the versatility of Davidic interpretations made available to Lyra through the literal/historical sense of the psalms. For Lefèvre there is only one sense to Scripture, the literal, but now it has nothing to do with pastoral or moral values; rather, Lefèvre's literal sense is the one that applies to Christ. Lefèvre thus differs from St. Augustine. While not erecting "parallel" senses as did Lyra, Augustine admitted that the literal or historical meaning of the psalm should be the basis for eliciting the allegorical meaning. Thus he was able to give some intrinsic value and worth to the Old Testament. Lefèvre denies the need for allegorizing as he denies the value of the "rabbinical" literal sense of Scripture. He claims he does not need to allegorize—as did Augustine—since literally the psalms refer to Christ, about

Whom the prophet always spoke. Hermeneutically different though Lefèvre is from St. Augustine, yet his David, no less than Augustine's, is Christological: that is, only Christ and the New Testament can give David meaning.

As in the case of St. Augustine, and unlike that of Nicolaus of Lyra, the most frequently found concept of David in Lefèvre's rather succinct *argumenta* to the psalms is that of David as the *typos* of Christ. A consideration of the temporal history of David's life makes it apparent to Lefèvre that David is the figure of Christ. The betrayal of Christ by Judas, one of His beloved followers, is found under the veil of Absalom's apostasy from his father, David. Each betrayer met a similar fate by hanging. David returned to Jerusalem as the honored victor; similarly, Christ emerged gloriously from His sepulchre. The events, then, portended by this psalm (and the more elaborate version in the Second Book of Samuel) are figures of the events that are found in the Gospels concerning the betrayal and ultimate victory of Christ.[21] In another argument, Lefèvre glosses the fiftieth verse of Psalm 16: "Great deliverance giveth He to His king and showeth mercy to His Anointed, to David and to his seed forevermore." These words, we are told, are not spoken about the Old Testament David whom Lefèvre calls a "type." Rather these words speak of the second and true David, Jesus Christ, the real shepherd of men.[22]

The tone of Lefèvre's Davidic exegesis is thus set. Only infrequently will he depart from seeing David as the type of Christ. He formulates David's type as Christ in such a way, also, that David loses all personality. It is not as if he sought the allegorical message hidden in the *gesta Davidica* as had St. Augustine, who at least had seemed to allow the idea that the Old Testament era was a different, if somewhat embarrassing, age which had a life of its own (and which meant that the allegorical lesson was necessary in order to reconcile the Testaments). The manner in which Lefèvre treats David is such that the contents of the Old Testament are rendered nugatory save for the fact that, according to Lefèvre, the books were written at the express command of the Holy Spirit solely for teaching lessons to be fulfilled in the New Testament. David is, in Lefèvre, a passive prophet who records what the Holy Spirit dictates.

This tone is not lessened in the other psalms which apply to Christ. David remains, throughout, Christ in disguise. In fact, David's change of countenance before Ahimelech is merely a facade for the false face Christ put on before His fellow Jews. For just as David changed his appearance when he appeared before Ahimelech, so did Christ mask His divinity with the cloak of poverty when He walked among the Jews. David is again not really David, but Christ; his demeanor before Ahimelech being really only a prophecy of the manner in which Christ would conduct Himself in the sight of the Chosen People.[23]

Nor are David's honesty and humility given any importance other than as the typologies that can associate David with Christ. Nicolaus of Lyra had stressed these qualities of David, but had applied them to the *viator,* the virtuous man. Not so Lefèvre. The link between David and Christ is straightforward. It is not David praying to God to be saved from death when Saul's hired men come to imprison and murder him in his own house. Rather, the true literal sense of the psalm is the prayer of Christ to His Father. Saul is truly the Hebrew people; David's house is, in fact, the sepulchre in which Christ was entombed; the guards sent by the king are the Romans who keep the vigil in front of that sepulchre. David's escape through a window has edifying meaning only when it is understood to be the foretelling of Christ's resurrection and escape from His tomb. The psalm, as usual, is not a song of David but of Christ.[24]

David's prayers asking to be liberated from the persecutions of his enemies have neither the literal immediacy nor the paralleling feature of the pious man seeking God's help in coping with the tribulations and temptations caused by demonic forces that they do in Lyra's interpretations. David's prayers, according to Lefèvre, are either simply the utterances of Christ praying to His Father in Heaven, or David's prayers about Christ. When the Ziphites (I Samuel 26) approached Saul, saying, "Does not David hide himself among us?", David represents Christ praying in the garden; the Ziphites carry the *persona* of the traitor Judas; Saul, Abner, and their associates represent the princes, priests, and their fellow Jews. David's prayer, which deals with the events described in I Samuel 26, reflects the situation in which David and Abissai come at night upon the sleeping Saul, his spear stuck in the ground at his head, with Abner and the people lying about him. This, of course, is the base literal sense that contributes nothing and only detracts from the "sweetness" of Scripture. The edifying literal significance of this psalm is that it prefigures Christ rising up from prayer in the night to find those who were guarding Him asleep and the Jewish people blind to His true nature.[25] Likewise, the psalm David wrote thanking God for his deliverance from Saul and all his enemies would be unrewarding reading if the reader did not realize that in Psalm 17 David thanks God not only for his victory but also for the Messiah Who is to come.[26] A psalm, which could have been explained, as Nicolaus of Lyra might have, as the thanksgiving of the pious man for God's aid, becomes instead a prophetic prayer of gratitude for the Messiah; and Psalm 39 is not about Christ, but is Christ speaking through the prophet to the faithful Christians.[27] There is no sense here of the *viator;* there is only the prophet.

As we have seen thus far, David does not emerge as a distinct personality, even in his role as prophet. David's psalms either refer literally to events found in the gospels, or they offer thanks with foreknowledge of the Advent of Christ, or, finally, they are psalms through which Christ Himself speaks. True, the concept is one of David as prophet. But as such he is quite indistinct from the other psalmists, such as the sons of Korah or Asaph.[28]

Consequently, when we turn to Psalm 35, we find once again that David's victory, spoken of on the trivial level of the psalm, is literally a song celebrating Christ's victory on the Cross. The prophet, David, sings not of himself as the servant of the Lord, but of Christ, the Son of the Eternal Father, Who conquered the world and Satan. It was Christ who balanced injustice with justice, perfidy with obedience, defilement with virtuousness, and the sins of men with His own blood.[29] Similarly, David represents Christ throughout His Passion. David's flight from Saul into the cave, his humility and simplicity contrasted with Saul's invidious nature, are veils for the story of Christ's Passion at the hands of the irreverent and haughty Jewish people. Christ's prayers to His Father under these circumstances are foretold in David's prayers for release from the persecution of Saul.[30]

Even some of the words spoken by David in his psalms are, according to Lefèvre, identical to the words uttered by Christ. In Psalm 62, for example, David says in the first verse, "Deus, Deus Meus." These words, in Hebrew, are the very ones which Christ cried out to the Father on the Cross at about the ninth hour (Matthew 27:46). In Hebrew, Psalm 62 begins "ELOHIM ELI ": "ELOHIM" is plural, and "ELI " is singular, meaning "my God." Thus, David uses the words of Christ, and he uses the singular and plural for the secret of the Trinity and the mystery of the triune God, in order to distinguish their substances and to assert their consubstantiality.[31] David's words, therefore, foretell of the mystery of New Testament theology and, in so doing, prophesy Christ's own words. Certainly the fusion of David into Christ's figure—and the consequent loss of his identity as a man worthy in his own right—could not be carried further. David is a shadow.

And so he remains in those psalms wherein he speaks not of or for Christ, but for faithful Christians. The public nature of David's characterization is made quite clear in Lefèvre's "argument" to Psalm 24. Praying to the Lord, David speaks in the person of the people faithful to God. When he says, "May innocence and uprightness protect me," he does not speak for himself, for he is not a private person; the "me" is really a word in the mouth of the Holy People.[32] Once again, then, David as a holy man in his own time is submerged beneath Lefèvre's concept of the prophet: one who speaks antecedently for others. Indeed, it would almost appear that David is not given the dignity of being a prototype of the Holy People. The Spirit speaking through him, he approximates a puppet who voices the words and sentiments of a people that he would not recognize save for the inspiration of the third member of the Trinity. This "puppet" concept of David, however, is not consistently pressed by Lefèvre. We see, for example, in Psalm 144 that David's praise of God is spoken by David both as a private person and as the figure of the pious. Thus, precariously, David remains a type who prefigures, and he fails to become more than merely a cat's-paw.[33]

Lefèvre's David is also the prophet of the Holy People as they represented their desires. In this case the pious people he represents are not Christians, but his own Jewish nation of the Old Covenant who eagerly awaited the coming of the Messiah.[34] It is somewhat unusual to find Lefèvre linking David with his own historical period; inasmuch as he does this, David is not a prefiguration of what is to come, although his representative prayer has a Christological end. On the other hand, the emphasis in this laconic "argument" falls not on David as an individual, but on David as a type of the Jews who knew that their spiritual life would be incomplete until the substitution of the New Covenant for the Old. Here, then, is typology without the sense of the *viator* that is found in Nicolaus of Lyra's expositions. Yet, just as when David represented the faithful praying to Christ, David usually is not a type of the Old Testament believers who, though they did not have true Christian faith, excelled in the virtue of hope; rather, he is a prefiguration of the complete believers of the New Testament and Christianity. Thus, in Psalm 139 when David prays for victory, he is instructed by the Spirit to speak on behalf of good Christians against heretics—apostates from the Christian fold.[35] The difference between Psalms 66 and 139—the former wherein the prophet represents his own people and the latter wherein he is the prototype of the Christian faithful—is exemplified by the wording of Lefèvre's arguments for each psalm. In Psalm 66 Lefèvre states, "Propheta loquitur in persona piorum . . ."; in Psalm 139, he says, "Psalmus, deprecatio in spiritu. . . ." The first might not be called true prophecy, for David merely sums up the most ardent desire of the ancient Hebrews. In the second, however, the Holy Spirit informs David's words and thus he engages in prototypal prophecy. The reader might not be amiss in concluding that the real David had no concern for heresy—at least such concern is never alluded to by Lefèvre—while only the David who is the mouthpiece for the Holy Spirit is able to rise to such heights of pious care.

Consequently, when David writes Psalm 22 he reflects prophetically the thoughts of Christians who are thankful for the gifts Christ has bestowed upon them. They rejoice in Christ's lordship over them, the beneficial nourishment of His doctrine and of His sacraments which are the very food of life.[36] He must compose, *in spiritu*, one supposes, because the essentials of religious life and experience are lacking to David and all Old Covenant people. Lefèvre never constructs a parallel situation between an Old Testament believer like David and Christians. Perhaps the attitude of the French humanist toward the literal sense of Scripture was determined by the same conviction as that which informed his exegesis of David as the representative of the Holy People. The belief that the Jews and David could only hope for Christ's Advent, that their own religious life was devoid of value, prompted Lefèvre to make David a prefiguration of the Holy People of Christ only in his (David's) words, only through the inspiration of the Holy Spirit.

Without such divine inspiration, David could have done no more than register hope; he could not have been viewed as a *viator*. So, too, the literal/historical sense of the Old Testament is base and lacks sweetness.

Lefèvre does once allow David to stand for himself, without the addition of any figuration. The circumstances, however, are unflattering, even though the psalm is termed a "human prayer." The occasion of Psalm 50 is the intimacy between David and Bathsheba and the attendant murder of her husband Uriah. Nathan came to David to issue God's warning and reprimand. Lefèvre then refers the reader to the eleventh and twelfth chapters of II Samuel. He next remarks that the psalm is a human prayer, that it is David alone who speaks, and, "Since this psalm contains a human prayer, not a prophecy, it is not difficult to understand it."[37]

If we think back to St. Augustine's comments on this incident,[38] we will recall that the exegete had blushed even to bring up the subject of David's heinous sins. But he did, anyway, and the result was a rather lengthy psalm commentary which Augustine devoted to a Christological exegesis. Once again with Lefèvre we find that the Old Testament patriarchs provide occasion for embarrassment, although Lefèvre does not admit as much. Instead of attempting to view the sins involved in some higher light, as had Augustine, Lefèvre flatly throws the burden of guilt on David by dismissing the psalm as a human–perhaps all too human–prayer. But why? Could not Lefèvre have twisted the psalm so it would elicit a higher, more edifying meaning? Or might he not have followed the example of Nicolaus of Lyra[39] when that scholar discussed David and Bathsheba, and have derived a moralizing pastoral message for the instruction of the Christian sinner who is, like David, a *viator* capable of sin, and, like David, eventually repentant of his sin?

Historical "ifs" and "might have beens" are notoriously hypothetical and usually non-productive. In this case, however, we might find illumination in a kind of negative proof, borrowed from the methodological thesaurus of our scientist-colleagues. The answer is that, yes, Lefèvre might have, could have, followed either the path laid down by St. Augustine or the trail blazed by Nicolaus of Lyra. Lefèvre did neither; he does not explain why, but it is permissible to search out his tacit motives. Perhaps he considered this psalm as a proof-text for his contention that the historical/literal sense of Scripture is unedifying. He certainly believed, as he stated in the psalm argument, that "it is not difficult to understand this Psalm." Simply put, David fornicated and murdered–these are certainly actions easily comprehensible to the reader. Nor are these actions especially interesting, save later to remark, as Lefèvre does, that David had to be punished by God for his sins. These are things any Christian knows: sin and divine punishment. In a sense, this exposition may be taken as Lefèvre's gesture to David as a *viator*. He finds it uninteresting and he has no use for formulating some consoling lesson as Lyra had done. How better to demonstrate that Lyra's literal sense is base and unprofitable. At worst, it might even have been such a psalm as that which had disturbed the monks whom Lefèvre visited. Viewing David as a sinner and a *viator*, emphasizing thereby the literal meaning, leads nowhere for Lefèvre. His laconic comments show the poverty of Lyra's method. Lefèvre's disparagement of the primary literal sense of Scripture perhaps helps to elucidate why he does not explain away this psalm in the manner of Augustine, who at least had founded his exegesis on the historical event. Had Lefèvre used Augustine's method, however, he would not have been able to stick a barb in Nicolaus of Lyra's exegetical method.

All of this, of course, is pure conjecture. It is, however, an entirely plausible explanation of Lefèvre's handling of Psalm 50. Our negative approach has merely shown what Lefèvre could and might have done. We realize that, rejecting Lyra's literal (and parallel) approach to Scripture (as Lefèvre did in his preface), he would not have been untrue to his hermeneutical technique had he chosen to make David speak *in spiritu*, as he does in almost every other psalm, and arrived at a more Augustinian solution of the difficulties posed by the psalm and II Samuel 11-12. That Lefèvre failed to achieve this latter result could have been due to neglect; but we think not. Rather, this "failure" offered Lefèvre the opportunity to castigate, by implication, Lyra's method while he displayed the unedifying simplicity and barrenness of the "bad" literal sense of Scripture, which is in a sense uninformed by the fruitful inspiration of the Holy Spirit.

This failure in Psalm 50 either to allegorize Christologically or to moralize, as did Lyra, about the *viator* in a state of sin appears to be all the more deliberate when we read Lefèvre's "arguments" to Psalms 51 and 31. We find in these two psalms, respectively, the concepts of David as the just man and as the penitent man. In Psalm 51, Lefèvre describes the unjust and wretched man as figured by Doeg the Edomite, who both reported to Saul that David rested in the house of Ahimelech and killed the priests of Nob at the command of Saul. David, who speaks under the inspiration of the Holy Spirit, says Lefèvre, is the just man whose description may be found under the superscription of "Beatus vir" in the first psalm. And, in Psalm 31, Lefèvre tersely remarks that David speaks in the person of the man aggrieved by his sins.[40]

To be sure, the concepts found in these two psalms are base. No full descriptions of the qualities David figures are offered (except to refer the reader to Psalm 1). All the reader knows is that David is the prototype of the just and penitent man. The fact that the concepts are enunciated, however barrenly, is suggestive. We know, first of all, that Lefèvre could relate David to moral concepts. We realize, then, that the way had lain open to Lefèvre to utilize these concepts when discussing David's adultery and homicide in Psalm 50.[41] He, like Nicolaus of Lyra, could have displayed David as the sometimes virtuous, sometimes sinful *viator* who repents his waywardness. Since Lefèvre chose not to attach the concepts of virtuous and penitent man to his exposition of Psalm 50, we judge this choice to have been deliberate and discretionary.

Lefèvre realized that, following Nathan's reproach, David said, "I have sinned against the Lord," to which Nathan replied, "The Lord also hath put away thy sin; thou shalt not die." (II Samuel 12:13.) The importance and efficacy of penitence is intrinsic in the tale of David's sins, just as Lyra pointed out. It must also have been clear to Lefèvre.

Lefèvre knew David as just and penitent, but this awareness is strangely lacking in the commentary on Psalm 50. We believe this to be further substantiation of the conclusions offered for that psalm. Psalm 50 served Lefèvre's purpose of extolling his own hermeneutic at the expense of Lyra's literal approach which served an exemplary and moralizing purpose.

Lefèvre d'Etaples assumes a strange, though not enigmatic, position in the tradition of psalm exegesis. Strange, because his role is one of exegetical retrenchment. He uses several of the Davidic concepts common to the tradition and especially to Nicolaus of Lyra. David as Christ-figure, as the type of the pious man and of the Church, as the penitent and just man, and as the sinner are all within Lefèvre's arsenal. Yet he explicitly avoids Nicolaus of Lyra's pastoral and historical parallelism in the preface to the *Quincuplex psalterium;* and in his psalms he explicitly, as in Psalm 50, rejects Lyra's fruitful literalism by demonstrating how easily understood is the base (or real) literal sense, and also how obvious is its lesson about sin and divine punishment. Strange, too, is Lefèvre's momentary digression (or so it seems) to discuss David the just and penitent man. This conceptual foray remains brief because, for Lefèvre, the important message of the Psalms is the prophetic one through the inspiration of the Holy Spirit. Truly, when Lefèvre stressed the "intention of the author" in his preface, the author he referred to was the divine author of Sacred Scripture.

Lefèvre's use of his concepts of David illuminates a theory of prophecy very different from that by which Nicolaus of Lyra operated. Lyra's David was the greatest prophet because of the constant infusion of the grace of the Holy Spirit. This would not appear, on the face of it, to be at variance with Lefèvre's phrase, "Propheta loquitur in spiritu." The dissimilarity between the two modes of prophecy is put into greater relief, however, when one analyzes each scholar's expositions of the psalms and of David. David receives, in Lyra's mode of interpretation, what might be better termed a constant infusion of spiritual grace of the sort that can be expected of a *viator*. Lyra's David is a spiritual man, living from day to day— through many experiences—constantly oscillating about the pole of virtuousness and religious awareness. Lefèvre's prophet, David, does not stand as a *viator*, nor as a model to men of faith. He utters, rather forecasts, what is to come in the Christian era without seeming to partake of it.

These remarks lead us also to rather obvious conclusions concerning Lefèvre's concept of the nature of the universal historical David—and of the Jewish people living under the Old Covenant. We find David as their spokesman, hoping for, desiring, the Messiah's Advent.[42] David's—and the Jews'—religion is one of hope, but not of fulfillment, moral or theological. Nicolaus of Lyra had not posited theological fulfillment for the Hebrew religion: that could only come with Christ. But Lyra at least held the Jews and their David to be morally fulfilled in their religion, so much so that David could be offered as an example to the Christian fold. Lefèvre's David is incomplete in every religious sense save for the gift of prophetic enunciation which was vouchsafed to him.

Lefèvre's David, then, remains a religious pigmy. So does the ancient religion of Israel. The Old Testament as a whole, it would be logical to conclude, is almost as Marcion had described it: a book of scant value, whose brazen immoralities made it embarrassing to use, if not dangerous, as part of the canonical literature. Its saving grace devolves for Lefèvre from the intention of the author informed by the Holy Spirit, the factor which "saves" the Old Testament by lifting it above its inherent religious poverty through the interpretational method of the double literal sense.

We said at the beginning of this excursion into the Davidic interpretations of Lefèvre d'Etaples that Nicolaus of Lyra's method of interpretation was fragile. Its fragility is attested to by Lefèvre's commitment to the double literal sense which manages to undo all that Lyra had achieved: a burgeoning respect for the innate worth of the Old Testament and its religious life; growing understanding of David as a religious man, rather than as an exceptional prophet who was allowed to see beyond the dullish horizon of his contemporaries; and, most importantly, the literalism that turned David into a figure to be imitated, that made him applicable to the ongoing history of the Christian Church, that, finally, interpreted God's Covenant as something that varies in its completeness, but is nonetheless perennial.

Lefèvre must, indeed, have had reason to reject Nicolaus of Lyra's work. We have mentioned one of the probable motives at the outset of this chapter: veneration of the Church Fathers that caused Lefèvre's exegesis to simulate in its Christologically-oriented results the commentaries of Ambrose and Augustine. The most potent motive, however, was Lefèvre's desire to usher reform into the Church. Certainly a reformer might and does look to the laity; he might, like Lyra, try to provide moralizing Davidic lessons. But we are aware of Lefèvre's concern for the "sweetness" absent in the monastic life.[43] It was with the restoration of this "sweetness" that Lefèvre concerned himself. His order of priorities—reform of the monastic circles first—probably encouraged him to interpret David Christologically rather than pastorally, to interpret the Old Testament so that the higher literal sense dominated his expositions, so that Christ was seen rather than David.[44] The monks, their eyes turned to Christ when they read the Psalms, would be elevated to Christ. They would sense the "sweetness" of Holy Scripture once again. To our mind, the loss that accompanied this restoration was unfortunate.

# NOTES

[1]Oberman, *Forerunners*, p. 286; Preus, *op. cit.*, p. 88, and Chapter 6, *passim*.

[2]*Ibid.*, Chapter 7, *passim*. Preus claims that James Perez of Valencia was the first exegete truly to reconcile the Old and New Testaments because he shifted "the *definiens* of justification from grace and *caritas* to faith in Christ" through the Promise (p. 122). Yet, Preus admits that "there is a problem. It is not at all clear from Perez' prologue [to the Old Testament] whether he really means to say this—really understands this as the concrete situation of particular Old Testament men—or whether, finally, this is only a different form of spiritual exegesis in which the Old Testament people are merely *signa tantum* of the timeless 'homo mysticus'. . . . Were actual Old Testament people being justified by faith in Christ, or is this the spiritual 'meaning' of the Old Testament history as a whole, dehistoricized in terms of the universal Adam?" (p. 121). Moreover, Preus states that Perez is on the point of breaking through to the position of the mature Luther (see Chapter IV, below), but does not. At any rate, we believe that Preus' evaluation of Perez underrates the achievement of Lyra, who did establish David's faith and repentance, etc., as living realities.

[3]Jacques Lefèvre d'Etaples [Faber Stapulensis] was born in Etaples, Picardy, *ca.* 1461. He died in Nérac, French Navarre, in March 1536. A humanist Aristotelian with mystical inclinations, he was educated at the University of Paris. From about 1490 until his retirement from teaching in 1508, he lectured on philosophy at the collège du Cardinal Lemoine. He continued his scholarly work under the patronage of Guillaume Briçonnet at the abbey of Saint-Germain-des-Prés. When the abbot Briçonnet became bishop of Meaux, he called Lefèvre to Meaux to aid him in diocesan reform. Lefèvre remained there until 1525. It was during this period that Lefèvre made a French translation of the New Testament (1523) and of the Psalms (1524). Alarmed by the penetration of Lutheranism into France, the theological faculty of the University of Paris investigated Lefèvre's works and found eleven errors in his commentary on the Gospels (1523). Lefèvre was summoned before the *Parlement* of Paris on suspicion of heresy, but he fled to Strasbourg in the summer of 1525. Recalled by Francis I in 1526, he became the librarian at Blois and he also tutored the king's children. Under royal protection, Lefèvre completed his translation of the Bible (published at Antwerp in 1530). His last years passed in a tranquil manner at the court of Marguerite d'Angoulême, the Queen of Navarre and the sister of Francis I. Lefèvre was principally interested in the philosophy of Aristotle, the Pauline Epistles, patristic literature, and medieval mysticism. For fuller accounts of the life and works of Lefèvre d'Etaples, see: E. Amann, DTC 9.1:132-159; Renaudet, *op. cit., passim;* Eugene F. Rice, Jr., *The Prefatory Epistles of Jacques Lefèvre d'Etaples and Related Texts* (New York: Columbia University Press, 1972), pp. xi-xxv; and the articles cited in notes 4 and 18, below.

[4]Eugene F. Rice, Jr., "The Humanist Idea of Christian Antiquity: Lefèvre d'Etaples and his Circle," *Studies in the Renaissance*, 9 (1962), p. 129.

[5]Bainton, *art. cit.,* discusses the various exegetical techniques which were employed in the fifteenth and sixteenth centuries in order to explain away Old Testament immoralities.

[6]See above, pp. 16 ff.

[7]Roland Bainton, *Erasmus of Christendom* (New York: Charles Scribner's Sons, 1969), pp. 142-143. Bainton also remarks (p. 143) that Erasmus was no less displeased than previous exegetes with the immoralities found in the Old Testament; so much displeased, in fact, that he could almost have been a Marcionite. Indeed, Erasmus delved little into Old Testament commentary (he never became adept as a Hebraist, and was too intellectually honest and philologically concerned to attempt large-scale exegeses of the Old Testament; cf. Louis Bouyer, Cong. Orat., *Erasmus and His Times* [Westminster, Maryland: The Newman Press, 1959], pp. 111-112 and 123-125); and he wrote expositions only on a handful of psalms. One of the psalms he chose to comment upon was Psalm 1; but he chose it only because its first verse ("Beatus vir") allowed him to make a polite pun: "Beatus vir" became Beatus Rhenanus, a humanist colleague and friend. Lewis W. Spitz, *The Religious Renaissance of the German Humanists* (Cambridge, Mass.: Harvard University Press, 1963), pp. 216-219, briefly discusses Erasmus' attitude towards the Old Testament and the Psalms, an attitude partially formed by his admiration of Origen. There is a short but thorough study of Erasmus' hermeneutic: John W. Aldridge, *The Hermeneutic of Erasmus* (Richmond, Virginia: John Knox Press, 1966).

[8]The preface to the *Psalterium David* (Paris: Simon de Colines, 1524) is dedicated to Jean de Selve; the "exhortation en la fin" of the *Psaultier de David* (Paris: Simon de Colines, 1525) is addressed to Lefèvre's Christian readers; and the preface to the *Quincuplex Psalterium* (Paris: Henri Estienne, 1509) is dedicated to Cardinal Guillaume Briçonnet. Critical editions of these epistles may be found in Rice, *Prefatory Epistles*, Epistles 142, 140 and 66. The most famous of Lefèvre's Psalters is of course the *Quincuplex Psalterium*. As Rice, *art. cit.*, p. 146, points out, the bulk of this

text is an edition of a medieval triple Psalter (a *Psalterium iuxta Hebraeos, Gallicanum et Romanum*).  The three versions are set up in parallel columns.  To these Lefèvre added a *Psalterium vetus* and a *Psalterium conciliatum*.  The former is the version the churches used before Jerome's revisions; since Lefèvre constructed the *Psalterium vetus* from the *lemmata* in Augustine's *Enarrationes in Psalmos,* this is one proof that Lefèvre knew Augustine's commentaries very well.  The *Psalterium conciliatum* was the Vulgate "corrected" from Jerome's *Psalterium iuxta Hebraeos.*

[9]Lefèvre, *Psalterium David,* Preface; ". . . quid aliud est divinae scripturae lectio quam quaedam animi nostri felix ad Deum peregrinatio?  Neque enim per aliud quodcumque studium propius ad Deum nos accedere contingit.  Et quis neget hunc ad Deum vere esse accessum, cum ipsum in ea loquentem audiamus?  Nam sacra scriptura (modo quis recte diffinire velit) nihil aliud est quam quaedam Dei loquela qut loguelae eius expressio.  At ita ferme comparatum est, ut qui aliquo peregrinantur compendio maxime gaudeant, ut quam citissime possint optatum pertingant terminum.  Et nescio an usquam magis sit Dei loquela et non fluxae sed consubstantialis loquelae eius (quae Christus dominus est) expressio quam in psalmis Davidicis." (Cf. Rice, *Epistles,* p. 471.)

[10]Lefèvre, *Psalterium David,* Preface: "Itaque tu et ipsi pro incomparabili animi vestri candore opus ipsum suscipite, non nosipsos, non nostros qualescumque labores attendendo, sed *Davidem ipsum, organum spiritus sancti* ad has sacras hymnidicasque odas Deo concinendas, sed patrem misericordiarum et Christum ipsum, de quibus hi divino afflatu sunt psalmi. . . .  O quam magnifice accrescit fides, . . . cum in ipsis videamus spiritum sanctum nihil non omnibus saeculis clarissime cercentem, omnia Christi mysteria praedicere ab incunabilis eius usque ad . . . [iustum] Dei iudicium. . . ." (Our italics: note that Lefèvre calls David "the organ of the Holy Spirit.")  Cf. Lefèvre, *Le psaultier de David,* Une exhortation en la fin:  "Et ces louenges sont faictes par lesprit parlant par David deuant laduenement de nostre seigneur Jesuchrist pres de mil ans. . . .  Doncques par ces louenges si long temps faictes deuant son aduenement, contenans son aduenement, sa nativité, son adoration par les roys, sa conuersation en terre, ses faictz, les congregations et conseilz contre luy faictz, sa mort et passion, sa resurrection, son ascension, sa session à la dextre de dieu son pere, la mission du sainct esprit et de ses apostres par le monde, du salut de tous fait par luy, et autres diuins mysteres. . . ." (Cf. Rice, *Epistles,* pp. 473, 488.)

[11]Lefèvre, *Psalterium David,* Preface: "Et quis ambigat psalmos ipsos de Christo esse, cum ipse apud Lucam [Luke 24:44] dicat, Necesse est impleri omnia quae scripta sunt in lege Moysi et prophetis et psalmis de me?  Et David de seipso novissima verba locutus etiam dicat, Dixit David filius Isai, dixit vir cui constitutum est de Christo Dei Iacob, egregius psaltes Israel.  Spiritus domini locutus est per me, et sermo eius per linguam meam? . . .  Et adeo nemo id possit inficiari, ut etiam Iudaei ipsi testentur, non psalmos modo sed et prophetas omnes de tempore Messiae locutos.  Auctores sunt Rabbi Ioanna et Rabbi Salomo, cuius haec sunt verba, Omnes prophetae non prophetaverunt nisi de diebus redemptionis et diebus Messiae. . . .  Christus dominus est totius scriptura spiritus.  Et scriptura sine Christo scriptura sola est et littera quae occidit; . . ." (Cf. Rice, *Epistles,* pp. 473, 475, 476.)

[12]Lefèvre, *Quincuplex Psalterium,* Dedicatory Epistle.  We have used the English translation of Lefèvre's dedicatory epistle by Paul L. Nyhus, in Oberman, *Forerunners,* pp. 297-301.  When appropriate, we will give the original Latin equivalent of our discussion, which will be cited as "Lefèvre, Ded. Ep."  Later, when we discuss his comments on the psalms in the *Quincuplex Psalterium,* we will use the following citation:  "Lefèvre, Ps. ___, fol(l). ___."  The quotation to which this note refers is from Oberman, *Forerunners,* p. 297.

[13]Lefèvre, Ded. Ep.: "Tunc coepi mecum ipse cogitare ne forte ille non verus litteralis sit sensus, sed . . . sit res pro re et sensus pro sensu inductus.  Ilico igitur me contuli ad primos duces nostros [the Apostles, Evangelists, and Prophets] . . . et videor michi alium videre sensum, qui scilicet est intentionis prophetae et spiritus sancti in eo loquentis, et hunc litteralem appello sed qui cum spiritu coincidit; . . ." (Cf. Oberman, *Forerunners,* p. 298. Rice, *Epistles,* pp. 193-194.)

[14]Lefèvre, Ded. Ep.: ". . . non videntibus autem, qui se nichilominus videre arbitrantur, alia littera surgit, quae (ut inquit apostolus) occidit et quae spiritui adversatur.  Quam et Iudaei nunc sequuntur, in quibus etiam nunc impletur prophetia. . . .  Et huiusmodi sensum litteralem appellant non prophetae profecto, sed quorumdam 'Rabinorum suorum,' qui divinos David hymnos maxima ex parte de ipsomet exponunt, de pressuris eius in persecutione Saulis et aliis bellis quae gessit, non facientes eum in psalmis prophetam, sed per eum visa et facta narrentem et quasi propriam texentem historiam.  Cum tamen ipse de se dicat: 'Spiritus domini locutus est per me, et sermo eius per linguam meam'. . . ." (Cf. Oberman, *Forerunners,* p. 298. Rice, *Epistles,* p. 194.)

[15]Lefèvre's attack on the rabbinic exegetes (see note 14, above: "Et huiusmodi sensum litteralem . . .'Rabinorum suorum' ") is a criticism of Lyra as well (cf. Oberman, *Forerunners,* p. 305, n. 6).  This is especially true since Lefèvre knew the rabbinic literature mainly through his reading of Lyra's *Postillae.*

[16]This need of God's illumination in order to arrive at a correct and pious understanding of Holy Scripture approaches, if it is not the equivalent of, Luther's assurance that his scriptural exegesis was guided by the Holy Spirit and right reason.

[17]Lefèvre, Ded. Ep.: "Quapropter duplicem crediderim sensum litteralem. Hunc improprium, caecutientium et non videntium qui divina solum carnaliter passibiliterque intelligunt, illum vero proprium, videntium et illuminatorum. Hunc humano sensu fictum, illum divino spiritu infusum. . . . Ad quod consequendum brevem in psalmos expositionem Christo adiutore tentavi, qui est clavis David et de quo illi in hac psalmodia per spiritum sanctum, ut dictum est, constitutum erat." (Cf. Oberman, *Forerunners*, pp. 298-299. Rice, *Epistles*, p. 194.)

[18]Be this as it may, Lefèvre's concern for restoring "sweetness" to monastic life and its attendant hermeneutic corresponded happily with his reformatory goal. Unlike the Protestants to whom we are about to turn, Lefèvre aimed at restoring the piety and evangelical simplicity of the early Church and Fathers. (The Protestants, on the other hand, found in the Psalms authentication for their doctrines.) The "sweetness" that Lefèvre sought to restore was deeply imbedded in the mystical tradition.
Both before and after he joined Briçonnet in Meaux (1521), Lefèvre was profoundly interested in and influenced by the spiritual, mystic literature which he considered especially appropriate in the Cloister. He saw the aim of the monk to be the same as that of the mystic: the achievement of union with the One. Indeed, Lefèvre called this union the sweetest fruit of the contemplative (and therefore the monastic) life. When Lefèvre joined the reforming experiment of Briçonnet at Meaux, the Meaux reformers began to distribute and popularize French translations of the New Testament and the Psalms; this effort was part of their total evangelical program to reform the secular and religious clergy and to sponsor the reading and homiletic explaining of the sacred text. Thus, Lefèvre's ideal of reform involved "genuine understanding" of Scripture. Moreover, Lefèvre asserted that such understanding was impossible when men tried to attain it by means of human reason: "artifices, disputes, ratiocinations," and the scholastic *viae*.
Lefèvre's belief that the "sweetness" of monastic (and lay) life lies in union with the One, i.e., in finding Christ in, for example, the Psalms, is attested to by Lefèvre in the following manner: "May kings, princes, magistrates and the peoples of all nations reflect on nothing else, embrace nothing so much, manifest nothing to the same extent as Christ, the vivifying Word of God and His holy Gospel. And may this be the sole effort and desire of all: to know the Gospel, to follow the Gospel, and everywhere to advance the Gospel. And may all hold firmly to what our ancestors and the early Church, red with the blood of martyrs, perceived: that to know nothing except the Gospel is to know all things: extra evangelium nihil scire est omnia scire." (Quoted by Eugene F. Rice, Jr. in Charles Trinkaus and Heiko A. Oberman, eds., *The Pursuit of Holiness* [Leiden: E. J. Brill, 1974], p. 473.)
On Lefèvre's concept of reform and his attitude towards the mystics, see *ibid.*, pp. 473-474; Eugene F. Rice, Jr., "Jacques Lefèvre d'Etaples and the Medieval Christian Mystics," in J. G. Rowe and W. H. Stockdale, eds., *Florilegium Historiale: Essays Presented to Wallace K. Ferguson* (Toronto: University of Toronto Press, 1971), pp. 95, 97, 99-100; Henry Heller, "Nicholas of Cusa and Early French Evangelism," *Archiv für Reformationsgeschichte*, 63 (1972), pp. 8 & 17; and Anthony Levi, S. J., "Humanist Reform in Sixteenth-Century France," *Heythrop Journal*, 6 (1965), pp. 447-464.

[19]Lefèvre, Ded. Ep.: "Secundum psalmum, 'Quare fremuerunt gentes et populi meditati sunt inania? Astiterunt reges terrae et principes convenerunt in unum adversus Dominum et adversus CHRISTUM eius' et sequentia. Ad litteram exponunt Hebraei de Palestinis qui insurrexerunt in David, Christum domini. Verum Paulus et ceteri apostoli, spiritu Dei repleti, ad litteram de CHRISTO domino, vero MESIAH et vero Dei filio (ut et verum est et decet) exponunt. . . . Et longum esset per singulos psalmos ostendere quem Hebraei astruunt litteralem sensum nequaquam illum litteram velle, sed figmentum esse et mendacium." (Cf. Oberman, *Forerunners*, pp. 299-300. Rice, *Epistles*, p. 195.)

[20]Lefèvre, Ded. Ep.: *"Sensus igitur litteralis et spiritualis coincidunt.* Non quem allegoricum aut tropologicum vocant, sed quem spiritus sanctus in propheta loquens intendit. Et huic eliciendo sensui. quantum spiritus Dei dedit, invigilavimus." (Our italics. Cf. Oberman, *Forerunners*, p. 300. Rice, *Epistles*, pp. 195-196.)

[21]Lefèvre, Ps. 7, fol. 13 recto: "Nichil absonum est David gessisse figuram Christi; Absalonem et populum Israel, Iudae, principum et cohortis. . . . David latet in campestribus: Dominus in sepulchro. Absalon crine pendet: Judas fune fauces stringitur. Redit David in Hierusalem, victor honoratus: Dominus de sepulchro surgit gloriosus ad suos rediens devictis hostibus et solutis inferni doloribus. Et multi huiusmodi ex historia secundi regum concinnare potes. . . ."

[22]Lefèvre, Ps. 16, fol. 236 recto: "Quinquagesimoquinto versu non pro primo et typico sed pro secundo et vero David, de quo Hieremias, 'Servient domino Deo suo et David regi suo quem suscitabo eius.' Et Ezechiel, 'Non erunt ultra duae gentes nec dividentur amplius in duo regna, neque polluentur ultra in idolis suis, et ero Deus et servus meus David rex super eos, et pastor unus erit omnium eorum.' "

[23]Lefèvre, Ps. 33, fol. 55 recto: "Titulus:  Ipsi David quando commutavit os suum coram Abimelech.  Psalmus de Christo domino quando commutavit faciem suam, quando divinitatem suam dissimulavit, quando contexit formam pauperis accipiens coram Abimelech in conspectu iudaeorum in conspectu regni patris sui.  Id enim Abimelech significat.  Propheta in spiritu inducit Christum de patre loquentem et suos hortantem."  Lefèvre here agrees with Augustine.

[24]Lefèvre, Ps. 58, fol. 91 recto: "Titulus:  Ad victoriam ut non disperdas David humilem ac simplicem quando misit Saul et custodierunt domum eius ut interficeret eum. . . .  David Christi domini, Saul populi hebraici; Domus David: sepulcri domini; missi ad custodiam:  custodum sepulcri; demissio David per fenestram egressionis Domini sepulcro clauso figuram gessit. . . .  Psalmus de Christo domino.  Propheta inducit Christum ad patrem."  Lefèvre's interpretation of Psalm 15 also demonstrates how little he conceives of David in human terms, for David is really Christ praying to the Father: "Titulus:  Humilis et simplicis psalmus David.  Psalmus de Christo domino qui vere humilis est et simplex. . . .  Propheta in spiritu.  Inducit Christum ad patrem" (fol. 24, recto).

[25]Lefèvre, Ps. 53, foll. 84 recto & verso: "Titulus:  Ad victoriam in psalmis eruditio David cum venissent Ziphei et dixissent Saul, 'Nonne David absconditus est apud nos.'  Pro titulo legatur caput xxvi primi regnorum.  David personam gessit Christi orantis in horto; Ziphei Judae traditoris; Saul, Abner, et complices, principum sacerdotum et cohortis. . . .  '[E]t inimicos meos videt oculus meus':  respicit quod dicitur capite 26 primi regnorum.  Venerunt ergo David et Abisai nocte ad populum.  Et invenerunt Saul iacentem et dormientem in tentorio, et hastam fixam in terra ad caput eius.  Abner autem et populum dormientes in circuitu eius; quod et Christum nocte resurgentem, clypeatos hastatosque custodes suos dormientes et cecum populum hebraicum reperisse figurare potest."

[26]Lefèvre, Ps. 17, foll. 28 verso & 29 recto: "Titulus:  Ad victoriam servo Domini David qui locutus est Domino verba cantica huius in die qua eripuit eum Dominus de manu omnium inimicorum eius et de manu Saul.  Psalmus de Christo Domino.  Propheta in spiritu inducit eum ad patrem. . . .  'Propter haec tanta beneficia tua confitebor tibi in nationibus, laudationes tuas notas faciam in gentibus, . . . nomini tuo psalmam dicam; nomini tuo canam laudem,' magnificans salutes regis eius: 'Christi tui quem constituisti regem,' et faciens misericordiam Christo suo David: 'Messiae tuo desiderabili et semini eius. . . .'"

[27]Lefèvre, Ps. 39, fol. 66 recto: "Titulus:  Ad victoriam psalmus David.  Psalmus de Christo Domino.  Propheta in spiritu Christum de patre loquentem inducit ad fideles."

[28]When Lefèvre comments on the psalms attributed to the Sons of Korah and to Asaph, he says that they speak *in spiritu* too.  They are thus no different from David as prophets; consequently, the individuality of David and his functions are virtually subordinated once more to the *sensus propheticus* which informs all the psalms.

[29]Lefèvre, Ps. 35, fol. 59, recto: "Titulus:  Pro victoria servi Domini David.  Psalmus de Christo Domino.  Propheta in spiritu loquitur.  Adverte:  Circa titulum pro victoria servi Domini.  Pro victoria Christi Domini pueri patris eterni, qui vicit mundum et Sathanum compensata iustitia pro iniustitia, obedientia pro perfidia, sanctimonia pro inquinatione, et tandem fuso suo preciosissimo sanguine pro omnium noxa.  Confidite inquit:  ego vici mundum."

[30]Lefèvre, Ps. 56, fol. 88 verso: "Titulus:  Ad victoriam ut non disperdas David humilem et simplicem quando fugit a facie Saul in speluncam. . . .  David humilis et simplex, Christus Dominus in passione.  Saul invidus, malivolus et superbus, populus hebraicus. Spelunca, gloriosum Domini sepulcrum.  Propheta in spiritu Dominum inducit ad patrem orantem."  See also Ps. 9, fol. 18 recto: "Circa titulum ad victoriam super passione Domini, quia hic psalmus quaedam confessio et gratiarum actio est bonorum que saluificam domini passionem sunt secuta. . . ."  Here the historical circumstances which prompted the psalm appear to have changed.  However, the Christological intention remains the same.

[31]Lefèvre, Ps. 62, fol. 95 recto: "Adverte:  Primo versu, 'Deus Deus meus,' pro quo Hieronymus ex Hebreo traduxit 'deus fortitudo mea.'  Id 'Deus meus' in Hebreo habetur idem verbum quo Dominus ad patrem in cruce circa horam nonam clamavit, 'Deus meus, Deus meus.'  Sic enim in Hebreo hic psalmus incipit, 'ELOHIM ELI' ubi revera 'ELOHIM' plurale est, et 'ELI' singulare, ad secretum trinitatis et Unitatis Mysterium ad discretionem hypostaseon et consubstantialitatem earum."

[32]Lefèvre, Ps. 24, foll. 42 recto & verso: ". . . Oratio ad Christum Dominum.  Propheta in spiritu loquitur personam gerens populi fidelis. . . .  Adverte:  Vicesimo versu, rectus ex Hebreo disceretur simplicitas et rectitudo adheserunt michi, nam David non est privatus sed in persona populi sancti loquitur: quod sequenti versu insinuatur ex quo cognoscitur rectius ultimum versum in nostra translatione hebrea vetusta et greca stare quam in romana ubi adiungitur 'me' particula anceps aut pro privato aut pro multitudine.  Et si malumus legere ut septuaginta innocentes et recti, rectius adhuc legendum adherebunt michi quam adheserunt, tum ex Hebreo tum ex precedentis versus vocabulo non erubescam."

[33]Lefèvre, Ps. 144, fol. 225 recto: "Titulus: Hymnus David. Psalmus, laus Dei et Christi eius regis eterni. Propheta in sua et piorum loquitur persona."

[34]Lefèvre, Ps. 66, fol. 98 verso: "Titulus: Ad victoriam in psalmis canticum carminis. Psalmus de Christo Domino. Propheta loquitur in persona piorum Christi Domini adventum magno affectu poscentium."

[35]Lefèvre, Ps. 139, fol. 219 verso: "Titulus: Ad victoriam psalmus David. Psalmus, deprecatio in spiritu contra haereticos. Populus fidelis inducitur."

[36]Lefèvre, Ps. 22, fol. 38 verso: "Titulus: Canticum David. Psalmus de Christo Domino. Propheta in spiritu loquitur in persona ecclesiae, populi fidelis, et electi. 'Dominus regit me': Christus dominus pascit me doctrina et pabulo vitae. 'Et nichil michi deerit': erit michi spiritualium bonorum sufficientia in loco pascue."

[37]Lefèvre, Ps. 50, foll. 81 recto & verso: "Titulus: Ad victoriam psalmus David, cum venit ad eum Nathan propheta, quando intravit ad Bersabee. Pro titulo legatur undecimum et duodecimum caput secundi regum. Psalmus de David, humana deprecatio. David loquitur. Et cum hic psalmus quid humanum contineat, non prophetiam, non est in eius intelligentia multum laborandum."

[38]See above, pp. 16-17.

[39]See above, pp. 34-35.

[40]Lefèvre, Ps. 51, fol. 83 recto: ". . . Ut primus psalmus continet descriptionem iusti et beati: ita hic iniusti et miseri qui figuratur per Doec Idumaeum. Per David vero figuratur iustus. Propheta loquitur in instructione spiritus." Also, Ps. 31, fol. 52 recto: "Titulus: Eruditio David: . . . Instructio pro penitentibus in spiritu monstrata. Propheta loquitur in persona penitentis."

[41]See Lyra's discussion, pp. 34-35, above. We should note that Lyra had emphasized David's penitence in such a way that David's unfortunate wanderings from godly paths served a pastoral purpose, that of instructing the virtuous Christian that sin is perhaps inevitable; rehabilitation *coram Deo* depends on the sinner's repentance, which restores the covenant between the individual and God. Moreover, Lyra had made this pastoral lesson without failing, at the same time, to portray David as a man of intense faith.

[42]David also represents the Jews praying in the synagogue (Ps. 143, fol. 223 verso: "Titulus: David. Psalmus, laus et deprecatio synagogae. Inducitur synagogae fidelis populus.") Since Lefèvre, unlike Luther and, especially, Melanchthon and Calvin (see Chapters IV-VI below, *passim*), does not distinguish David and the faithful Jews from the unfaithful Jews, it seems to us that Lefèvre sees the Old Testament Jews as a "*signa tantum* of the timeless 'homo mysticus' " (see note 2, above), whereby it is debatable whether the Jews were justified by faith in Christ, and it is likely that they are seen by Lefèvre as providing the spiritual meaning of the Old Testament history. If this is the case, then Lefèvre discredits the contemporary Old Testament validity of David even more.

[43]See above, p. 51.

[44]For the edification and reform of mendicants and seculars, Lyra's exegesis was more appropriate. For the monastic milieu, patristic and Lefèvrian exegeses were more fitting. Lefèvre's exegesis corresponds to the monastic tradition of *lectio divina* (cf. Smalley, *op. cit., passim*).

# PART II

# DAVID AND THE REFORMATION

## Chapter IV
## The Reformation and the Recovery of the Prophet

In Part I we have charted the course of the shifting concepts of David in the commentaries of our three expositors. Afraid, as Luther was later to say, that "if the Old Testament could be understood in itself, then Christ had died in vain,"[1] Augustine viewed David as the figure of Christ and, when not of Christ, at least as an allegorical symbol who contained little worth in himself except as a kind of Silenus–figure which contained some Christian teachings that would be fulfilled with the Advent of Christ. Lyra, on the other hand, abandoned this allegorical approach and viewed David "literally" as the man himself. Lyra agreed with Rashi that David himself spoke in the psalms.[2] While not entirely rehabilitating David as a man of theological importance, the Franciscan exegete employed what can properly be called a "David *moralisé*"[3] who served as an example to the Christian faithful. Influenced by Lyra's exegesis, Lefèvre d'Etaples contributed a spiritualized understanding of the prophet David who "spoke in the Spirit about Christ." Except that Lefèvre's David was an exceptional prophet before the Age of Grace, there was no reconciliation of the Old and New Testaments theologically and no feeling, as there had been in Lyra's expositions, of David as an image of the faithful Christian.

It is in the commentaries of our selected Protestant reformers that we find the full recovery of David as a real man of faith and as a theological spokesman, on the same plane, both to his own people and to Christians. The Protestant commentators went beyond Lyra's moralizing schema, although they certainly benefited from his emphasis on the historical or literal importance of David's actions and words; and they perceived David as a man who was sanctified by the Holy Spirit rather than as an otherwise mute mouthpiece through whom the Holy Spirit spoke.

We shall find that the Protestants "evangelized" David and with him the Old Testament. David and the faithful Jews have the gift of the Holy Spirit: wisdom. David teaches the Jews about true doctrine, about justification by faith alone, the forgiveness of sins, and true worship. Underlying these, David believes in the promises of God and is, then, a man of faith, hope, and prayer, as are the faithful Jews. With the "reformed" commentaries on the Psalms, David becomes theologically relevant, and the Old and New Testaments no longer have to be forced into agreement either by allegory or by unwitting prophecy, for the Old Testament faith and promise become identical with the faith and promise contained in the New Testament. The faithful and hopeful David and Jews live under the same Covenant, they know Christ through God's promises, and they hope for the fulfillment of the promises in the same way as do true Christians.

One might object, when reading the following examination of the Protestant David, that there is a historiographical paradox in the reformers' David and Old Testament. Believers in the linear progression of history to the Last Judgment, the sixteenth-century reformers yet weave into their linear view a curious cyclical pattern. Theirs, of course, is not the cyclism of Machiavelli, who believed that later civilizations could equal the *virtù* of Rome, but could never surpass it. Naturally the Protestant divines considered the history of the world to be fuller and richer after the Advent and glorification of Christ. However, as we shall see in our examination of the concepts of David, there is an identity between the faith, hope, and promises of the people of the Old Testament and those of the New Testament. The doctrines to be learned, the faith to be preached, and the crises that the faithful must face are repetitions of those which David and the other Old Testament "sons of God" encountered.

Nor is this identity between the Testaments to be wondered at, for to the reformers the Law of the Old Testament and of the Gospel is the word of God,[4] and the works of the Law, existing in both periods, are of equal—that is to say, of no—value.[5]

Why do we find that the Reformation Psalm commentaries which we have studied portray a David and Old Testament which are clear and theologically important by themselves, without having to be authenticated at every turn by the New Testament and Christ? The author believes that there are three motivations underlying the newly applied concepts of David and of the Old Testament. It is impossible to offer absolute proof for the first, for it rests on possible and probable psychological factors which caused the Protestants to identify themselves with David. The second causative motivation is the mature hermeneutic of Martin Luther, through which David became a figure of theological venerability. The third motivation evolves from the problem faced by the Protestants when they jettisoned, at least in theory, the previous Catholic tradition.

There is no more treacherous ground for an historian to tread than to hazard a psychological explanation of the past. Yet it does seem appropriate to suggest that the new view we shall find of David and the Old Testament was in part psychologically motivated. The very situation in which the various reformers found themselves could well have influenced their perception of David and of the history of the Jews. Viewing the history of the Christian Church as a process of rise, decline, and rebirth, it should not be unexpected that the reformers cast more appreciative glances at David and his people. David restored true doctrine and worship, he contended with both internal and external enemies of the Church, he preached to Jews who were a remnant, those who remained in the faithful synagogue.

The reformers also found themselves surrounded by enemies, external and internal (though there are different degrees of the expression of this struggle against material foes in the reformers we shall study). They felt themselves to be the "faithful remnant" which was preaching true doctrine to a religious world that had become lax and had fallen away, and the anguish of the spirit which is so apparent in Luther (and which is also found in other reformers) nicely parallels the anguished cries of David. The historical resemblance between the Age of Reformation and the time of David could in this way have contributed to the realization of the Protestant and Protestantized David in the expositions of Luther, Melanchthon, Calvin, and Beza.

There is indeed a certain amount of evidence that some reformers did become caught up with David in a personal way. In the Peasants' War of 1524-1525 Thomas Müntzer encouraged his troops by convincing them of the invincibility of the tiny few who were supported by God's justice; he equated their struggles with those of Gideon and David of old.[6] Philip Melanchthon delivered his inaugural lecture to the University of Wittenberg on August 29, 1518. Luther, of course, was present. As he watched and heard the unimposing, stammering, and strident-voiced Greek scholar win over his audience with his address on the reform of studies at the university, Luther remarked that the audience forgot Melanchthon's crude appearance and "saw in him only the David who was destined to go forth against the Goliath of Scholasticism."[7]

The case of John Calvin is perhaps the most striking of all. The preface to his *Commentary on the Psalms* indicates Calvin's complete self-identification of his career with that of David. We might cite it as a very special and unusual concept of David: David as the figure of John Calvin. Explaining the reasons why he undertook the writing of an exposition on the Psalms, Calvin tells the reader:

> I began to perceive . . . that this was by no means a superfluous undertaking, and I have also felt from my own experience, that . . . I would furnish important assistance in understanding the Psalms. . . . And as David holds the principal place among the writers of the Psalms, it has greatly aided me in understanding more fully the complaints made by him of the internal afflictions which the Church had to sustain through those who gave themselves out to be her members, that I had suffered the same or similar things from the domestic enemies of the Church. For although I follow David at a great distance, and come far short of equalling him, . . . I have no hesitation in comparing myself with him. . . . [I]t has . . . been of very great advantage to me to behold in him as in a mirror, both the commencement of my calling, and the continued course of my functions; so that I know the more assuredly, that whatever the most illustrious king and prophet suffered, was exhibited to me by God as an example for imitation. . . . But as he was taken from the sheepfold, and elevated to the rank of supreme authority; so God having taken me from my originally obscure and humble condition, has reckoned me worthy of being invested with the honorable office of a preacher and minister of the Gospel.[8]

After narrating his conversion both to the Gospel and to the ministry of the Word, Calvin compares his struggles to the tribulations and calumnies which David sustained from the Philistines and other external enemies, as well as from those within the Church. He refers indirectly to the doctrinal challenges by Pierre Caroli and the Anabaptists in 1537.[9] The years between 1541 and 1555, when Calvin struggled for supremacy in Geneva against the Perrinists and other so-called *libertins,* were also paralleled, Calvin thought, by the obstacles David had encountered when he had set about restoring the true religion. Both bore vicious slanders from these enemies within, and so Calvin could "complain with David," "Yea, mine own familiar friend, in whom I trusted, which did eat of my bread, hath lifted up his heel against me"; and again, "For it was not an enemy that reproached me . . .: but it was thou, a man mine equal, my guide and mine acquaintance. We took sweet counsel together, and walked into the house of the Lord in company."[10] Thus, Calvin points out in the text of his commentary that David, as was applicable to his own experience in those years, "calls to God's tribunal . . . the degenerate Jews who, circumcised in the flesh, boast that they belong to the holy progeny of Abraham."[11]

The foes within the Church, however, were not restricted to Geneva. Like David, Calvin was for peace, but when he spoke, they (the Lutherans) were for war. Calvin explains this historical parallel with David's ministry as follows:

> In a distant country towards the frozen ocean, there was raised . . . by the frenzy of a few, a storm which afterwards stirred up against me a vast number of persons, who . . . have nothing to do but by their bickering to hinder those who are laboring for the edification of the Church. I am speaking of those who, boasting mightily of the Gospel of Christ, nevertheless rush against me . . . because I do not embrace their gross and fictitious notion concerning a carnal way of eating Christ in the Sacrament. . . . Certainly if such persons were possessed of even a small portion of humanity, the furor of the Papists

which is directed against me . . . , would appease the most implacable animosity which they may bear towards me.  But since the condition of David was such, that though he deserved well of his own people, he was nevertheless bitterly hated by many without a cause, as he complains in Psalm 69:4 . . . , it afforded me no small consolation when I was groundlessly assailed by the hatred of those who ought to have assisted and solaced me, to conform myself to the example of so great and so excellent a person.[12]

Certainly, then, Calvin's comparison of himself to David bears witness to a sense of historical identity between David and the Genevan reformer in their labors for their faiths.  We can also detect a similar identification by other reformers with David as they were caught up in what they believed were parallel crises, duties and feelings.  But "to conform myself to . . . so excellent a person" indicates a relationship that is more than casual and even more than psychological.  In our explorations of the concepts of David in the Reformation we shall find that Melanchthon and Beza sought, as did Calvin, to imitate the excellent David.  We shall note that these reformers desired *conformity* with David for a reason unknown in Augustine, Lyra, and Lefèvre:  because the Protestant commentators saw in the Psalms and in David the manifestation of the doctrine of the Promise.

David became for the reformers both a preacher of the Promise, of the trust in justification by faith alone, and the man who experienced the revivifying spirit which spells the end of the flesh and sin.  His faith, consequently, became the faith of the reformed religion and his hope for deliverance is also that of the reformers.  And with this realization came, for the first time in the millennium of struggling with the Old Testament, the novel idea that not only David but also the Old Testament were theologically valid and could stand alone without the New Testament.  Gone now are the typologies of the Middle Ages.  To be sure, the reformers still speak of David and the faithful Jews as "types," but they intend something different:  not "types" as shadows, but as the first examples of beliefs and teachings that remain the same under the New Covenant.  It was Martin Luther who first realized that the faith and promise of the Old Testament, as seen through David, were *the* Faith and *the* Promise.

In his recent study, *From Shadow to Promise,* James S. Preus has traced Martin Luther's hermeneutical transformation as he progressed through his lectures on the Psalms between 1513 and 1516.  Preus analyzes how Luther gradually came, in the *Dictata super Psalterium,* to a revolutionary evaluation of the faith of the Old Testament.[13]  Our purpose now is to summarize Preus' arguments in order to demonstrate that Luther indeed was the progenitor of the concepts of David and of the attitude toward Old Testament faith which we shall find in our subsequent study of other reformers' expositions of the Psalms.

Luther's Old Testament hermeneutic gradually changed as he worked on his university lectures on the Psalms.  This metamorphosis is traceable by following Luther's development through the seven Penitential Psalms in the Vulgate:  Psalms 6, 31, 37, 50, 101, 129, and 142.  In his explication of the first four of these psalms, Luther remains wedded to a medieval hermeneutic.  For example, in the exposition of Psalm 6, the psalmist is absent and no indication is given of what the words mean to him.  Rather, the subject of the psalm is Christ, for it is an *oratio Christi.*  Without sin Himself, He suffers for us.  Moreover, there is a tropological identity between the subject of the psalm, Christ, and the penitent man.[14]  While Luther does not interpret Psalm 31 Christologically, the subject is Christian spiritual understanding:  the knowledge that Christ came as our Savior and that without Him all men are in sin.  This spiritual understanding, Luther declares, is a gift of the Holy Spirit.  Although the psalmist is credited here with speaking *in spiritu,* David has no relevance except as a *Christian* theologian.[15]  Thus, Luther's explanation of Psalm 31 and of the role of the psalmist is nearly identical with Lefèvre's definition of the literal sense.

Luther's technique becomes very different when he reaches Psalm 101, the prayer of the pauper anxious about the reality of God's presence and help. Preus demonstrates that Luther first explicated this psalm in 1513, but added a gloss in 1515. In this gloss Luther explains that the pauper is the people before the Advent of Christ, and that the prayer is an urgent petition for the coming of Christ. The pauper's prayer has, moreover, significance for the Christian: tropologically, it is the Christian's prayer for Christ's spiritual advent, when the faithful man experiences temptation.[16] As Preus rightly remarks, " . . . the Psalmist's own words, spoken out of his own circumstances, are the basis of theological interpretation." The object of the psalm is Christ, the subject is now the faithful people before the Incarnation, who passionately longed for the Messiah. Nor is the Christian spoken of in terms of his typological resemblance to Christ, but rather to the Old Testament believer. Finally, the literal sense of the psalm corresponds to the historical situation.[17]

The expositions of Psalms 129 and 142 complete the development which occurs in the *Dictata super Psalterium*, wherein the Old Testament attains theological independence: independence, because Luther, having discovered the faithful synagogue's real faith and trust in the promises of God, no longer need apply the psalms and David allegorically or prophetically—in the sense of the Holy Spirit teaching Christian doctrine through the mouth of a two-dimensional prophet who is little more than a passive medium. Whether living before the Incarnation or after it, the faith, hope, trust and prayers of the Old and New Testament faithful are identical.[18] From this point, the subjects of the psalms are the "faithful remnant" of the Old Testament who await the promised Messiah and his eternal benefices; it is they who suffer temptations and trials and who look forward to deliverance. The application of this "faithful remnant" concept, whether applied to David or to all faithful pre-Advent Jews, makes them a people of the Promise, filled with faith, or rather, Reformation faith, in the form of trust and hope.[19] When applied morally to the post-Incarnation faithful, we shall find in Melanchthon and Calvin that they also await with faith the fulfillment of the Promise which will be displayed in earthly deliverances and the establishment of the eternal kingdom. The Old Testament, the Psalms, and David thus became substantial rather than merely prefigurative *exempla* for the sixteenth–century Protestants who also have faith and trust, and await the future advent of the *liberatio* which only Christ can provide.

The revolutionary aspect of Luther's exegesis of the later psalms in the *Dictata* has gone unrecognized by eminent historians of biblical scholarship and of the Reformation. Guided by Luther's rejection of the historical understanding of the Psalms in the preface to the *Dictata* and by his criticism of Nicolaus of Lyra's employment of that technique, Gerhard Ebeling sees only Luther's antithesis of the letter and the spirit.[20] Ebeling understands this antithesis in terms of *figura* or *umbra* and *veritas,* and thus, for him, Luther opposes the Old and New Testaments and their peoples. Yet Ebeling's citations indicate that he reached this conclusion on the basis of a consideration of Luther's earlier psalm expositions, that is, those before 1515. But, as we have seen, it is only in the later explications and glosses that Luther discovered the faith in God's promises which made David and the "faithful remnant" worthy of emulation precisely because they were existentially on the same level as Christians in their trust in, and expectation of, the fulfillment of the promises.[21]

E. Gordon Rupp comes basically to the same conclusion as does Ebeling: Luther's psalm commentaries rejected Lyra's literal interpretation. He adds,

> But we must remember that Luther was concerned with the Psalms, and that a literal interpretation of the Psalms would leave many of them baffling indeed, so that even Lyra himself made frequent use of tropology.[22]

We may note, however, that Rupp also documents his argument by referring to the early expositions in the *Dictata*.[23]   Rupp also fails to see that it is not whether Luther (or Lyra) employs a tropological method that is crucial, but rather the route to the tropological explanation.   As we have seen, Luther's more mature methodology in the psalms is to fasten upon the historical situation of David (or his people) and to find the identity between their milieu and strivings and those of Christians who also live under the Promise.   The habit of adding a tropological explanation, found both in Luther and Lyra, represents less a concession on Luther's part to medieval exegesis than a turn by Luther to the novel aspect of Lyra's exegesis.   For both of them came to realize the identity between the Old and New Testaments— morally, in the case of Lyra, and theologically, in the case of Luther.

Luther's shift from a Lefèvrian hermeneutic to a profound concern for the Old Testament *sensus litteralis* can also be seen when one compares his marginal comments in his copy of Lefèvre's *Quincuplex Psalterium* to his preface to the German Psalter.[24]   Luther's marginalia display a close intellectual harmony with Lefèvre's commentary and, therefore, a distaste for Lyra's attempts to explain the psalms' contents "time-historically" for David's time.[25]

In his *Adnotationes,* written in 1513, Luther consistently interprets the Psalms according to the *sensus propheticus.*   He argues, for example, that Christ speaks in Psalm 7.   Only Christ can, as He does in the Gospels, call out "Lord my God," for men say "our God."   Thus, the pronoun "my" always indicates that Christ or His *persona* is the speaker.   Similarly, Christ's words are heard in verse 4 ("O Lord my God, if I have done this, etc."), expressing His innocence when the Jews accused Him of seeking to take over the kingdom.[26]

Not only does Luther someti...es find Christ speaking in the Psalms, but he also insists that David's words foretell future events.   Accordingly, the title of Psalm 17 ("A Psalm of David . . . who spoke unto the Lord the words of this song in the day that the Lord delivered him from the hand of all his enemies, and from the hand of Saul") misleads the reader, for David does not speak of his own deliverance, but of Christ's Passion and Resurrection.[27]   Christological also are Luther's interpretative notes on Psalms 55 and 56. The former represents the Crucifixion and Christ's return to the Father, while the latter refers to Christ's flight into the sepulchre from the synagogue.[28]

Even though the representative marginal notations that we have cited indicate Luther's reliance on Lefèvre's exegetical method, we must not assume that Luther's interpretations in the *Adnotationes* are slavish imitations of Lefèvre's.   He occasionally disagrees with Lefèvre and sides with Augustine or Nicolaus of Lyra.[29]   Yet, even when Luther agrees with Lyra, it concerns the dating of the psalm's composition, not its meaning.[30]   To Luther, the Psalter is prophetic; its words refer to Christ.

When we contrast Luther's remarks on the Book of Psalms in his preface to the German Psalter with his *Adnotationes,* we find an entirely different mode of expression.   His approach to the Psalms in this preface is "time-historical," for he perceives them as "a faithful record of what the saints did and said: how they communed with God and prayed to Him in the old days [i.e., pious Old Testament times], and how such men still commune with Him and pray to Him."[31]   Luther's emphasis is thus upon the faith and piety of the psalmists, not, as it had been in the *Adnotationes,* on the mystery of Christ.

One could accurately paraphrase Luther's message in this preface by saying that the Psalms exhibit the proper response of faithful men to God's goodness and love.   He describes the Psalms as "heartfelt utterances," in which the Old Testament saints "lay bare their hearts and the deepest treasures in their souls." The Psalms are "charming and delightful flowers which grow out of all kinds of beautiful thoughts about God and His grace." Their words therefore reveal true and profound adoration and thanksgiving as well as equally deep-felt penitence. In sum, the Book of Psalms

> enables us to see into their hearts and understand the nature of their thoughts; how at heart the Old Testament saints took their stand in varying circumstances of life, in danger, and in distress. . . . What the Book of Psalms gives us in richest measure in regard to the saints is the fulness of certainty as to what they felt in their hearts, and what was the sound of the words which they used in addressing God and their fellowmen.[32]

The sixteenth-century reader of the Psalms will, according to Luther, learn, and should strive to emulate, the equability in mind and word of the Old Testament saints. The imitation of their tranquility amid the storms of life as well as its joys, will lead the reader "into the fellowship of the saints," that is, the "holy Christian Church."[33]

Luther thus views the Psalter as a witness to the deep faith of the pious Old Testament Jews. Thinking perhaps of his earlier, Lefèvrian exegesis, Luther sadly remarks that before, in "the dark times, what a great treasure it would have been held to be, if a man could have rightly understood one single Psalm."[34] Because he now "rightly" understands the Book of Psalms, the edificatory literature on the saints, which had been written in those "dark times," pales in comparison with the Psalter:

> No book of moral tales and no legends of saints which have been written . . . are to my mind as noble as the Book of Psalms. . . . In comparison with the Book of Psalms [these] other books . . . depict holy men all with their tongues tied; whereas the Book of Psalms presents us with saints alive and in the round. It is like putting a dumb man side by side with one who can speak: the first is only half alive. . . . The moral stories and legends of the saints whose words are never given, advocate works that no man can imitate, works that are, in most cases, the beginnings of sects and factions, that lead and even drag one away from the fellowship of the saints.[35]

These words indicate Luther's and other Protestants' attitude towards the psalmists (including David), and they allude to the contributive role that the problem of tradition played in the rehabilitation of David. Having jettisoned the teaching authority of the Roman Church and its doctrine of salvation, the Protestants had to look elsewhere, to Sacred Scripture itself, for the proof of their theology and faith. If, then, the Protestants found in the words of David (whose psalms formed part of Sacred Scripture) a faith identical to theirs, if they found expressed by David the messianic hope of deliverance, then they would be able to substitute a new but venerable tradition of faith and teaching to replace the Roman tradition which they had eschewed; and the validity of their faith and teachings would be authenticated, not by mere human arguments, but by that very trust in the Promise they found expressed in the Book of Psalms.

## NOTES

[1] Preus, *op. cit.*, p. 149.

[2] Hailperin, *op. cit.*, p. 53.

[3] Lyra's *postillae*, then, might be compared with the popular, late medieval *Ovide moralisé*.

[4] Jaroslav Pelikan, *Luther the Expositor: Introduction to the Reformer's Exegetical Writings* (St. Louis: Concordia Publishing House, 1959), p. 65.

[5] *Ibid.*, p. 242.

[6] E. Gordan Rupp, *Patterns of the Reformation* (Philadelphia: Fortress Press, 1969), p. 244.

[7] Robert Stupperich, *Melanchthon*, trans. by R. H. Fischer (Philadelphia: Westminster Press, 1965), p. 32.

[8] John Calvin, Preface to the *Commentaries on the Psalms*. The preface is completely translated in John Dillenberger, ed., *John Calvin: Selections from His Writings* (Garden City, N. Y.: Anchor Book, 1971), pp. 22-26. In the following discussion of Calvin's preface, we shall quote from this English translation.

[9] John T. McNeill, *The History and Character of Calvinism* (New York: Oxford University Press, 1967), pp. 141-142; cf. also, François Wendel, *Calvin: Origin and Development of His Religious Thought*, trans. by Philip Mairet (New York: Harper and Row, 1963), pp. 53-55.

[10] Psalms 41:9 and 55:12-14. For details on Calvin's arduous rise to supremacy in Geneva, see McNeill, *op. cit.*, pp. 159ff; and E. William Monter, *Calvin's Geneva* (New York: John Wiley & Sons, 1967), Chapter 3. Calvin had been escorted to Geneva in 1540 by Ami Perrin, and he experienced deteriorating relations with the Perrin faction in Geneva until his final break with them in 1548 (*ibid.*, pp. 70 & 80).

[11] John Calvin, *Commentarii in librum psalmorum* (Amsterdam: Jacobus Schipper, 1667), Ps. 5:10, pp. 14-15.

[12] Quoted in Dillenberger, *op. cit.*, pp. 29-33.

[13] As he studied and commented on the Psalms, Luther also began to formulate his doctrines of justification and *coram Deo*. See E. Gordan Rupp, *The Righteousness of God: Luther Studies* (London: Hodder and Stoughton, 2nd edition, 1963), pp. 130-157 for a full analysis of Luther's development as he wrote his first commentaries on the Psalms.

[14] Preus, *op. cit.*, p. 167. *D. Martin Luthers Werke: Kritische Gesamtausgabe* (Weimar: 1833ff.) 55/I. 38. 3-6 (hereafter cited as WA, followed by volume, page, and line references): "Oratio Christi pro suis passionibus et peccatis membrorum suorum ut mediatoris inter deum patrem et homines."

[15] Preus, *op. cit.*, p. 167. WA 3. 172. 24-27: "Scire ergo filium dei esse incarnatum pro salute nostra et extra eum omnes esse in peccatis, hec est eruditio ista, intellectus iste: quod nemo nisi per spiritum sanctum cognovit."

[16] Preus, *op. cit.*, pp. 169-170.

[17] *Ibid.*, pp. 170-171.

[18] *Ibid.*, pp. 171-173. In Psalm 129 David speaks *in behalf of* the Old Testament faithful for Christ's Incarnation; it is, as well, a prayer for any sins. Thus, Luther sets David clearly within the Old Testament ambiance; we may note here the difference between Luther and Lefèvre who said that David represented (*in figura*) the Jews praying in the synagogue (see above, Chapter III, note 42). Furthermore, the Jew *sub lege* is identical tropologically with the Christian *in peccato;* the same analogy applies between the Jew praying for the coming of the Messiah and the Christian entreating forgiveness of sins. Cf. WA 4. 418. 35 - 419.18: "Est autem expressa petitio redemptionis populi a peccatis. . . . Ideo primo intelligitur de redemptione per Christum facta toti generi humano. Sed quia omnis, qui est in peccato, est adhuc sub lege, ideo moraliter est oratio pro quibuscunque peccatis."

[19] Preus, *op. cit.*, pp. 174-175 and *passim*.

[20] Gerhard Ebeling, *Luther: An Introduction to His Thought*, trans. by R. A. Wilson (London: Collins, 1970), pp. 98-100 and notes.

[21] In our examination of Luther's sermons on individual psalms, written in the 1530's, we have found ample support for Preus' position, as opposed to Ebeling's. For example, when discussing Psalm 101, Luther starts his exegesis by referring to the Old Testament event (David against Goliath). Moreover, his explanation never leaves the Old Testament milieu: "When David wanted to beat Goliath, they wanted to teach him; they put armor on him and equipped him (1 Samuel

17:38-39). . . . But David could not wear this armor. He had another Master in mind. . . . For he was no apprentice either, trained in this craft; he was a master, created for it by God." (Trans. in Jaroslav Pelikan, ed., *Luther's Works* [St. Louis: Concordia Publishing House, 1956], Vol. 13 [*Selected Psalms II*], p. 156.) In his sermon on Psalm 101:4, Luther remarks: "In addition [David] sought, demanded, . . . and commanded everywhere that the Word of God be preached in its truth and purity and that God be properly worshipped. . . . He himself composed psalms as a model of how they should teach and praise God . . . . Under his reign more people were properly trained in Scripture than ever before or after. David is a model and master of the way one should seek God's kingdom and His righteousness and of the way to keep people loyal to the Word of God and His preachers." (*Ibid.*, pp. 188ff.) David, then, is a model because he had true faith. These are themes which we shall develop in Chapters V and VI.

[22]Rupp, *Righteousness of God*, p. 133.

[23]*Ibid.*, pp. 133, n. 4 (referring to WA 3. 335. 33) and 134, nn. 1-3 (WA 3. 11. 14; 3. 11. 33; 3. 13. 17).

[24]Luther's *Adnotationes Quincuplici Fabri Stapulensis Psalterio manu adscriptae* (1513) were discovered in 1885 in the Dresden Library. This copy, with the marginal comments in Luther's own hand, was destroyed in the bombing of Dresden at the end of World War II. The edition to which we refer is in *D. Martin Luthers Werke: Kritische Gesamtausgabe*, Vol. 4 (Weimar: 1886), pp. 463-526. The preface to Luther's German Psalter was written for the second edition of the Psalter in 1528. The German text is available in Hanns Rückert, ed., *Die deutsche Bibel*, WA 10$^1$, pp. 98-104; a Latin version of the preface exists in a Wittenberg, 1529 edition; and there is a French translation of the preface in Rice, *Epistles*, Epistle 149. We have used the English translation from the Weimar edition by B. L. Woolf in *Reformation Writings of Martin Luther*, Vol. II (London: Lutterworth Press, 1956 [reproduced in an authorized facsimile by microfilm-xerography in 1967 by University Microfilms, Ann Arbor, Michigan]), pp. 267-271.

[25]Cf. editor's introduction to the *Adnotationes*, WA 4, pp. 463-466.

[26]WA 4. 474. 10-20: "Sic enim in Evangelio Christus vocat 'Deus meus.' Sed nos dicimus 'Deus noster.' . . . Unde hoc pronomen 'meum' semper mihi indicat loquentem Christum aut in persona eius loquentem. . . . 'Domine Deus meus, si feci istud etc.' Solus Christus potest hec verba dicere proprie et non David, cui fuit predictum, quod ista pateretur ex domo propria propter peccatum in Uriam. Igitur omnis persecutor querit occasionem, quomodo accuset pium: sic enim Iudei contra Christum querebant, scilicet quod regnum appeteret. Et ipse sciens suam innocentiam dicit: 'Si feci istud.' "

[27]WA 4. 481. 27-29: "Et tamen ea que ponuntur infra, non fuerunt facta in David liberatione, sed in Christi passione et resurrectione. Ideo de Christo sunt intelligenda."

[28]WA 4. 499. 1-7: ". . . Et sine dubio sensus est de Christo crucifixo et titulo crucis insignito, qui tunc longe abiit per mortem ad patrem. Tunc enim tenuerunt eum Allophyli i.e. alienigene Iudei, generatio adultera. Et in figura sui hoc David previdens de Christo sic loquitur." WA 4. 499. 13-15: "In tituli inscriptione: 'Michtam' ut supra, quando fugit Christus in sepulchrum a facie Saul, i.e. abutentis synagoge, cuius ille erat figura." Notes in a similar vein are made on Psalms 1, 3, and 50 (WA 4. 466, 472, and 496-497).

[29]For example, to Lefèvre's comment on Psalm 7 that Absalom prefigured Judas, Luther remarks: "Rectius b. Augustinus Iudam per Achitophel intelligit psalmo eodem presente" [referring of course to Augustine's translation of "Achitophel" as "ruin of his brother"] (WA 4. 475. 8-9). To Lefèvre's comment on Psalm 7 that the historical situation which occasioned the psalm was David's flight from Absalom, Luther objects (WA 4. 474. 28-30): "Sed meo iudicio dorsum huius psalmi aptius Lyra exponit de Saule. Quia sic verba optime consonant. Non enim David optabat ista mala filio Absalon, sed magis flevit."

[30]Thus, Luther adds to his remark on Lyra (note 29, above): "Sed adhuc melius de Christo" (WA 4. 474. 30). Commenting on Psalm 3:6 ("dormivi et soporatus sum"), Luther writes: "De Davidis autem somno nequaquam. . . . Item si dormivit, quid mirum si exurrexit? Certe mirum, si non exurrexisset, magis fuisset. Igitur bene Burgensis [Paul of Burgos] exponit contra Lyram, non obstante ignivomo illo Matthia [Matthias Döring] calumniatore eius" (WA 4. 472. 35 - 473.2). See also WA 4. 482. 20-25 and 496. 32-35, where Luther says that Lyra's exegesis is in error because it is in disagreement with St. Paul's exegesis.

[31]Woolf, ed. and trans., *op. cit.*, p. 268.

[32]*Ibid.*, p. 269.

[33]*Ibid.*, p. 271.

[34]*Loc. cit.*

[35]*Ibid.*, pp. 267-268.

## Chapter V
## David Theologus

### David Restored

Both Nicolaus of Lyra and Lefèvre d'Étaples viewed David as a member of an inferior Covenant which had given way to the fuller and richer Dispensation of the New Testament. Yet both commentators were able to affect a seemingly happy reconciliation between the Psalms and the New Covenant by founding their interpretations of the former upon the "literal" sense of Scripture. However, since the literal sense implied two different hermeneutical techniques for Lyra and Lefèvre, their images of David also differed.

Starting from a consideration of the literal and moral meanings of David's words, Lyra interpreted David both as a prophet and as a *viator.* David the prophet had been given special illumination concerning the coming of Christ and the institution of His kingdom. David the *viator* was a religious man under the Old Covenant, who, as a pilgrim between birth and death, struggled to perfect his life. David strove to be alienated from the allurements both of this imperfect world and of the *demones* (the fallen angels and their agents, e.g., Saul, who themselves were *alieni,* but in a different way: as Gregory the Great said, they were *a flore aeternae haereditatis alieni.*").[1] David desired both for himself and for his people the order, purity, and harmony which form the "flower of the eternal heritage." Lyra's *viator David* gave rise to a tropological interpretation through which the now pedagogical David instructed, by his example, what conduct and habit of faith should be striven after by crusaders, bishops, clerics in general, and laymen.

Lefèvre's David, on the other hand, was a prophet *par excellence.* The Holy Spirit speaking through him, David prophesied about Christ's Advent and the shape and nature of His kingdom and church. David's words, interpreted according to the *sensus propheticus,* proclaimed a future Covenant which he had experienced only through divine illumination.

Although Lyra and Lefèvre exemplify modes of reconciling the Old and New Testaments, through which David's prophecies and moral teachings could be applied to Christian teaching and conduct, their exegetical paths completed neither the reconciliation of David with the Christian man nor the reconciliation of the Old and New Testaments. One may find an important insight into the nature of Renaissance art instructive in developing this point. The eminent art historian Erwin Panofsky based his interpretation of the Renaissance upon the overcoming of what he termed the "principle of disjunction."[2] In art, the disjunction between the classical figure portrayed and the theme exemplified by the figure remained, until, in the early modern era, both theme and figure were at last conjoined as they had been in classical times.[3] This phenomenon can be traced in two obvious examples. On the famous pulpit by Nicola Pisano there is a figure of Hercules. He represents not the theme of the pagan demi-god but that of the Christian virtue of fortitude. Secondly, Dido and Aeneas, portrayed in twelfth-century book illuminations, are given their classical theme—the lovers who are to be tragically separated, enjoying each other's company before the departure of Aeneas and the immolation of Dido. Yet, although the classical theme is present, the dress of Dido and Aeneas and the setting in which they are placed are decidedly non-classical.[4] It was only with the rehabilitation of the correct classical texts, in which both the figures and the theme exemplified were described, that Renaissance artists, instructed by humanists, accomplished the reunion of classical figure and theme.[5]

As was suggested above, we believe that Panofsky's theory about the incompleteness of previous renascences and the full reunion of classical figure and theme has its corollary in the exegetical writings on David which we have studied. Nicolaus of Lyra had come close to the reunification of the figure of David and the theme, i.e., the true nature of David. As a *viator* Lyra's David spoke about his efforts to perfect his life, but the "principle of disjunction" governed Lyra's *postillae*. In the curious medieval inability to realize historical differences and changes, David was construed as the model of various medieval personages who were unknown to him. Thus, David, in the garb of an Old Testament *viator* under a different Covenant, was dressed up in medieval clothing and situations. On the other hand, Lefèvre's David was actually taken out of his Old Testament setting and, through Lefèvre's understanding of the *sensus propheticus* as the literal sense, David spoke not about himself or his own situation but of Christ and His kingdom and people. In Lyra, then, the moral striving of the figure was maintained but the garb was changed, while in Lefèvre, the setting was prophetically changed because David spoke about the future, although he did this in his role as Old Testament prophet.

What we noted in the last chapter concerning Martin Luther holds true for the three remaining commentators whom we shall discuss: Melanchthon, Calvin, and Beza.[6] Melanchthon and Calvin, though adhering to different churches, are almost identical in their treatment of David. As a consequence the discussion which follows in this chapter will be somewhat redundant. On the other hand, in order to demonstrate that the mid-century Lutheran and Calvinist views of David are basically identical and that their identity stems from the same hermeneutical foundation, rather full expositions of their views must be undertaken.

Melanchthon and Calvin both believe that the Psalms and David can be applied to Christians in the sixteenth century. In this sense they are no different from Nicolaus of Lyra or Lefèvre d'Etaples. Yet they also believe that this contemporary application of David can be accomplished without twisting and distorting David's words allegorically or morally in order to give the psalms theological and consolatory value. Furthermore, in their commentaries upon the Psalms, Melanchthon and Calvin achieve what Panofsky noted about Renaissance art--the abolition of the "principle of disjunction." As we shall see, the two reformers begin their exegeses with David's words and they leave the words in their historical setting and what they considered to be their original meaning. Their application of the words to Christians thus does not betray the existential David, the events in which he was caught up, or his faith and Covenant. The application of the words is based upon the belief that there is no real distinction between the two Covenants, save for the substitution for Old Testament sacrifices of the sacrifice of Christ (which does not affect David since he is already messianic) and the extension of Christ's kingdom to the farthest reaches of the world.

Thus, as in the case of the Renaissance attitude towards classical antiquity, Melanchthon and Calvin are able to effect a *rapprochement* between David and Christians through what they see as a realization of identical theological values and historical crises. This was the result of no mere imposition on the past of present values, but rather the result of the perception that the reformed theologies and churches shared a messianic faith with David and the other Old Testament prophets.

It will seem that the reformers evangelize the Psalms and David since they find the theology of the Reformation expounded in the Psalms. Indeed, it cannot be doubted that this is the case. However, we believe that this discovery of the evangel in David is not so much due to the imposing of alien ideas upon David as it is due to the nature of Protestant theology itself, which shares with the Psalms a forward-looking concept of promise, hope, and eventual deliverance.

The basic premise behind the theology of the classical Reformation is the concept of the Promise. God has promised—and this promise has been effected through Christ—that He will be gracious to those whom He has chosen. The elect are given faith which causes them to depend totally upon God, a dependence that is well-founded and is strengthened by the trust that God will not forsake His promise. Thus, the elect, though they can never be without sin in God's eyes, are considered just by Him through the working of His freely-given grace rather than through their works. The despair of the elected sinner is conquered by the assurance of God's benevolence towards those who depend totally upon Him.[7]

Melanchthon's and Calvin's attitudes towards David are governed by this economy of salvation and they can allow David to abide in his time and in the literal meaning of his words because they find in David that messianic looking-forward which is the foundation of the Reformed theology. Thus, for them, the Psalter becomes almost the equivalent of the New Testament Gospels, and David shares the same sonship of God and brotherhood with Christ which the elect within the Reformed churches share. We shall also endeavor to argue that, on a number of theological and behavioral issues, David is to the reformers the *preceptor* of the Church and that he is a preceptor, not because he is able to overcome the inferiority of the Old Covenant by the special gift of prophecy, but because he shares the trust in the Promise and the Calling, on the basis of which he may instruct the "whole Church."

### Melanchthon and David

Since Melanchthon believes that penitence and faith are stirred by the awareness of iniquity, David's words in Psalm 28 (verse 1)[8] exemplify, according to Melanchthon, David's recognition of his own iniquity and his trust in "the promise of the Gospel." These words

> deplore his impurity and they recognize the just wrath of God. . . . Saul, Judas, and innumerable others have succumbed in such great griefs as these, but David, Ezechias and others, sustaining themselves in the thought of the Promise *or of the Gospel,* know that remission of sin is promised.[9]

Melanchthon contrasts David's relief from these terrors to the confusion of the ancient wise men, such as Cato and Brutus, who, ignorant of the Gospel, did not take refuge in God. They did not know that human affairs are in the care of God, and so they did not foresee deliverance from their confusion and iniquities.[10] Again in Psalm 116, David rejoices because God heard his prayer. Melanchthon remarks that David composed this prayer in the midst of the punishments which followed his adultery, and he adds that "it is the cry of faith." It teaches that we ought not to despair because of our sins; instead, the prayer consoles and sustains us in the promise of mercy. Melanchthon continues,

> David is moved by the consciousness of his fall. . . . He is not able to depend on his merits, but he looks to the free promise of the forgiveness of sins and salvation. Thus he struggles out of the depths with faith. Such examples show the true purpose of these psalms, especially for the godly, whose minds are not filled with carnal security; rather, the godly experience the same tremblings and faith.[11]

There are several important points to be noted in Melanchthon's comments on these two verses.  The first is his equation of the Promise with the Gospel.  He shows that he considers David to have known through the Promise what Christians know through the Gospel.  This is further buttressed by Melanchthon's comparison of David to Cato and Brutus (as well as to Saul and Achitophel), for it suggests that he perceives David as a member of the "faithful remnant" who knew the Promise and thence the Gospel. He specifically indicates that since not all Jews had this faith, David belonged to the Church, the True Israel.[12]  Moreover, again unlike the "wise" pagans and the faithless Jews, David trusted in the Promise, recognized that God's providence is effective everywhere and that salvation comes not from works, but from God alone.[13]  Furthermore, because David's trust was placed not merely in the expectation of the promised Messiah, but also in the promise of eternal salvation, his faith was that of the Restored Church. If David had been only a prophet through whom the Holy Spirit spoke, he would have known the promise of redemption in his mind.  However, Melanchthon asserts that David's assurance of gratuitous mercy, like Paul's, was held firmly in the heart,[14] a part of his existential experience and a sign of the indwelling of the Holy Spirit.

David, then, had inward confidence that his salvation came from God alone.  Yet he did not cease his tremblings.  The righteous man must always consider himself a sinner *coram Deo,* for although the sinner is gratuitously saved, Satan continues to prompt the Flesh to revolt against the interior Spirit.  Consequently, sin remains "even now," after faith and election have been given.  The man who claims that he is by nature upright, is a liar.[15]  Since continuing sin, such as David's adultery, can lead to a diminution of faith, continuing sanctification is necessary.  David also had from God the promise of sanctification,[16] the vivifying Spirit which Christ sends to the elect.  The Holy Spirit buoyed up David's faith and gave him patience so that he did not kill Saul when he had the opportunity, nor did he seize the throne of Israel before the appointed time.  The thought of mercy, thus strengthened, sustained David in all his trials, whether against sin or against Saul and Goliath.[17]

The promise of sanctification serves the two purposes of endowing the faithful man with the strength to continue to rely upon the promise of earthly and heavenly deliverance, as well as to submit to the will of God until such deliverance.  The disturbances caused by the obstinacy of the Flesh against hope and faith continue throughout the lives of David and all the faithful.  The promise of the indwelling Spirit sustained David so that he was able to cry out, "I will not die, but I will live and tell the works of the Lord."  Melanchthon says,

> David *felt* that he was delivered from his enemies, and he grew in faith and in spiritual gifts.  Thus the Son of God, Who is the head, fills all in all.[18]

The most significant of these spiritual gifts which signify advancement in faith and trust in the promises of salvation and sanctification is the acquisition of the "free spirit" which, as Melanchthon defines it, is the will to obey and to morally change.  David, thus consoled by the Promise, was intent upon following the Cross.[19]  Since David apprehended God as his protector through the sacrifice of the promised Messiah, he, as a member of the "faithful remnant," knew that God wishes a similitude to exist between the head of the Church and its members.  Although Melanchthon describes the sufferings of David as a "type" of the Passion of Christ, it is clear that the typology described is not that which we have seen in our exegetical tradition.  We have noted how, formerly, the great men of the Old Testament provided prophetic examples of the afflictions Christ would sustain and thus would give meaning to, *via* the fulfillment of the prophetic umbrae.  When Melanchthon speaks of David's afflictions as a "type" of

Christ's, he intends a richer meaning of that word. Rather than portending fulfillment and validity only after Christ's crucifixion, death and resurrection, Melanchthon's use of the term "type" is generic; that is, the members of the True Israel before and after Christ's advent know that they are called to bear the Cross.[20] Implied here is a vision of sonship and brotherhood: the faithful elect are sons of God by adoption and brothers of Christ in suffering.

The call to bear the Cross intimately connects with the Promise. Whether the calling is manifested in the penitent bearing of one's own sins or of the calumnies and persecutions of the impious, who have only human wisdom which cannot comprehend the wisdom of faith, the faithful trust in the promise of deliverance. Godly men every day see the scandal of the success and power of the wicked, the men of Flesh. The impious mock and triumph over the faithful, but in this the similarity with the suffering Christ is most apparent.

The traditional exegesis suffered from a glaring deficiency. When David and other Old Testament prophets, patriarchs and kings pointed as figures to Christ, there existed the inherent embarrassment, though never recognized or admitted, of using mere men to portend divine actions and characteristics. But Melanchthon's concept of David's similitude to Christ's human sufferings overcomes this problem, for he need not reconcile David as a figure to Christ's divinity. Rather, through faith in the promised sacrifice of the Messiah, David knew that his and his Church's imitation of Christ entailed suffering the barbs of the world whose wisdom is folly. Moreover, David spoke to the faithful about his own calling, divinely appointed by the Messiah, and thus David's sufferings were made theologically legitimate by the Promise. Here, then, there is no empty shell that will be fulfilled in Christ, but, in its place, a vibrant calling which was sanctified no less for David than it is for the faithful of the Christian era by the deliverance that shall be (and is) obtained through Christ's sacrifice.

Furthermore, David's strength in the calling followed from faith; and necessarily so, because deliverance is not always immediate. Just as in the case of sin, where the faith of David rested on the promise of the non-imputation of liability for his iniquity and of the gratuitous imputation of saving righteousness,[21] so too did liberation from the persecution of the foolish world rest on the promise of eventual deliverance, even if only in the next life. David's heart was further gladdened by the assurance of the eventual punishment of the mockers of faith who, blasphemous, then seemingly directed the affairs of the world. As Melanchthon says:

> But even if some are punished lightly in this life, as Tiberius, nevertheless it is certain that those who are not turned to God will suffer eternal punishments in the future. . . .
> . . . . . . . . . . . . . . . . . . . . . . . . . . . . . . . . . . . . . . . . . . . . . . . . . . . . . . .
> Although the elect also die and suffer very grievously before they die, . . . as David and John the Baptist, yet they are delivered. . . .[22]

Faith in the promise of redemption and safekeeping, as it applies to the calling, further distinguishes David and those of the calling from men who are merely God's instruments. Melanchthon, of course, believes that all men are under God's instrumentality, but he divides those who are unknowing instruments from those who are aware that they are serving God. Among the latter group is David, who knew and responded to the Calling. The confidence that resulted from this inward awareness of calling was once more founded upon trust in the Promise, as seen in David's words, "I shall not die, but live, and declare the works of the Lord."[23]

Melanchthon's comparison of Scipio and David clarifies these general points. Scipio and David were both great conquerors, their victories obtained at the will of God. Scipio, however, did not know that he had been aided by God, nor that death is abolished by faith. Instead, Scipio thought that his victories and triumphs were contingent upon chance. No matter how elaborate his preparations for battle, Scipio always reflected upon the commanders of the past who had lost their lives on the field of battle; and so, he enjoyed confidence neither about his personal safety nor about that of the cause and republic he served. Both the longevity of his existence and the durability of his state seemed completely fortuitous to Scipio.

David, however, experienced none of these terrors. For he and all the faithful know that through the Promise or the Gospel they will survive death. Moreover, David recognized his calling and had no trepidations, even if he should die in battle, concerning the perpetuity of the Church which he served. Through faith in the promised resurrection and its agency, he was confident that he would share eternal triumph and glory in the House of the Lord.[24]

Not only do David's recognition of his calling and his trust in, and expectation of, the promised ultimate victory distinguish him from other men. His assurance of justification by faith alone and his faith in the promise of sanctification, all of which we have discussed above, set him off, as a member of the Old Testament "faithful remnant," from the Jews who did not trust in the Promise, and from the pagans whose epicurean opinions left them in ignorance of the Gospel as well as of God's universal providence.[25] More than this, Melanchthon draws the parallel between David and the reformers from the example of David's true worship and teaching.

Most of the ancient Jews were like Saul, who was tied to the Law. They sacrificed and attended religious observances, but since their ceremonies emanated from a belief in the efficacy of good works in "buying" salvation, they had not that trust in the Promise that David exemplified. Unlike David, they could only despair, for they could not hope their prayers would be heard favorably by God.[26] David knew the Promise, and he felt faith and the workings of the Holy Spirit within him. In his calling, moreover, David was a propagator of the Gospel and "taught the Gospel out of the House of the Lord." Thus, David's ministry of the Gospel distinguishes him not only from the "wicked priests, Pharisees and Sadducees" in Jerusalem but also from sixteenth-century popes, bishops and priests who "crush the Gospel and teach only the shadow of the Law,[27] . . . who do not bless[28] . . . and who use force against" the House of the Lord:

> This definition of the Church teaches that priests who are against the Gospel are not
> the Church nor are they teachers of the Church. Furthermore, the duty of a teacher
> of the Church derives from this definition: namely, to bless . . . and not to fabricate
> new laws or new types of worship.[29]

Thus we find, as we end our analysis of Melanchthon's concept of *David theologus promissionis,* that the reformer views David as an evangelist because of his faith in the promises. Consequently, he draws the historical parallel (and even identity) between David and the reformers as members of the "faithful remnant." As we shall see after our discussion and review of Calvin's conception of the theological David, the perception that the true Church is *always* a remnant makes David, in both Melanchthon's and Calvin's eyes, a powerful exemplar and teacher of the sixteenth-century Church (his Church), especially *in tempore belli.*

## Calvin and David

John Calvin thought very highly of St. Augustine and warmly acknowledged his debt to the African Father. His respect and indebtedness to Augustine, however, were not without limits. Calvin stated that Augustine was unsurpassed by any other patristic authority for the explication of doctrine, especially since Calvin was able to find in Augustine's theological teachings so much that was similar to his own.[30] Yet, Calvin found the Father's abundant use of allegory too "subtle," and in exegetical matters he preferred to keep to the literal sense of Scripture and the "simplicity" of exegesis typified by the works of St. John Chrysostom.[31] Not having Augustine's enthusiasm for allegory, Calvin could never approve of the former's interpretations of the meaning of the names of Saul, Jacob, and Paul, and, we might add, the explanation of David's name. Calvin reserved his praise for Augustine's commentaries on the four major prophets and on Matthew, Mark, and Luke, but his praises were less frequent for the Augustinian exegesis of the Pentateuch, the Gospel of St. John, and the Psalms.[32]

Given this antipathy to allegory, we should not be surprised to discover that Calvin approached David *via* the literal sense. Just as he was not prepared to accept Augustine's interpretation of John the Baptist's baptizing as being a hollow ceremony,[33] so, too, Calvin explained David and the Psalms interiorly, from the words and situations themselves. David thus acquires theological stature, as he had in Luther's and Melanchthon's commentaries, both as a teacher of "true" doctrine and as a recipient of saving grace.

We believe, however, that Calvin's evangelical David is more than the result of a preference for literal to allegorical interpretation. As in the case of Melanchthon, Calvin benefits from a greater appreciation of David's words and their historical relevance and applicability to the reformed faith and milieu. Having remarked how Calvin perceived a historical parallel between David's ministry and his own,[34] it will be of some value to examine Calvin's preface to his Psalm commentary more carefully.

Calvin calls the Psalter "an anatomy of all the parts of the soul," within which one finds all the emotions. Indeed, this complete description of the emotions is exactly what makes the Psalter so advantageous to him who would read and study it. As Calvin says, the reader finds in the Psalms

> all the griefs, sorrows, fears, doubts, hopes, cares, perplexities, in short, all the distracting emotions with which the minds of men are wont to be agitated.[35]

Yet opposing these agitations of the soul, the Psalms are above all "genuine and earnest" prayers which emanate from David's and the other psalmists' needs and from "faith in the promise of God." Truly, these psalms are compositions inspired by the Holy Spirit, but not because the Spirit speaks through otherwise mute and hollow spokesmen, but rather because the authors are men who stand on the battleground between the "invitations of God" and the "impediments of the Flesh."[36] The Spirit, then, was within David who belongs to the elect; and faith having put forth its power, his prayers entreated further sanctification which could overcome the fleshly obstacles and would allow the soul to "rise up to God."[37] Finally, declares Calvin, the Psalter provides examples of God's "unparalleled liberality" toward His faithful and His Church, as well as experiences and testimony of God's providence and love. The Psalter is, therefore, an exemplary book whose examples of real faith and trust may help sixteenth-century Calvinists lead a godly life while bearing the Cross which is the proof of man's obedience to God.[38]

In sum, Calvin's preface to his *Commentary on the Psalms* demonstrates that the Psalms contain the faith and prayers of men (including David) whose experiences are instructive for all members of the True Church. The parallel that Calvin drew between David and himself[39] shows also that, inasmuch as David and he felt the same struggle between the Flesh and the call of God, as well as the same type of struggle against the enemies of God, he values David and the Psalms precisely because they portray, in their own words and time, the plight of the individual member and the Church at all times in history. Furthermore, Calvin's vision of David as the man of faith and teacher of that faith in the Promise determines his delineation of what we have termed the "theological David."

As was true for Melanchthon, Calvin's David exhibited his membership in the True Israel through his realization that the fear of God is the beginning of wisdom. *Anfechtung* is the existential situation which teaches the faithful that the Law is conjoined with the Promise. Although God's election of the sinner is from all eternity, the fact of election is revealed in the juxtaposition of the terror of God's judgment to the hope of undeserved and unearned mercy; indeed, this very recognition of iniquity and absolute reliance on God's loving-kindness begins the process of sanctification which continues throughout the sinner's life. David's experiencing of terror and promise quelled his pride, and, as we shall see, the consciousness of sin, through sanctification, continued to crush the arrogance of the Flesh, leaving David desperate, in terms of his own worth, and consoled and joyous in the promise of gratuitous election.

Calvin finds David's recognition of sin in the words of Psalm 32: "For day and night thy hand was heavy upon me: my moisture is turned into the drought of summer." Calvin says:

> David explains whence he has such great anguish: namely, he clearly sensed that the hand of God was set in a hostile manner against him. For this is the worst thing imaginable, to be crushed by the hand of God so that the sinner feels that he is judged by God, Whose wrath and severity contain innumerable deaths beyond eternal death. Hence David complains that his moisture is dried up not only because he recognizes the misfortunes that have befallen him but also because he knows their cause and source [i.e., God]. For then all the strength of men wastes away when God appears as judge and lays them low and casts them down with the signs of His wrath. . . . The text shows that David was consumed with confusing griefs and was pulled apart by drawn-out torments until he was tamed. . . . It seems to rage against us, . . . since we know that our arrogance is indomitable unless it is constrained by the severest wounds.[40]

David, then, does not advise the Christian of the need and purpose of encountering God as the judge of man's sins without his own realization of their inevitability, for, as Calvin tells the reader, the context—David's words—reveal that he himself felt God's anger. Nor will any contemporary member of the Church find David's extravagance of language misplaced in describing his overwhelming and self-recriminating anguish, since the Christian likewise truly contends with the fear of eternal death.[41]

David's confession of his transgressions in Psalm 51:5,[42] prompted by his desire for reconciliation with God, distinguishes him from those who do not earnestly pray to God because they are not at all terrorized by His judgment of iniquitous man. Although they may ornament their praises of God, Who remits sins, with rhetorical brilliance, they, unlike David, do not care for God's grace; they are, Calvin intimates, mockers of God in that they are *hommes d'affaires religieux* and they see the Law as contractual rather than as condemning. David, on the other hand, rightly understood the Law; through his fear of God he prayed with faith and trust in the Promise:[43]

David hoped for light only from the promises of God. For the unbelievers, although they desire God's favor, do not raise their eyes to His light. For the nature of man is always downward onto the earth, unless it be raised upwards by the Word of God. Hence, therefore, David begins to feel the assurance of God's grace, since God, Who is true and unable to deceive, promised that He would always assist His servants.[44]

After 1539 Calvin no longer asserted that the recognition of sin preceded the gift of faith. Instead, the consciousness and affliction of sin followed from faith (and therefore election) so that in no way could it be construed that the confession of iniquity was a human means of gaining justification.[45] Thus, we may understand that David's confession of his guilt and penitence were the effects of his election. From the gift of faith also flowed continuing regeneration through sanctification.[46] We find that David's experience of regenerative sanctification is identical with that which Calvin describes for the Christian elect.

David's words are witness to the need of and the faithful desire for sanctification.[47] Calvin explains that even though David's initial despair was due to his apprehension of the Judgment of God and that he was consoled by the promise of God's mercy, he was not without human weakness; in other words, the Flesh still contended with the Spirit. The resulting irresolute wavering of faith could only be bolstered by fixing all the senses upon God; through prayer which brought calm to David's mind and which continues to mitigate the irresoluteness of all the faithful.[48] Moreover, David's foolish cries, resulting from his humanly inferior attempts to ascend to God, do not signify that David is not a member of the elected and True Israel, since they were uttered out of a benign ministry to instruct other men of faith, despairing under the weight of their sins, that progress along the path of sanctification lies only in the refuge of God and His grace.[49]

Consequently, then, Calvin firmly draws the parallel between the Christian and David. To say, for example, that David prophetically offers only a metaphor of the doctrine of sanctification would be completely to misunderstand the burden of Calvin's exegetical argument. David surely suffered the anguish of knowing that he was still a sinner, an anguish exacerbated by the promise of God's gracious elective decree. Thus David himself implored God for sanctification and the deeper understanding which only the Holy Spirit could give. He felt, even from the degree of sanctification that God had already given him, that he as a man was still far distant from the goal of complete regeneration; and he acknowledged that the attainment of this goal is purely a divine gift.[50] David therefore bears a very poignant instructive value for sixteenth-century Calvinists: if David, given the gift of faith, hope and trust in the immutability of God's Promise, felt anguish over his incomplete righteousness and understanding, the members of the contemporary Church should not despair, nor should they in their disquietude, even at the moment of death and judgment, cast about for human aid—such as the Law or the Catholic sacraments; rather, they should, like David, ultimately rest secure and trust in God's providence alone.[51] Just as David prayed for sanctification and the strengthening of faith, so should all other members of the Church. David, as one of the elect, had a ministry to fulfill, that of giving succor, through the record of his experiences of faith, to those who would come after him. If one were to claim that David's real faith, as Calvin describes it, was not the foundation of his ministry, then one would have to deny Calvin's *Institutes,* the attestation of *his* faith, as well as Calvin's perception in his preface to the Psalms that his own ministry paralleled David's.

Calvin finds proof for David's calling[52] in David's words in the psalms.[53] Moreover, Calvin argues that David's calling took two forms: first, the realization that he was, in his own time, a servant of God; and second, as we have intimated above, that his calling also partook of a ministerial function.

Like the Apostles, David called himself a servant of God, for he wished to testify to the Calling; in David's case, that of being a king. Calvin, no less than Melanchthon, perceives David's brotherhood with Christ both in his submission to the mandate of the Father and in suffering. David's stewardship over Israel was not gained, says Calvin, through any ambitious inclination; indeed, had his rule been selfishly motivated, he would not have sustained the internal and external attacks against his person and the kingdom. Rather, David became king at the command of God, and the cognizance of his divine calling enabled him to suffer the tempests which erupted throughout his reign. David's calling, moreover, is further attested to by his complete lack of *hubris*. He, who was so powerful and victorious, called himself simply God's servant, for he was unimpressed by his regal dignity.[54]

This very lack of pretence is self-renunciatory and unworldly. Most kings, "if they are not born fools, become fools" because of their too fulsome regal self-absorption.[55] Not so David. He was a shepherd to his people, caring for their welfare as well as for their piety. In this faithful obedience to the duty imposed upon him by God, David was the image of Christ, not because his kingly rule was the prophetic shadow of Christ's, but because he bore the yoke of Christ conferred on him by his calling. Performing his pastoral duties of bearing the Cross and caring for the spiritual and physical safekeeping of his people, David attributed the source and purpose of his power to God.

As always, David's calling is also preceptorial. His example is, of course, instructive, for it teaches all kings that their role should also be one of shepherdship. They too should, if they would testify to their calling, put on the evangelical yoke, conduct themselves moderately, and be upright. However, David's example, it seems, is intended more for an instructive critique. According to the logic of Calvinist theology, a tyrannical prince *ipso facto* does not have the Calling, is not elect, and cannot, since he does not have the aid of the Holy Spirit, imitate either David or Christ. Thus, the example of David's vocation is one which can only serve to mortify tyrants.[56]

David's preceptorial ministry is seen positively, however, in Calvin's explanation of the exemplary value of David's calling to the elect. The Calling is not an isolated, private vocation, but, like David's, it necessitates bearing witness to God's truth in the public forum. Since the unregenerate always oppose God's wisdom, the elect must expect and be prepared for malicious attacks and slanders. In order, then, to imitate David's conduct in his public duty, the saints also need to bear the person of Christ and accept the Cross with its attendant sufferings. The great examples of David's and the Savior's callings further teach the sixteenth-century elect that they should expect no immunity from such tribulations:[57] their consolation lies in the promise of sanctification and of deliverance from their earthly terrors. Yet this assurance must not puff them up in self-congratulatory pride, for, just as David did, the Calvinists must attribute the ability to endure suffering, as well as the glory of their calling, to God. They, too, are humble servants of the Lord. We see, then, that Calvin cites David's calling, as it applies to the faithful, not for its special regal function but because his vocation is just one of many; and because it is one of numerous manifestations of the Calling, David's attitude to, and conduct under, the Calling teaches all other saints the spirit in which they are to fulfill their vocations, and it consoles them to realize that humility and suffering are perpetual attributes of the Calling whose purpose is self-renunciation and imitation of Christ.[58]

The testimony of both Calvin and Melanchthon, then, is that David's Old Testament faith was rich and complete. Because of the role the Promise played in reformed theology, David returned home to his own times, no longer forced to be allegorized or tropologically moralized. Gone also is the embarrassment that had formerly derived from, for example, David's adultery; for, after all, sinfulness, while it is always reprehensible, is an attribute of man which can only be overcome completely in the next life. In this life it is only God, said the reformers, Who makes the Spirit overcome the Flesh through the process of sanctification.

No longer morally or theologically embarrassing, the pristine David was now available to help guide the Reformation Churches through the trials and tumults of religious strife.

## NOTES

[1] Gregory the Great, *Moralia* XXI, 8. Quoted in Ladner, *art. cit.,* pp. 234-235. Ladner points out that the concept of the pilgrim *viator* and the dual use of *alienus* are common in early Christian and medieval thought.

[2] Erwin Panofsky, *Renaissance and Renascences in Western Art* (New York: Harper Torchbook, 1969), pp. 84-85 and *passim.*

[3] Jean Seznec, *The Survival of the Pagan Gods: The Mythological Tradition and its Place in Renaissance Humanism and Art,* trans. by Barbara Sessions (New York: Harper Torchbook, 1953), demonstrated, with some qualifications, that much the same phenomenon can be found in the literary and artistic traditions of the classical deities.

[4] Panofsky, *op. cit.,* p. 86.

[5] Another example of this completion of renascence in the Renaissance may be found in E. H. Gombrich, "Botticelli's Mythologies: A Study of the Neoplatonic Symbolism of His Circle," *Journal of the Warburg and Courtauld Institutes,* 8 (1945), pp. 7-60.

[6] Since Beza, to paraphrase the criticism of Nicolaus of Lyra, is in his exposition of the theological David the "ape of Calvin," he shall not be discussed in this chapter. We shall save our discussion of his uses of David until Chapter VI, for the parts where his exposition goes beyond the model of Calvin.

[7] For Calvin's and Melanchthon's theologies, see François Wendel, *op. cit.;* Robert Stupperich, *op. cit.;* Clyde L. Manschreck, *Melanchthon: The Quiet Reformer* (New York: Abingdon Press, 1958).

[8] Ps. 28:1 (KJV): "Unto thee will I cry, O Lord my rock; be not silent to me: lest, if thou be silent to me, I become like them that go down into the pit."

[9] Philip Melanchthon, *Commentarii in psalmos* (coll. 1017-1472), in *Corpus Reformatorum,* 13 (1846; reprinted, New York: Johnson Reprint Corporation, 1963), col. 1059. (Our italics.) Hereafter cited as "Melanchthon, CR 13, Ps. ___ , col(l). ___ ."

[10] Melanchthon, CR 13, col. 1060.

[11] Melanchthon, CR 13, coll. 1394-1395.

[12] These views are not atypical of Melanchthon. They can be found throughout his commentaries, but particularly in his expositions on Psalms 6, 42, 51, and 59.

[13] Melanchthon, CR 13, col. 1393, also says that "David's terrors are true penitence" and that David's example "shows clearly that faith must rest on mercy alone . . . and that we should not be dejected and crushed by the sight of our weakness. This is the very teaching of the Gospel . . . and must be distinguished from the preaching of the Law."

[14] Melanchthon, CR 13, col. 1335.

[15] Ps. 116:11: "All men are liars." Melanchthon, CR 13, coll. 1408-1409.

[16] Ps. 32:8: "I will instruct thee and teach thee in the way which thou shalt go: I will guide thee with mine eye."

[17]Melanchthon, CR 13, coll. 1237-1238: "Nonus versus: 'Intellectum tibi dabo, etc.' Est promissio sanctificationis et gubernationis. . . . 'Consilium tibi dabunt oculi mei,' id est, meis oculis, mea sapientia tibi adero ego . . . et confirmabo te Spiritu sancto, . . . ut David regitur consilio, . . . et confirmatur Spiritu sancto, ut dolorem patientia vincat." Also Melanchthon, CR 13, Ps. 118, col. 1448.

[18]Melanchthon, CR 13, Ps. 118, col. 1448. (Our italics.) Again we find that the emphasis is on inward strength and faith, even though the agitations of the flesh continue and deliverance from enemies is not immediately at hand.

[19]Melanchthon, CR 13, Ps. 51, col. 1230. (Comment on verse 12: "Redde mihi laeticiam salutaris tui. . . .")

[20]Melanchthon, CR 13, Ps. 59, col. 1141.

[21]Melanchthon, CR 13, Ps. 32, col. 1235: " 'Beatus cui Dominus, etc.' . . . Sentit ergo David, sember in hac vita reliquum esse peccatum in hominibus, quod possit obiici, propter quod homo esset reus poenae aeternae, si non remitteretur reatus, sed ita homines esse iustos, id est, acceptos Deo, quia non imputantur peccata credentibus."

[22]Melanchthon, CR 13, Ps. 32, coll. 1238-1239. Also Ps. 59, col. 1359: "Thus, many of the elect, such as David . . . , are tested by afflictions for a while, indeed they are also oppressed and killed by the wicked, and yet they hold the promises by faith, that God at some time will glorify them and heap punishments on the impious."

[23]Ps. 118:17 (KJV).

[24]Melanchthon, CR 13, Ps. 118, coll. 1437-1439. Melanchthon also discusses the calling and its faithful confidence in his exposition of Ps. 20 (CR 13, col. 1047). Melanchthon considered Scipio a good man, but desperate because he did not have faith in eternal life, nor did he recognize God's providence. In Ps. 20, Melanchthon compares David to the "wicked" King Achab. Achab experienced none of the fear of Scipio, for the former trusted in his military preparations and dared not hope for God's help and presence.

[25]We have seen above how David differed from Cato and Brutus. Melanchthon also contrasts David with Themistocles who relied on outward fortifications for the building of his city rather than on the aid of God. Melanchthon, CR 13, Ps. 110, coll. 1171-1172.

[26]Melanchthon, CR 13, Ps. 114, col. 1386.

[27]As we see, Melanchthon does not denigrate the value of the Law. He concurs with David that "the fear of the Lord is the beginning of wisdom" (CR 13, Ps. 111:10, col. 1171), and that the dread of God's judgment, rightly understood, is the first sign of faith. Those who teach the shadow of the Law are those who know God only as a terrible judge and not as the Merciful One Who imputes righteousness and gives faith to the elect.

[28]We have rendered "benedicebant" and "benedictionem praedicare" as "bless" for ease of translation. However, Melanchthon defines "benedictio" as the "teachings of the Gospel, by which, on account of Christ, grace and eternal life are given." (Col. 1463.)

[29]Melanchthon, CR 13, Ps. 118, coll. 1462-1463: "Ecclesia est domus Dei, in qua benedixerunt nobis patres et Prophetae. . . . Cum enim inquit David: 'Benediximus vobis ex domo Domini,' id est, nos, qui sumus in domo Domini, benediximus vobis, docuimus hanc benedictionem, et eam magnis certaminibus propagavimus, Intuere animo stantes in templo patres, . . . Isaac, Iacob, Moisen, Davidem, Eliam, Elisaeum et alios. Omnium haec una vox est: 'Benediximus vobis de domo Domini.' . . . Haec est vox, quae de Dei voluntate erga nos in Ecclesia sonare debet. Sed hanc vocem non sonant pontifices et episcopi, qui oppresso Evangelio docent umbram doctrinae legis. . . . Ideo nec benedicunt, nec sunt pars domus Domini, sed vi grassantes in ea, tyrannidem exercent, sicut erant in domo Domini Ierosolymis pontifices impii, Pharisaei et Sadducaei. . . . Ex hac definitione Ecclesiae satis intelligi potest, pontifices adversantes Evangelio non esse Ecclesiam, aut doctores Ecclesiae. Praeterea quod sit officium doctoris in Ecclesia, ex eadem descriptione intelligi potest, scilicet, una cum Prophetis et Apostolis benedictionem praedicare, non fingere novas leges aut novos cultus. Est autem benedictio ipsa vox Evangelii, qua propter Filium Dei, deleto peccato, restituitur gratia et vita aeterna, ut supra saepe de benedictione dictum est."

[30]Luchesius Smits, *Saint Augustin dans l'oeuvre de Jean Calvin*, trans. from the Dutch by Egbert van Laethem, Vol. 1 (Assen: Van Gorcum and Comp. N. V., 1957), p. 265.

[31]*Ibid.*, p. 266. Of course Calvin found little to agree with in Chrysostom's doctrinal writings.

[32]*Ibid.*, pp. 266 & 268.

[33]*Ibid.*, p. 267.

[34]See above, pp. 69-70.

[35]Quoted in Dillenberger, *op. cit.*, p. 23.

[36]*Loc. cit.*

[37]As we shall see below, sanctification plays an important role, as it did for Melanchthon, in Calvin's concept of David.

[38]Dillenberger, *op. cit.*, p. 24.

[39]See above, pp. 69-70.

[40]John Calvin, *Joannis Calvini, magni theologi, commentarii in librum psalmorum* (Amsterdam: Joannis Jacobi Schipper, 1667), Ps. 32:4 (KJV 32:4), p. 118. Hereafter cited as "Calvin, Ps. ___ , p(p). ___ ." " . . . explicat unde tantus moeror, quia scilicet Dei manum sensit infestam sibi esse. Hic enim malorum omnium cumulus est, urgeri Dei manu, ut sentiat peccator sibi cum eo judice negotium esse, cujus ira et severitas praeter aeternam mortem innumeras mortes in se continet. Hinc conqueritur David succum suum exaruisse non modo quod simpliciter reputaret sua mala, sed causam et fontem agnosceret. Tunc enim concidit totus hominum vigor, ubi Deus judex apparet, ac propositis irae suae signis eos humiliat ac prosternit. . . . Siquis roget de Davide, an callum obduxerat ad plagas, quas sciebat divinitus sibi infligi, responsio ex contextu petenda est: detentum fuisse et constrictum in perplexis doloribus, et lentis tormentis fuisse distractum, donec bene domitus mansuesceret. . . . [N]on frustra iterare castigationes quibus in nos videtur Deus saevire, . . . quam scimus esse [nostram ferociam] indomitam, nisi durissimis plagis cogatur."

[41]Calvin, Ps. 6:7, pp. 17-18: "Quanquam hyperbolicae sunt loquutiones, non tamen Poëtice amplificat David suum moerorem, sed vere et simpliciter, quam durus acerbusque fuerit, declarat. . . . Qui vero mediocriter experti sunt quid sit certare cum formidine aeternae mortis, nullum in his verbis excessum reperient."

[42]KJV, Ps. 51:3: "For I acknowledge my transgressions: and my sin is ever before me." There is often a discrepancy between Calvin's numbering of the psalms and verses and that of the King James Version.

[43]Calvin, Ps. 51:5, p. 199: "Atque hoc modo [David] testatur se nihil afferre simulationis: qualiter interdum magno verborum splendore, gratiam Dei in remittendis peccatis ornant, qui tamen eam frigide curant, quia non admodum ejus judicio tanguntur." Also Ps. 18:23, p. 61 on David and the Law: " . . . simul enim ac negligitur doctrina [legis], facile socordia obrepit et evanescit omnis Dei timor."

[44]Calvin, Ps. 43:3 (KJV 43:2), p. 167: " . . . Hinc ergo David fiduciam gratiae Dei concipit, quia Deus, qui verax est ac fallere non potest, servis suis se adfuturum sit pollicitus."

[45]Wendel, *op. cit.*, p. 248.

[46]For a description of this process, see *ibid.*, pp. 242-255.

[47]Ps. 38:11 (KJV, 38:10): "My heart panteth, my strength faileth me: as for the light of mine eyes, it also is gone from me."

[48]Calvin, Ps. 38:11, p. 149: "Verbum quo utitur David, Peregrinari, aut Vagari significat, hic vero pro agitatione capitur, quam generat anxietas ubi destituimur consilio. . . . Sed quum fides, ubi nos addicit Deo in obsequium, sensus nostros ejus verbo affixos teneat, objici potest quaestio, quomodo cor Davidis perculerit hic vagus error. Respondeo, quamvis suffultus Dei promissionibus in suo gradu consisteret, non fuisse tamen humanae infirmitatis expertem. Nec certe fieri aliter potest quin simulatque incidimus in aliquod discrimen, caro nostra varios circuitus nobis ingerat, et ad captanda consilia distrahat in multos errores: hic firmissimus quisque labesceret, nisi sibi frenum injiceret, quo retentus ac cohibitus fuit David, nempe sensus omnes suos verbi Dei cancellis inclusos tenens. Imo in precibus quietis plus satis experimur quam erraticae sint mentes nostrae, quas difficile est eodem tenore intentas ad finem usque dirigere."

[49]Calvin, Ps. 39:4 (KJV, v. 3: "My heart was hot within me, while I was musing the fire burned: then spake I with my tongue"), p. 152: "Itaque siquando in nobis ferveant magnae ustiones, memoria revocandum erit certamen hoc Davidis, ne . . . ad desperationem infirmitas nostra nos praecipitet. . . . Sciamus nos eodem tentationis genere exerceri quod plurimum molestiae Davidi exhibuit. . . . Nam in sua persona, humanae infirmitatis speculum nobis ante oculos ponit, ut periculo admoniti, sollicite sub umbram alarum Dei confugere discamus."

[50]Calvin, Ps. 86:11, p. 323, elaborates these points, whereby David admits that free will is inefficacious and asserts that only the light of the Holy Spirit can lift the veil of blindness from the human mind and heart.

[51]Calvin, Ps. 143:6, p. 520, describes David in his last hours: " . . . se deficere sentiens, sepulchroque propinquus, non tamen vacillanti animo huc et illuc circumspicit, sed manet in Deo solo defixus. . . . Semper vero notandum est, ut se alliget uni Deo, omnes alias spes ex animo rescindere."

[52]By the process of sanctification the elect are submitted to God. The indwelling of the Holy Spirit provokes the renunciation of self, resulting in the "imitation of Christ." Cf. Wendel, *op. cit.,* pp. 242-255, and especially pp. 249-250 for a full exposition of these points.

[53]For example, Ps. 18:1-2: "I will love thee, O Lord, my strength. The Lord is my rock, and my fortress, and my deliverer; my God, my strength, in whom I will trust; my buckler, and the horn of my salvation, and my high tower;" and Ps. 28:9 : "Save thy people, and bless thine inheritance. . . ."

[54]Calvin, Ps. 18:1, p. 56: "Servum Dei se nominans, de sua vocatione . . . testari voluit: ac si negaret se temere involasse in regnum, sed tantum Dei oraculo paruisse. . . . [I]mo in naufragiis hic unicus portus fuit, sibi de caelesti mandato probe esse conscium. . . . Interim digna observatu est ejus modestia, quod tot victoriis nobilis, . . . non alio quam servi Dei elogio se insignit: ac si hoc omni mundi praestantia magis honorificum censeret, fideliter munus a Deo injunctum obiisse."

[55]Calvin, Ps. 101:2, p. 368, sympathizes with the old adage that "either a fool or a king must be born." However, he inclines to the position that kings are not born foolish, but become fools because their position blinds them to their true duties whose reality is seen in the upright nature of David's rule. Calvin had already elaborated on this same theme in his exposition of Ps. 28:9, p. 105.

[56]This critique of tyrants is implicit in Calvin's comments on Psalms 101:2 and 28:9, *loci citi.* For example, unlike David, "Neque tamen mirum est, tam superbe et contumeliose calcari humanum genus, quod magna ex parte a ferendo Christi jugo abhorret." The polemical use of David is a theme which we shall treat in the next chapter, as it becomes especially important in understanding Theodore Beza's concept of David.

[57]Commenting on Ps. 18:1, *loc. cit.,* Calvin asserts, "Ergo Servi nomen ad publicum munus hoc loco (ut saepe alibi) refertur." Within this same context, he says, "Quod nobis cognitu non parum utile est, ne immunitatem speremus ab omni molestia, ubi sequimur vocantem Deum: sed nos potius ad duram militiam paremus."

[58]Speaking of the calling, Calvin says, for example (Ps. 69:23, p. 258), "Haec tria [Spiritus prudentiae, rectitudinis et moderationis] quum in Davide fuisse minime dubium sit, quisquis eum probe imitari cupiet, non temere caeco impetu prosiliat ad diras: deinde compescat turbidas animi sui passiones: neque sibi privatim sit addictus, sed studia sua affectusque ad quaerendam Dei gloriam adjiciat. Denique, ut veri simus imitatores Davidis, primum induere Christi personam necesse est. . . ."

## Chapter VI
## David and the Embattled Church


### Melanchthon and Calvin: David and the Remnant Churches

In our previous discussion of the concept of the "theological" David, we have seen that by reading and understanding the words of the Psalms "literally," Melanchthon and Calvin found in David a faith compatible with their own. We can never be certain that David's faith in the Promise was exactly as the reformers portrayed it. However, his utter dependence upon God's spiritual aid and his messianic hope and trust in the Promise accorded well, in the minds of the reformers, with their sense of *Anfechtung*, with their idea of the majesty of God, and with their equally messianic reliance on the fulfillment of God's merciful Word.

We have seen, also, that the Protestant commentators' perception of David as a man of true faith, belonging to the true Israel, made him a fit teacher both to instruct the sixteenth-century faithful by the example of his conduct and to console them in their agonies of developing faith and vocation. Finding testimony in David's words of his experience of faith, sanctification and calling, the reformers were able to view him as a new kind of prophet. David spoke about faith because, through the Promise and the gift of the Spirit, he enjoyed brotherhood with Christ; and he composed psalms because he knew that among his vocational duties ∴ as included the duty to instruct his posterity: the perennially remnant Church.

Melanchthon and Calvin plainly say as much. The purpose of David's psalms, as David himself knew, is to instruct the pious remnant—"us"—that it experiences the same struggles with incompletely developed faith. And so, also, it was to teach the sixteenth-century faithful of God's benefits and of His immutable will to save them that David recorded his own trepidations and trust in God's promises, lest they succumb in the despair caused by the recognition of their sins.[1] Moreover, both assert that, because of his true faith, David's prophetic duty was to watch over the health and zeal of the *whole* Church, to formulate its form of praying, and to teach the faithful that true worship and "works" involve anguish, faith, prayer, and hope.[2] Thus, Calvin could advise his readers to turn to the Psalms in order to find in them consolation and encouragement in true faith; thus could Melanchthon say that the Psalms are the true doctrine of the Church and the voice of the Gospel.

But David, as one of the Old Testament "faithful remnant," did not merely speak to the sixteenth-century "faithful remnant" about the doctrine of the Promise and true worship. He also spoke to them concerning, if we be allowed to coin a word, the plight of "remnancy."

Except for the moralized David of Nicolaus of Lyra, we have not found, in our investigation of selected Prereformation exegetes, a theological rehabilitation of and affinity with David such as we have discovered in the sixteenth-century reformers. It is also true that seldom, if ever before, had there been the occasion to perceive such a historical parallel between the situation of the post-Advent Christian Church and the pre-Advent "faithful remnant."[3] In the Middle Ages most of Europe was Roman Catholic, and, although there were heresies to contend with and the Infidel to defeat in the Holy Land and Spain, the Church did not necessarily need to perceive itself as being grievously oppressed. However, the mid-sixteenth-century reformers did indeed find their Church and themselves embattled. Consequently, it was for this reason that they found David historically relevant for themselves.

Yet we believe that the reformers' vehemence in equating their situation to David's could only have been possible after the reformers received David as one of their own theologically.[4] Since David was of the elect, they were able to regard his sufferings with empathy and see in them an exemplary witness to the fact that persecution is endemic to the True Church, that the world has always and will always abhor the "faithful remnant" who must accept their plight because the Calling entails bearing the Cross.

Thus David, because of his own experience of the Calling and his trust in the Promise, became a powerful model and example for the reformers, Melanchthon and Calvin. Citing what happened to David, how he conducted and expressed himself, and how the conduct of the sixteenth-century faithful was similar to his, Melanchthon and Calvin professed the innocence and probity of their followers' calling. This teaching could only bolster and instruct the faithful and cast odious shame upon their foes, the enemies of the True Church, indeed, David's sixteenth-century enemies.

In fact, the only glaring difference between the comments of Calvin and Melanchthon lies in the latter's more specific references to contemporary events. This contrast, however, is as much the result of differing political climates as of the two reformers' predilections about overtly naming those responsible for the trials of the Calvinist and Lutheran confessions. Melanchthon wrote his Psalm commentaries in 1542 and, again, between 1552 and 1555,[5] and thus they reflect the moods and events of those years: the events following the formation of the Schmalkaldic League in 1531, the intermittent warfare between the German princes and Charles V, the religious conferences which failed and were followed by the Schmalkaldic War of 1546-1547, the Turkish menace, and the Emperor's dalliance with the idea of imposing Philip of Spain as the King of the Romans, after the installation of Duke Ferdinand as Emperor.[6]

Thus, we find Melanchthon's expressions of horror, not unmixed with a feeling of German patriotism, at the Muslim menace to Christian Europe, Germany, and the True Church.[7] He lashes out at those who, in those years, acted perfidiously against the Church and its adherents: Stephen Gardiner, Bishop of Winchester, who re-emerged as a power in the Catholic faction under Queen Mary; Francis I who, in the Treaty of Crépy (1544), promised the Emperor that he would not enter into alliances with German Protestants.[8] Finally, Melanchthon sadly remarks the personal betrayal, so comparable to the example of the betrayal of David by Achitophel, of the Landgrave Philip of Hesse when, in 1547, Charles V imprisoned him.[9] More than this, however, Melanchthon's remarks often display his concern with German princely machinations.

Calvin, on the other hand, confines his comparisons of the persecution of David with that of Protestants to more obscure and general remarks. His reticence to implicate the French throne in the persecution of Protestants is entirely in keeping with the later Calvinist historiographical tradition. Although, after the *Affaire des Placards,* Francis I instituted the persecutions of Huguenots, the great *Histoire ecclésiastique . . . du royaume de France* was most careful to disclaim any opposition to the king who was not yet, although he would later be, portrayed as the instrument of Satan. Rather, the king, who at least had taken some interest in the rebirth of the liberal arts and in ecclesiastical reform, was misled by the *parlements;* his nefarious advisers were really the ones responsible for the persecutions.[10] Indeed, Francis had directly intervened in favor of the Protestants of Merindol and had issued *lettres de grâce* directing the Parlement of Provence to desist from the unjust persecution.[11] So, too, Calvin, as we shall see, usually speaks only of the wicked judges of the world who, without provocation, persecute the people of God.  We may perhaps legitimately infer that Calvin alludes to the culpability of the *parlements.*

With these differences of tone noted, we may now proceed to delineate how Melanchthon and Calvin invoke David to instruct sixteenth-century Protestants in their conduct and attitudes towards religious conflict.

The purpose of both Melanchthon and Calvin is first of all to demonstrate that the Church has always been a small group of remnant faithful who have been oppressed by the enemies of God and the Gospel. The Church, as Melanchthon describes it,[12] is small and weak.  The people of Christ, ever since the time of Abel, have suffered the "bite of the Devil" and the oppression of tyrants.  Yet this earthly condition of the True Church should not engender despair, for there always remains a remnant on earth to testify to the goodness and majesty of God.  Moreover, since the wicked did not even spare David calumnies and injuries, the persecution of David's heirs needs no explanation.[13]  David himself realized, from his own experience, that the impious would unceasingly hate the Church, and, for this reason, he wrote a prayer for his descendant-Church, expressing his anguish and anger against the wicked who, unlike the poor and unpretentious Protestant congregations which will be taught true doctrine, would establish with their titles, power and wealth, a false Church based on human authority and succession.[14]

Because of this parallel between the faithful David and the contemporary Church, the psalms of David, who conducted himself at every moment as a servant of God, provide important lessons in the period of its affliction:  the necessity of maintaining a good conscience and of professing the righteousness of the Church's cause, and the importance of restraint and prayer.

There is, of course, a distinction between the justice of the good conscience and human righteousness in the presence of God.  David was aware of this difference and so also must be the members of the sixteenth-century Church.  David never boasted of his righteousness as a man, for he knew that justification can only be and is the gratuitous gift of God.  Thus, the embattled elect, who no more than David have escaped occasions for sin, should not vainly claim they differ from other men, save through the mercy of God.

David only claimed the righteousness of the good conscience and that he defended a just cause.  Since his was a defense against the enemies of God, he knew that both his actions and the cause they served were just and indispensable.[15]  Nor was this common necessity and justice unknown to his adversaries, for he forthrightly asked them, "Do ye indeed speak righteousness, O congregation?  Do ye judge uprightly, O ye sons of men?"  As Calvin explains,

> David, relying on a good conscience, went forth publicly and refuted the calumnies
> with which they burdened him; and this refutation came by their own admission, as
> if he had said, "I have you who have slandered me as witness of my innocence.
> Does it not shame you to thus oppress groundlessly an innocent one?"[16]

Such public professions, while necessary, cannot be expected to influence the judges of this world any more than David's moved those whom Saul called together "under the appearance of counsel."  Saul's "congregation" of august judges were "sons of men," not of God, and therefore they were no more than a band of brigands who perversely treated David as if he were a common thief.  Recognition of the justice of the elect in professing the Gospel must not be sought from men who do not know that "the fear of the Lord is the beginning of wisdom."[17] And, just as David loftily and scornfully provoked his calumniators, so should Calvinists (and Lutherans) not esteem the judgments of men; rather they should, like David, rely on their innocent conscience and appeal to the tribunal of God.[18]

Calvin and Melanchthon view the slanderous and physical attacks upon David as another sign of his calling, for the primary purpose of the persecution of David was not motivated by personal animosity nor by a desire to kill him. His enemies' true aim in attacking him with arms and "lying tongues" was to eradicate the evangelical teaching to which David bore witness. The sixteenth-century remnant Church suffers the enmity of the impious for this same reason, and therefore the reformers insist that the experience of suffering conforms to the Passion of Christ Who also bore the Cross.[19] We thus find once again that, through the Calling and its tribulations, David and the Protestants prove their brotherhood with Christ's humanity.

If the example of David serves to hearten the Reformation faithful in the urgency and integrity of their calling, it also provides historic precedents for the proper attitude in the face of adversity. David's psalms ring out clarion messages of the efficacy of indefatigable faith and prayer to sixteenth-century Lutherans and Calvinists. The prayers of the faithful, beseeching the intervention of God's mighty strength, must, of course, follow David's example, and proclaim the righteousness of their cause before God and men, because it is only after the world and God know the justice which the godly serve that divine aid may come: or, as Melanchthon says, "We must not entreat God to aid unjust causes."[20] This seems to us to smack of semi-pelagianism, at least in the theater of worldly trials. We, however, do not wish to push this point, since this trace of the worth of human effort might be handily explained away as being due to the assurance of the Calling as well as of God's merciful intervention, which we shall discuss below. Concerning a parallel to this point, however, it is well to recall that Protestants

> . . . sometimes thought . . . that the doctrine of predestination . . . might produce a morally pernicious fatalism among ordinary people; it was wiser, therefore, as Jurieu said, . . . to "dogmatiser comme St. Augustin, et prêcher comme Pélage."[21]

Notwithstanding Melanchthon's and Calvin's seeming ambiguity, deriving from the sequential nature of the assertion of the good conscience and from the appeal to God's tribunal for suprahuman justice, both reformers agree that prayer remains a *sine qua non* for the members of the embattled Church. Indeed, if the faithful consider David's words, as for example those of Psalm 69:4, they will know that prayer bears testimony to true faith. Although obedience to the Calling involves, just as it did for David, the garnering of unfair rewards from the world in the form of open attacks and disgrace in the eyes of men, the people of God must display their faith in unceasing prayer. This is precisely what David's prayers teach.[22]

Since the persecutions which the sons of God sustain lack human remedy, they must follow David and await divine deliverance from their travail. Nor is this expectation an empty hope, for David's eventual earthly deliverance attests to the unwavering will of God to safeguard His people and to be present in His Church. David's prayers witness his trust in God's Promise and his realization that the power and efforts of his tormentors would be frustrated since God was on his side. Thus Calvin, summing up for us Melanchthon's advice, too: Let us take heed of David's constancy and perseverance in prayer, "so that our prayers will not grow faint, no matter how much the arrows of our enemies threaten us with death."[23]

Faith, hope, and prayer are, therefore, not only theological virtues; they are also the virtues of the Church in a hostile and pernicious world. The remnant Churches, whether that of David or those of Lutherans and Calvinists, cultivate (with the aid of the Holy Spirit) these virtues which provide what Calvin calls "invincible strength,"[24] in total dependence upon God. They also offer proof positive which exculpates the people of God from the nefarious and false accusation of sedition.

While princes and priests claim that they justly protect the commonweal from the traitorous ambitions of the reformed Churches, the members of those congregations can point to their resigned long-suffering, which is in conformity with David's, in order to dispel such false charges. Melanchthon and Calvin proclaim the innocence of their peoples' intentions, but they do so in somewhat different and instructive ways.

Calvin argues that throughout his trials David never gave occasion for the joint charge of impiety and sedition with which he was burdened by his enemies. Rather, his whole life was devoted to piety and uprightness. David's own words attest to his innocence and dedication, for he spoke of those "who hate me without a cause" and he said unequivocally that "thy loving-kindness is ever before mine eyes, and I have walked in thy truth."[25] Had he deviated from the path of righteousness, David would have been deprived of his defense against those who cast aspersions on the rectitude of his conduct. The very fact that David trusted in God's providence and aid deterred him from perversely acting against his foes. In his resigned conduct, then, David revealed once again that he was not of the sons of men. For it is the latter who are ignorant of God's providence. It is they who, although they may support a good cause, practice aimless deceptions and attempt to conquer evil, engendering even worse calamities.[26] The defense, then, against persecution is divine, not human. The sixteenth-century faithful must, like David, be servants of righteousness and have only God as their leader. Misfortune, disgrace, reproaches, even death, are the very test of the righteousness of the cause they serve.[27] Neither should this test of the Calling be considered ultimately burdensome or a cause for despair. The God Who remembered David's tears and responded to his prayers will not fail likewise to conserve the tears and count every drop of blood of the contemporary faithful and martyrs.[28]

Melanchthon also surveys the present plight of the True Church in Germany and compares it with the tribulations of David. Since the Church often disagrees with the highest authorities of the state, charges of sedition and blasphemy are never lacking. Just as David was falsely accused of attempting to overthrow the legitimate dynastic rule of Saul, so is the Church once again charged with the dismembering of civil harmony, the purposeless destruction of the unity of the Church, and the replacement of true modes of worship with invented idols. These are harsh accusations, and they have no foundation, for blasphemy and sedition overthrow the first table of the Decalogue.[29]

Even though David was unjustly persecuted by Saul, he urges reliance on God's protective presence to the faithful who come after him, and he teaches the sixteenth-century people of God to endure patiently their tyrannical magistrates. David might have opportunely allowed his men to slay Saul, but, instead, he forbade it. Human reason and natural law allow that a manifest tyrant may be killed; indeed, there have been many examples of just tyrannicide, not only in classical antiquity, but also in ancient Hebraic times. Moses slew the tyrannical Egyptian who, in Pharoah's name, ruled over the Israelites; and the wise and holy Abissai counselled David that tyrannicide would be no crime. Yes, says Melanchthon,

> . . . the opinion of nature is that the defense against atrocious injury is justified,
> and David is often used as an example of such an occasion. But David restrained

himself and did not kill Saul, which I esteem would have been permitted.  But often this rule should be followed:  consider not only what is allowed [by natural law], but also what is safer for the conscience and useful for example.[30]

Present consideration of this rule conforms to David's attitude.  He knew that he was called to be king over Israel and he realized that if he were to usurp the kingdom before the appointed time he would confirm the opinion of those who saw not Saul as the persecutor but David as the rebellious traitor. Moreover, although David knew that justice and reason allowed tyrannicide, he did not wish to provide an example for future abuses by men who, under the pretext of a custom established by his example, would claim that they were imitating him.

Let us observe, concludes Melanchthon, David's patient endurance and his hope and trust in divine help. Many anguished souls seek, without order, a violent remedy for persecution; but they only instill the desire for revenge and reap even worse evils.  The faithful recognize that the examples of David's many deliverances from his enemies were effected through the agency of God and that such examples teach God's benign concern for his Church.[31]

Although Melanchthon and Calvin seemingly arrive at identical conclusions concerning resistance to superior powers, the differences between their evocation of David and their use and development of his example attest to a profound difference in the elaboration of political theory by the fifteen-fifties.

The two reformers look to the parallel between the persecution of David and that of their Churches, and they find that his example counsels restraint.  As they both clearly state, the righteous defense of the evangelical cause is to rely on God's promise to protect and vindicate His remnant Church by punishing oppressive tyrants.  Calvin's assertions in these matters are unequivocal and he will admit no concession either to expediency or to the frustration caused by unabating persecution.  The Calling is the Calling; and as David bore the evangelical Cross, so must all "sons of God."

Melanchthon's handling of the same problem is, however, much more slippery.  Even though he upholds the inevitability of suffering as a result of the Calling, Melanchthon opposes to David's resignation the shield of human reason and natural law.  In so doing, he lays claim through David to the purely religious motivation of the beleaguered adherents of the Lutheran Church, unsullied by political ambition; at the same time, he leaves room for the imitation of Moses' and Abissai's actions.  Nor does Melanchthon clothe David's restraint in an unmixed fabric of holy forbearance.  Instead, he portrays a principled, yet expedient, David, who feared not the mere imitation in future ages of resistance on his part, but, rather, a rash and disorderly imitation.  It is as if David had been able to foresee warily, as Melanchthon could see retrospectively, the Anabaptists in Munster and the sometimes disorganized military activities of the Schmalkaldic princes.

In fact, Melanchthon's position, as we have shown it here, accords with the Lutheran theory of resistance that was cautiously developed by Bugenhagen, Melanchthon, and other leading theologians after the failure of the Schmalkaldic League in the fifteen-forties.  Besides incorporating theoretical elements of feudal and religious derivation (the feudal contract and Satanic tyranny), the Lutheran resistance doctrine viewed the Empire as a corporate unity.  Citing the Golden Bull of 1356,[32] which had affirmed the prerogative of the Electors as well as German particularism, and the ancient Spartan model of collegiality of power, the authority and responsibility, shared between the Electors and the Emperor, were defined in a corporate manner.  If the Emperor failed to perform his duties, the inferior magistrates, as members of the Estates and as nearly sovereign princes, had the right to resist the Emperor.  This duty to resist, moreover, was based on natural law and custom (the deposition of the Emperor Wenzel in 1400 providing a customary precedent).  Although Bugenhagen counselled that even women and children should resist Charles V, Melanchthon and other theologians strove to prevent inchoate resistance, and they firmly established, in order that justified resistance not take on the odious appearance of mass revolution, that resistance must be directed by the proper and lawful subaltern authorities.[33]  The equivocation we have found in Melanchthon's comments on David might, therefore, also have been partly the result of some indecision as to David's political role in the ancient Hebraic kingdom:  did David, destined by God to inherit the kingdom, exercise a role commensurate with that of the Ephors of Sparta and the imperial Electors?

However much this Lutheran resistance theory resembles the later Calvinist doctrine, it does represent a major departure from Calvin's own view.  Castigating tyrannical rulers, Calvin allowed almost no recourse to afflicted subjects.  Except for a single sentence in his *Commentary on the Prophet Daniel* wherein he suggested that the king had, by acting despotically, abrogated his authority, Calvin permitted only prayer and emigration, saying:

> It would be better to renounce all human bonds of social life and have everyone
> live by himself than to tolerate the confusion resulting from disobedience to the
> appointed superiors. . . .  We owe sentiments of affection and reverence to all our
> rulers, whatever their character may be.

Entertaining only momentarily the idea that a solution to persecution by the French monarchy might be available, as he wrote Coligny, through the conjoined action of the princes of the blood and the *parlements,* he nevertheless reprimanded the Huguenots for attempting to abduct Francis II from the influence of the Guise.  Speaking of the abortive Conspiracy of Amboise, he wrote:  "It would be better to perish than to soil the name of Christianity and the Gospel with such a horror."[34]  These sentiments, then, are faithfully echoed in Calvin's discussion of David's non-resistance to Saul.

Yet, even with these differences of approach to David's restraint, Melanchthon and Calvin insist on the probity of David's attitude and, by historical extension, the integrity of their own Churches in the midst of religious and political upheaval.  In either case, David, as a member of a previous faithful remnant, offered an exemplary model of rectitude and trust to the sixteenth century.

Indeed, as we have seen, David's bearing of persecution was entirely exemplary.  The reformers invoked both David's words and the events which precipitated them to demonstrate to their flocks that the present persecutions and attacks were not exceptional, but that all men of true faith, whether David or themselves, experience such tribulations.  Furthermore, the reformers' discussions of David and the ancient and modern embattled Churches revolved around the theological doctrines which they applied to David.  In this way, the reformers, by conforming the *verba et gesta Davidis* to their own times, used David to console Lutherans and Calvinists, to encourage them by the example of historical parallelism in the patient bearing of the Cross, and to suggest to them that, although God often works in hidden ways, the punishment of the impious may be postponed, but never lacking.  In fact, David's example must have been particularly encouraging, for the reader of the Old Testament would know that God miraculously delivered David from his enemies during his lifetime and triumphantly placed him on his appointed throne.

And yet, we should not think that Melanchthon's and Calvin's disquisitions on David were aimed solely at Protestants who might read their commentaries or learn of the value of David through preachers influenced by their expositions. The writings of the Protestant theologians did not go unread by learned Catholics, as the spate of polemical and apologetic religious literature in the sixteenth century attests. Thus, these Psalm commentaries could very well have been intended to serve a purpose almost identical to the *Loci communes* and the *Institutio christianae religionis,* which instructed the faithful and profane alike in the main elements of reformed theology. Furthermore, just as the first edition of the *Institutes,* with its dedicatory epistle to Francis I, endeavored to prove the evangelical purity of motive of the members of the Reformed Church in France, thus distinguishing them from the spiritualist and political madness of the Anabaptists, as well as relieving Calvinists from the embarrassment caused by the *placardistes,* David seems to reach out apologetically to Catholic readers and authorities.[35] If we might fabricate a statement of purpose in what we perceive to be the spirit of Melanchthon and Calvin, it would take the following form:

> In reading our commentaries on the Psalms, you will see David, a man of pure faith
> and calling, persecuted, as are we, without provocation or worldly ambition. You, who
> already know David, even if only through a veil of allegory, should take his faith to
> heart, recognize the truth of his and our faith, and cease troubling the wretchedly
> oppressed brothers of Christ.[36] He will not allow the tormenters of His faithful to
> go unpunished.

The promise of the deluge, whether in this life or in the next, is implicit even in the apologetic nature of their use of David. We will next meet David amid the diluvial torrent of the French Wars of Religion. While David will still bolster the integrity of the Calvinists, through the employment of a polemical device he will answer the question of what lies beyond the deluge.

## Beza and David *in tempore belli* [37]

Theodore Beza succeeded John Calvin in 1564 as the Moderator of the Company of Pastors. Both before and after this event, he played an active and exhortative role in the civil wars.[38] After the massacre at Wassy and the beginning of the wars in 1562, Beza served as chaplain, diplomat and propagandist for the Prince of Condé. He acted as Henry of Navarre's agent in Geneva after 1571 and, in 1574-1575, he visited the new Prince of Condé (who had taken refuge in German border towns) on several occasions as a counsellor and diplomat.[39]

Yet Beza's sponsorship of French Calvinists had actually begun in 1554 when, foreseeing the probable necessity of resisting increasingly oppressive French authorities,[40] he devoted a part of his *De haereticis* to a political theory which would justify such resistance.[41] Included in this work was a passage which asserted the right and duty of inferior magistrates to resist superior authorities in order to preserve the true (i.e., Calvinist) faith.[42] Beza further argued that since princes hold their offices by public consent, they must fulfill their contractual obligations by scrupulously observing the laws. Not only subservient to the laws of the polity, princes are also obligated to preserve the public's piety and morality as well as to guard themselves against any tinges of moral laxity. Should princes insult the political contract by abusing these public and private rules, then the subaltern "Christian magistrates" have the right to resist them.[43]

These brief remarks in *De haereticis* constitute Beza's first statement of his theory of resistance.  It was translated into French and published again in 1560, just after the failure of the Conspiracy of Amboise, as an anti-Guisard document attempting to show that Huguenot resistance was not directed against the king but against his evil counsellors who had "kidnapped" the king and ruled in his stead.[44]

Though *De haereticis* may be seen as an embryonic formulation of Beza's later *Du Droit des magistrats,* the line of descent from the former to the latter is not direct.  In 1558 Beza wrote his *Confession de la foy chrestienne;* it appeared in French in 1559 and in Latin and French editions in 1560.  A summary in seven points of reformed doctrine, Point V (*"De l'Eglise"*), ends with a section on the question of political resistance.  The 1559 edition is a regression from Beza's position in 1554:  Christian subjects must completely obey their governors, even in the case of tyranny; at best, they may passively disobey a magistrate who forces them to act against the will of God.[45]  The 1560 editions, on the other hand, recoup some of the ground given up the previous year.  In the same section, Beza (perhaps thinking of the Conspiracy of Amboise which had made the French Calvinists into an overtly political party) states that the general duty of each Christian to obey his magistrates is open to exception.  Even a private person, if he has the ability to do so, can offer resistance to the illegitimate usurper; yet, sometimes the power of the usurper is legitimatized by the consent of the governed, making all further resistance illegal.[46]

Tyrants present a more complex example.  Their power, gained *de jure,* is used improperly.  In this instance, Beza allows of legitimate resistance, as long as it is led by governmental members who possess a constitutional right to limit the powers of their superiors.  Beza gives as examples of such constitutional resistance leaders the seven Electors of the Holy Roman Empire and the members of the Estates-General. In so doing, however, he absolutely refuses this right to all inferior magistrates and private persons, who, at most, can only passively disobey.[47]

The 1560 version of the *Confession* is particularly important, as it was in this form that Beza's resistance theory was most widely known in the 1560's and 1570's.  Since his *Du Droit des magistrats* (to which we shall next turn) was not, unlike the *Confession,* published under Beza's name, very few people realized during that period that the more radical *Droit* was by the Genevan Moderator.  It has, furthermore, been asserted that this association of Beza with the "moderate" political doctrine found in the *Confession* and the disassociation of him from the more radical and anonymous resistance theory found in the *Droit* obtained until relatively recent times.[48]  However, as we shall show, Beza's radicalism did become publically known with the publications, under his name, of his commentaries on the Psalms between 1579 and 1581.

The theoretical bases for Beza's uses of David in his Psalm commentaries are found in his *Du Droit des magistrats.*  Reacting to the massacre of thousands of Huguenots on and during the days following St. Bartholomew's Eve in 1572, Beza appeared before the Genevan Council in 1573 to obtain its permission to print the *Droit* in Geneva.  Having just received an official French protest over François Hotman's *Francogallia,*[49] the Council refused to grant its *imprimatur.*  The moment was indeed one of great delicacy for the Genevans, for they found that Geneva was under attack:  two tracts had been published in 1572, asserting that the massacre had not been aimed against the Huguenots in general but only against Coligny and the militant wing of the Calvinists led by Beza.  These charges had to be refuted, for the Genevan authorities needed to persuade the various Swiss cantons (to which many Huguenot noblemen had fled) of the innocence of the victims, in order to enlist the cantons' aid both in recovering the *emigrés'* confiscated revenues and possessions and in negotiating with France to gain protection against attacks upon Geneva by the Duke of Savoy.  Moreover, the Genevan authorities were attempting to persuade the Polish Electors either not to elect Henry of Anjou king of Poland or to wring concessions of religious toleration from him, applicable both in France and in Poland, as the price of his election. Thus, it was useful for Beza's *Droit* to be published, but it was imperative that it not bear Beza's name or the imprint of Geneva.[50] Consequently, Beza's treatise was published anonymously in Heidelberg; the first edition of 1574 was in French.[51]

*Du Droit des magistrats* explains and defends the uprising of the Huguenots in defense of their faith and liberties. After offering the customary admonitions against too hasty revolt, Beza clearly suggests that the time for caution and restraint has passed, for, threatening bloody reprisals, the king commands godly Calvinists to attend Roman Catholic rites; yet,

> . . . the duty of all pious men requires not only that they should not carry out
> that command, but, further, that they should, in accordance with the example of
> Eliza and Elisha, even of the entire pure and true Church of old, join in pious
> gatherings, there to hear the word of God. . . .[52]

In these circumstances, neither flight nor martyrdom is called for. Instead, French Calvinists may lawfully oppose the king's injustice.

Beza describes two types of tyranny. The first is that of the *tyran d'origine,* the usurper who provokes a just national resistance on the part of all citizens. As he said in the *Confession,* such a usurper may yet become a legitimate ruler if and when he pledges obedience to the constitution of the country and obtains the free consent of its citizenry. More crucial to Beza's purpose is his definition of the *tyran manifest,* the actual and legitimate king who, because of his tyranny, no longer retains lawful power and legitimacy. Beza cautions that the intention of resistance to such a king should be to restore him to his senses and thus to reinstate him as *de jure* king.[53] Beza again hints that the occasion for this mild and restorative resistance is past. Indeed, the Valois tyranny is all the more flagrant and it requires an extreme form of remedy because the edict of partial toleration, granted in January 1562 (which Beza had helped to draft), had been abjured.[54]

Thus, the king's sacred promise to protect the people of God and to observe the laws he had guaranteed by his royal signature had been broken; his reign had become irretrievably abusive. Therefore, as Beza states in *Droit,* "those who have the power to create a king also have the power to depose him."[55] However, the lawful power to depose an abusive tyrant rests, not with men acting as individuals, but with the people led by the proper magistrates.

Who are the magistrates who may lead the Huguenots against the king? Historical examples would suggest ephoral authorities such as the Estates-General.[56] However, the Estates are sometimes unable to be convened and on other occasions they are unable to be freely convened. Failing this body, Beza argues that the "healthier part" of the subaltern magistrates–those who share in the government (and whose titles are hereditary) and those who are the elected magistrates of municipal governments–may answer the call of the pious:

> [Nothing] prevents private persons from going to the inferior magistrates and taking
> them to task concerning their duty; and if all of them or the healthier part of them
> are prepared to make use of such help from private citizens, I have already shown . . .
> what they are bound to render to God and to their country.[57]

Having thus restricted the source of lawful resistance to the healthier segment of the French population—the Calvinist faithful led by their aristocratic and urban magistrates—Beza is able to argue that, even though the goal is now to depose the king, their aim is nevertheless above reproach.  Even if the manifest tyranny of the Valois king has made it impossible to render him *de jure* king, the lawful and pious intent of the resistance is to install a (Huguenot) king with, one presumes, the free consent of the healthier part of the kingdom; a king who will keep his pact with the people and God, and also maintain the godly in peace and prosperity.  Thus, the pious intentions of the healthier segment of France would render the revolt righteous, and the Huguenot king, whom the Catholics might regard as a *tyran d'origine*, would be *de facto* and *de jure* king because he had been elected by the free consent of that same healthier part.[58]

Beza's *Du Droit des magistrats* has the appearance of a high-minded study of the question of resistance.  Its allusions to the massacre of 1572 which prompted it are oblique, and Beza's theory is based on the contractual obligations entered into by a governor and the governed[59] which he had previously sketched out.  The *Droit* was therefore perfectly appropriate to its apologetic purpose, i.e., the assertion of the Huguenots' innocence to the Swiss and other European peoples; nonetheless, it also served to justify the Huguenots' resistance after the St. Bartholomew's Eve Massacre.  Its author was unnamed, so that the direct ties of this work (whose villain was no longer the Guise but the king) to Beza could not be detected.

This excursion into Beza's actual and theoretical contributions to Huguenot resistance has not been idle.  With this background we shall the more readily understand the role his David played in the larger scenario of the French Religious Wars.  We have examined another previously unknown source of Beza's political doctrine of resistance.  This is his commentary on the Psalms, contained in each of seven editions of the Genevan Psalter which appeared between 1579 and 1581.[60]  Beza's commentary is in the form of "arguments" which explain the meaning and relevance of each of the psalms (hence our calling them his commentaries on the Psalms).

While it has been impossible for us to determine precisely when Beza actually composed the commentaries,[61] internal evidence suggests that they were written no earlier than 1576.[62]  The fact that we have found no evidence indicating that the Psalter with Beza's commentaries had been published, even anonymously, outside Geneva prior to 1579 leads us to the conclusion that Beza probably wrote them in late 1578 or early 1579.[63]  However, this latter dating, which we find attractive and compelling, cannot be advanced with absolute certitude.

It is certain, however, that the date of the commentaries' first publication was timely, for, by 1579, there was need for new political messages[64] to meet the changing political situation.  To be sure, the Peace of Monsieur in May 1576 would seem to have ended temporarily the civil wars, but we know that the pacification of the kingdom was not entirely successful:  even before the outbreak of the seventh civil war in 1580, "the situation in France remained critical, if not dangerous."[65]  Moreover, the continuing minority status of the Huguenots militated against their ever attaining domination in the Estates-General, a hope which Beza had still entertained in the *Droit*.  The imposition of reality on this latter hope probably explains why Beza no longer mentions the Estates in his commentaries as well as why his emphasis there seems to be entirely on inferior magistrates such as Henry of Navarre.[66]  Yet what is strange is that four of the editions in which Beza's new political message appeared between 1579 and 1581 were clearly identified as being from Beza and Geneva.

We have already explained why the Genevan authorities refused to permit the publication in their city of incendiary political works such as the *Droit,* and why they did not wish this work to be published elsewhere under Beza's name.[67]   It is true that by late 1579 the political exigencies which had obtained in the years immediately following the St. Bartholomew's Eve Massacre no longer existed to the same degree.   The issue which had remained outstanding for the longest time—the negotiations with the other Swiss cantons and, through them, with France to safeguard Geneva from French and Savoyard invasions— was settled by the Treaty of Soleure, according to which Geneva gained the protection of Bern, Soleure and Zurich.[68]   Even at the penultimate moment before the treaty was ratified by Henry III, the General Council had (30 July 1579) learned of the illegal publication by Claude Juge outside Geneva of Goulart's *Mémoires de l'estat de France* (containing Beza's *Droit*) and had apologized to the French court.[69] However, permission was given by this same body on 16 March 1579 to publish the Psalter with Beza's commentaries.   It would seem, then, either that the Council did not know about the commentaries or, more likely, that it thought the political message (hidden in a *prima facie* non-political work) would not be readily detected by the French court.   And, by the time the fourth Genevan edition came out in 1581, its appearance was felicitous from the Calvinist point of view.   The Treaty of Soleure was in force; French sensibilities, which might have been affected by the edition in the vulgar tongue, probably did not have to be so carefully considered after the treaty had been signed.   Secondly, Beza's 1581 French Psalter with commentaries would reach out to a larger Gallic public who could not have been expected to miss their applicability to the situation in France.[70]

This applicability, however, was short-lived.   Henry III adopted a *politique* position after 1580 and the prospect of the eventual succession of Henry of Navarre to the French throne seemed more and more likely.   In this altered situation  the overt thrust of Huguenot propaganda could not remain the same.[71] Accordingly, Beza's *Droit* was not published in Geneva after 1581; and his commentaries on the Psalms were only published three more times in that city, between 1593 and 1597—and then for what appears to have been an instructive lesson to the new king, Henry IV.[72]

As long as they retained their usefulness, though, Beza's commentaries were a potent ideological tool, as can be seen in his treatment of David.   The premise which undergirded his exhortatory and propagandistic application of David to the French civil wars was identical to that which had governed Melanchthon's and Calvin's earlier concept of David:   his true and evangelical faith, which made him a member of the True Church of old.   Since it has already been shown how the earlier reformers rehabilitated David, there is no need to exercise the reader any further on that count.   Instead, we shall move directly to a discussion of Beza's contribution:   David *in tempore belli.*

Beza's portrayal of the earthly appearance and plight of the remnant Church parallels and reiterates what had been previously stated by Melanchthon and Calvin.   If the Huguenots would only reflect upon the hostility to David, they would recognize that the Church's enemies are similar to David's; for, at all times, the True Church resembles a bird which must constantly evade the snares of hunters.   Persecuted, as was David, the contemporary faithful are likewise emboldened by the promise of God's eventual punishment of those who vex His people.[73]   Furthermore, no less for Beza than for the other two reformers, David's reliance on his own innocence and his appeals to God are instructive to Huguenots when their enemies equate the defense of their calling with treason.   Patient forbearance and prayer testify to the purity of their motivations.[74]

Thus far, Beza has not deviated from the path Melanchthon and Calvin had paved. However, in others of his comments he passes from general statements to references to particular events which culminated in the need to revolt.

Between 1561 and 1572 Catherine de' Medici had "flirted" with the Huguenot leaders, Antoine of Navarre, Admiral Coligny, even Beza himself, and intermittently invited and welcomed them to court.[75] Although Beza fails to name explicitly either himself or Navarre and Coligny in his arguments to the Psalms, we believe that he could not be alluding to anything other than the experiences of those eleven years, for, unlike Melanchthon and Calvin, Beza puts great emphasis on David's experiences at court.

Referring to David's presence at Saul's court, Beza remarks on the extreme difficulty of maintaining one's purity of religion and conduct in the ambience of an intriguing and tyrannical court. David exemplifies the proper response of a servant of God to such a demoralizing environment. Neither did he waver in his allegiance to his calling, nor did he succumb to court pressures which would have had him attend polluted and legalistic religious rites:

> To the contrary, David shows in this Psalm that, although there were all the
> afore-mentioned difficulties to bear in Saul's court, . . . he will nevertheless
> continue in his duty, and he shows that he intends to frequent all the more
> assiduously the holy assemblies which had no stain of idolatry.[76]

Persevering in his duty and religion, David advanced in the court to a position second only to Saul. But it was at that moment that the envious hatred of the king and his courtiers cast him down from his high office and drove him from the court.[77]

Beza's reference to David's tribulations in Saul's court allows him to make two points *vis-à-vis* the conduct of the Huguenot captains in the French court between 1561 and 1572. First of all, Beza says that David vowed to continue in his *"charge"*, a word which carries a double meaning: the duty of the Calling and, especially, the fulfillment of a public office. It seems, then, that Beza would make David into an intermediate Christian magistrate[78] whose duty it was to be the tribune of the pious and to intercede for them in the councils of the kingdom. Indeed, Beza's description of David's constancy of faith is intriguingly similar to François Coligny's steadfastness before Henry II in 1558. According to the *Histoire ecclésiastique des églises réformées au royaume de France* (which was published in 1580 and drew from Beza's voluminous correspondance and *aides-mémoire*), the Duke of Guise had informed the king of Coligny's adherence to the reformed religion and of his attendance at its rites. Severely reproached by the king, Coligny replied:

> Please, Sire, do not find it strange that, if after having done my duty in your service,
> I take pains to seek my salvation. . . . Even if I had been there [at the "pré aux
> Clercs," a public place near the university, where the Huguenots worshipped], I
> would not think I had done anything wrong against God or your Majesty; for as
> much as I have inquired diligently I have found that they only sang the Psalms of
> David and prayed to God in this perilous time to appease His wrath against us and
> to give us a good peace. . . .[79]

Not only does David's continuing faith even in the court of Saul parallel that of the Huguenot leaders (such as the Colignys) in the French court, but his very presence there attests to the fact that the intention of the Huguenots in that period was not social disruption. Immediately after Beza praises David's refusal to forsake his calling and public duty, he adds that David's attitude might be contrasted with the Anabaptists who yield to the pressures of the world and absent themselves from public offices and affairs.[80] In the context of the Beza-inspired *Histoire ecclésiastique,* we find that Beza implicitly argues that the David-like presence of the Calvinists in the French court betokened a desire to restore the religious purity of the realm and to safeguard the people of God.

Secondly, we believe that Beza uses David's situation in Saul's court to jab at the apostate, King Antoine of Navarre, as well as to offer some mitigating explanation for his betrayal of the Huguenot cause in 1562. Elevated to high station, David had not considered the sudden changes which could occasion his downfall; yet when the tempest did come, he recalled God's promises of deliverance and did not despair. Continuing, Beza says,

> And we know how in these so sudden changes, it sometimes happens that those
> who have shown themselves to be among the virtuous make terrible mistakes,
> and finally give way completely.[81]

Certainly, the reference to Navarre is obscure since it is covered by the treachery of other erstwhile Huguenots. Perhaps Beza is recalling the slackening of Huguenot enthusiasm after the St. Bartholomew's Eve Massacre.[82] Yet, as we have shown, the quotation follows the discussion of David's activities in Saul's court; in this context, it would seem that Beza specifically intends a reference to Navarre. The contemporary reader of this passage, moreover, could not have missed the allusion to that most infamous of betrayals. At the same time, he would have learned that, invidious as Navarre's apostasy was, the embarrassment it caused for the Huguenots could be at least partly alleviated by pleading the crushing burden of living in a tyrannical court: all in all, a rather slick piece of casuistry.

Thus, through the application of David to recent events, Beza to some degree parallels his discussions in *De haereticis* and in *Du Droit des magistrats.* He has equated David's forthright devotion to the pure worship of God with the Huguenots' similar dedication, and he has demonstrated (Navarre aside) the religious rather than seditious nature of the Huguenots' employments in the court. Yet, just as in the *Droit* and, in a different way, the *Histoire ecclésiastique,*[83] Beza's commentaries subtly move to the breaking point: the massacre that culminated years of persecution.

Psalm 52, says Beza, was occasioned by Saul's massacre, at Doeg's suggestion, of the innocent priests of Nob who were David's friends. David composed the psalm to console himself and all the faithful who were shocked by the event, as well as to sustain them with a reminder of God's promise to protect His Church. Innocent, moreover, of any provocation, David feared that false accusers might make him seem responsible for the perpetration of the massacre. Beza concludes:

> The Psalm is as useful now as it was then, since there is never a lack of kings or
> princes who cruelly persecute the faithful pastors of churches, nor is there a lack
> of sycophants who inflame the rage of princes . . . against the children of God.
> One need look no further than those sustained and barbarous persecutions of an
> infinity of poor lambs of Christ in the kingdom of France. The Lord has seen it
> and He will demand an accounting for it.[84]

Since the arguments to the Psalms do not appear in any edition before the Latin Psalter of 1579,[85]
Beza, writing this comment sometime between 1576 and 1579, surely intended to use David's reference
to the slaughter of the innocent priests as a parallel not only to previous atrocities (such as the massacre
at Wassy) but also to the massacre on St. Bartholomew's Eve; this reference would, of course, also have
been apparent to the French reader. Moreover, David's fear of being burdened with the responsibility
would allude to the Catholics' attempts to cite Huguenot provocation of the event,[86] while the faithful
Calvinists and Beza would have recognized Catherine de' Medici (and perhaps Henry of Anjou) in Doeg
and Charles IX in Saul.

"God has seen it and He will demand an accounting." With these words Beza foresees the punishment of
the Valois court and the eventual victory of the Huguenot cause. Thus far, we have only investigated
David's role as an apologist for the Huguenot leaders and their revolt. It is apparent, however, from Beza's
fulsome polemical use of David that the psalmist was extremely useful in contrasting the evil ways of the
Valois court with the righteous manner in which the kingdom would be governed after the installation of
Henry of Navarre.[87] Nor were only the evil advisers castigated by this polemic; the time had come for the
king himself to be repudiated.[88]

The attack on the Valois monarchy revolves around Beza's description of the Davidic kingship. In passages
which recall for us the duties of kings in *De haereticis* and in *Du Droit des magistrats,* Beza explains that
David described his rule in terms of the Calling. To be sure, this is again no more than Calvin had done.

True kings must acquit themselves of their duties, duties which serve the welfare of their subjects as well
as the glory of God. In this spirit, David had declared that his regal position and his capacity to fulfill
his obligations to God and man were singular gifts of God, given through the indwelling of the Holy
Spirit. Because of his awareness of the true purpose of kingship, and with the aid of the spirit of
wisdom, David established a model kingdom which restored the pure worship of God and defended the
godly subjects within it.[89]

Having established David as the model and prototype of truly sacred kings, Beza exceeds the limits imposed
upon David by Melanchthon and Calvin. As we shall show, Beza projects a similar kingship for France
and, unlike his predecessors, makes David the nodal point for the transition from the impious and corrupt
Valois to the reestablishment of the Old Testament kingdom of David. The promise of the accompanying
deliverance of the pious consequently does not await the end of time and the eternal perdition of the
wicked; nor does it vaguely allude, as in Calvin, merely to an eventual humiliation of the persecutors of
the true faith. Beza promises, through David, the closely impending earthly establishment of the Kingdom
of God. Let us retrace our steps for a moment, so that Beza's vision of the sequence of events leading
to this restitution can be more clearly perceived.

For years, the seemingly hapless children of God have been persecuted without surcease,[90] and over the
same period of time they have, even as David taught, prayed for their magistrates and for deliverance.
But for which magistrates have they prayed? Certainly not for the king:

> When God does raise up such kings [as David], one must recognize that they are
> singular [and infrequent] gifts of God. . . . David lists the beneficences which come
> to peoples to whom it pleases God to give such magistrates, so that they may know
> what good has befallen them, and so that they may know that it is for themselves
> that they pray when they pray for their Lords and Magistrates.[91]

The Valois monarchs had already proven that they were not kings who acquitted themselves of their godly duties. The people pray, then, for kings like David, who, in fulfilling their divine and public charges, will safeguard the *"gens de bien."* Even though the Huguenots have unceasingly prayed for such magistrates, the enemies of God still rage. The faithful have held their impatience in check, but that patience awaits victories, as those of David over his foes, which will advance the glory of God; for the gradual display of His judgments upon the wicked will be better noted by the world than if God were to destroy His Church's enemies all at once.[92]

Moreover, the parallel that Beza has already drawn between the activities of David and the Huguenot leadership in the courts of tyrants served to equate them with the intermediate magistrates whom he had discussed in *Du Droit des magistrats.* While few if any French Huguenots who read Beza's commentaries on the Psalms were also aware that he was the author of the *Droit,* and could thus trace the connections between them, there is no doubt to the modern reader that Beza orchestrated them harmoniously within his own mind. Thus, when Beza devotes his lengthy argument accompanying Psalm 101 to David's meditation on his and his successors' future conduct, after he shall have assumed the regal office promised him by God, Beza also describes the attributes of the Huguenot magistrates[93] who will assume, through the same promise, the theocratic government of France.

David promises, says Beza, to uphold and exercise the virtues from which devolves the entire implementation of righteous government: clemency and judgment. Gentle and kind to the pious people of God, he will, on the other hand, severely cast down the faithless members of the kingdom; for

> . . . judgment, according to scriptural usage, means inflexibility and severity which
> is proper to exercise towards the hardened and obstinate, rather than a certain
> laxity and passive cooperation [with evil men], which not only loosens the firmness
> of the laws, but also completely dissolves and destroys it.[94]

David, then, will not subordinate the laws to the will of the wicked, for this would, as Beza suggested in *De haereticis* and *Du Droit des magistrats,* shatter the contract which binds the king to the service of his sovereign subjects.

But David pledges still more. He gives his future royal word that he will govern his private and public life in the manner which befits a king whose obligations extend below to the people and above to God. There will be no dichotomy between what he will command and expect of others and what he will exact of himself, nor will he fail to extend this same rule to his own dynastic house.[95] David's self-discipline will serve as an example to the restored earthly Israel.

Kings cannot govern the state alone. They have customarily been required to collect around them men who act both as advisers and as a sensory apparatus, gathering information needful for the making of governmental decisions. All too often, however, kings have utilized these counsellors and their plans in order to satisfy their own appetites. Since the collusion of evil advisers and the king's own infirmity as a man could only disturb the careful regimen of the royal person and kingdom, David vows that he will eschew such nefarious types; more than this, he will banish them from his sight and crush them. In the place of those who have slandered and contrived against the pious, in the place of those same evil men who have, in the past, encouraged kings in their desires to rule ignobly, David promises to recruit and employ only virtuous men, whose advice will serve the best interests of the kingdom and of the pure worship of God.[96]

David as polemic device rides in tandem with David as future king of France, the New Israel. Opposing the prospects for the future to the dismal past, Beza musters and ennumerates all the abominations of the Valois in a powerfully destructive attack against the recent monarchs of France. From Henry II, whose insatiable lust for Diane de Poitiers made him an easy prey for the Guise from Lorraine,[97] to Henry III, who, disguised, cavorted through the streets of Paris with his *mignons*; from Henry II's misrule and persecution of the Huguenots, to Catherine de' Medici's Italian duplicity and constant intrigues with the Guise; all of them, monarchs, advisers, and the Queen-Mother, are caught up in this scathing attack which condemns the Valois monarchy and brands its members as utterly irredeemable outlaws and tyrants.

Modern historians have been somewhat more kind to the Valois than was Theodore Beza.[98] Captivated by the righteousness and truth of his religion, he could not see—or perhaps could not admit—the very strong political element in the French Wars of Religion, which pitted two aristocratic factions against each other and the crown. No, Beza saw only God in His glory about to triumph over Satan. And he pledged, as did David, reflecting on the faults of Saul and the disorders which resulted from them, that God's servant from Navarre would swear for himself and his sucessors by solemn oath that God would be purely worshipped in His holy city, His Church—in France.

Victory, restoration of Davidic kingship, the security and prosperity of the remnant Church: the promise which God kept with David will again be fulfilled. But even though David's heirs pledge that they will be true kings, that they will reward the faithful and punish the obstinate, will the future King David be accepted as anything more than a usurper, a *tyran d'origine*? Beza answers affirmatively, for again the historical parallel between David and the Huguenots shows what will occur when the last enemies will have been defeated. After a series of civil wars, David was anointed, by the common consent of the people, as king of Israel. Beza refers to the description of this election in II Samuel 5 and I Chronicles 2. It is to these chapters that we must turn to discover who pronounced David the lawful king. The first passage speaks only of the tribes of Israel who are the bone and flesh of David; the second passage calls these tribes the sons of Israel. Beza's own words are ambiguous:[99]

> . . . apres les guerres civiles d'environ huit ans, toutes les *lignees du peuple*
> s'assemblerent d'un commun accord pour l'oindre Roy sur eux (2 Sam. 5 et 1
> des Chron. II). . . .[100]

Collating these three versions with Beza's political argument in the *Droit* that the sovereignty resides among the "healthier part" of the realm, we conclude that his meaning is closer to that found in Chronicles: "the sons of Israel," seen in the Protestant tradition, would imply the faithful. The Huguenot king's legitimacy will be based on his covenant with the "*gens de bien*," and so, no matter what Catholics might think of him, he will be *de jure* king. Against this king there can be no lawful revolt.[101]

Through the historical parallelism which Beza perceived between the condition of his remnant Church in France and David's in ancient Israel, he was able to accommodate David in a way not seen before in the *Droit* to Huguenot political theory. The Huguenots and David fulfilled their duty to act as checks on the manifest tyranny of an odious monarchy; but their immediate reward was increasing persecution. Moreover, David's assumption of the promised throne and his electoral ratification guaranteed, to Beza at least, the success of the Huguenot cause and the public (or semi-public) proclamation of the future monarch's legal right to rule. Finally, the absorption by the Huguenot leadership of the duties and goals of Davidic kingship demonstrated that their resistance and revolt aimed not at social disruption (which Beza had condemned in the *Droit*), but at the restoration of a divinely led government and kingdom.

Only one obstacle remained: how to make this powerfully apologetic and polemical David and his biblical authority countenance and proclaim the revolt of the Huguenots against the Valois and their wicked advisers. Prevented perhaps by his own fear of the irascible mob, Calvin had been unable to see anything other than restraint in David's conduct, nor could Melanchthon find any way around David's forbearance toward Saul. Lutheran political theory allowed just resistance to a tyrant; natural reason and natural law, Moses and Abissai, taught that even tyrannicide might be permitted *in extremis,* but never David.

By the time he wrote his commentaries on the Psalms, however, Beza had explored David's words, and he discovered in the Psalms the passage which opened the route and lent David's authority to a Huguenot revolt which acted as God's instrument for the destruction of His enemies. The words of Psalm 109 are extremely important:

> Hold not thy peace, O God of my praise;
>
> For the mouth of the wicked and the mouth of the deceitful are opened against me with a lying tongue.
>
> They compassed me about also with words of hatred; and fought against me without a cause.
>
> For my love they are my adversaries; but I give myself unto prayer.
>
> And they have rewarded me evil for good, and hatred for my love.
>
> Set thou a wicked man over him: and let Satan stand at his right hand.
>
> When he shall be judged, let him be condemned: and let his prayer become sin.
>
> Let his days be few; and let another take his office.
>
> Let his children be fatherless, and his wife a widow.
>
> Let his children be continually vagabonds, and beg; let them seek their bread also out of their desolate places.
>
> Let the extortioner catch all that he hath; and let the strangers spoil his labour.

Let there be none to extend mercy unto him;
neither let there be any to favour his father-
less children.

Let his posterity be cut off; and in the
generation following let their name be blotted
out.

Let the iniquity of his fathers be remembered
with the Lord; and let not the sin of his
mother be blotted out.

Let them be before the Lord continually,
that he may cut off the memory of them from
the earth.

Because that he remembered not to shew mercy,
but persecuted the poor and needy man, that
he might even slay the broken in heart.

As he loved cursing, so let it come unto him:
as he delighted not in blessing, so let it be
far from him.

As he clothed himself with cursing like as to
with his garment, so let it into his bowels
like water, and like oil into his bones.

Let it be unto him as the garment which
covereth him, and for a girdle wherewith he
is girded continually.

Let this be the reward of mine adversaries
from the Lord, and of them that speak evil
against my soul. . . .[102]

Commenting on this psalm, Beza reminds his reader that David never bore personal anger against Saul. On the contrary, his words denote holy indignation and his desire for the glory of God and for the restoration of the kingdom which God had promised him. We too, Beza continues, know those who band themselves against the Church and, led on by their private hatreds and dynastic disputes, ceaselessly inflame kings whom they have bewitched to execute barbarous cruelties against the innocent people of God. And then the threat:

Would that, I say, such people know, although the Church does not *explicitly* use
this Psalm against them, that nevertheless neither they nor theirs may fare any better
than is represented in this Psalm, *indeed even in this life,* if God does not give them
the grace to repent and cease such wickedness, which would be much more desirable.
However, that which one can see even now to have befallen some, indicates very
well what those who so maliciously attack the innocent can expect.[103]

"If God does not give them the grace to repent:" these are the words which distinguish the Huguenots' holy indignation from selfish wrath and their calling from selfish ambition. Such conditional words are also necessary, lest God's ways be thought to be knowable by men. Even so, David's psalm is a prayer which the Huguenots *implicitly* use in order to call on God to lead them to victory in this life; a victory which will destroy the royal mother and son who so grievously sinned against the Huguenots and, thereby, God, and whose images are so easily discernible in the words of this prayer.[104] And David will smile upon the accomplishment, by God's instruments, of the long-awaited and just punishment of the House of Valois.

Thus did Beza's David play a magisterial role in justifying Huguenot revolt in France. He showed that the French Wars of Religion were the cyclical repetition of the timeless struggle of the remnant Church against godless kings and priests; and his words finally came to countenance the overthrow of the Valois and the accession of the House of Bourbon.

It was vital that this latter justification be found, for Beza's use of David as a historical predecessor of the Huguenot leadership removed the need to appeal to the Estates (which Beza had still thought necessary in the *Droit*). Of equal importance, this justification necessitated the discovery of Davidic authority for the establishment of a new dynasty. Beza's use of Psalm 109 insured that Henry IV would not ride into Paris alone.

God having cast down their enemies, David and Henry IV rode into their respective capitals. David's return to the holy city of Jerusalem presaged a long life still to come, lived in holy zeal for the pure worship of God, and succoured by the timely ministrations of obliging maidens. Henry IV's life in Paris must not be imagined to have been less delectable than David's; but, when Navarre made his *joyeuse entrée* into what was to have been his and the Huguenots' holy city, he was greeted by the tolling of cathedral and church bells rung by papistical priests. Beza, who had mightily aided the Huguenot cause and had, with sure hope, awaited the coming of the earthly kingdom, had not foreseen that the Davidic Henry would become, if not another Saul, at least a second Absalom, portending the eventual return of his Church in France to the status of a faithful and persecuted remnant.

## NOTES

[1]Melanchthon, CR 13, Ps. 116, coll. 1394-1395: "David movetur conscientia sui lapsus . . . : non potuit niti meritis, sed intuetur promissionem gratuitam remissionis peccatorum. Hac una se erigit et sustentat, accipit remissionem, et expectat veniam ac liberationem. Ita fide eluctatur ex inferis. Talia exempla monstrant veram sententiam horum Psalmorum, praesertim apud pios qui non habent mentes carnali securitate ebrias, sed aliqua certamina experiuntur pavorum et fidei." Also, CR 13, Ps. 34, col. 1240: ". . . sciamus hunc Psalmum consolationem esse, quia gratiarum actio scripta est ad alios consolandos, ut fide petant, et expectent similes liberationes." Calvin, Ps. 116:11, p. 431, speaking of the wavering of David's and all the elect's faith, says: "Consilium [nobis] Davidis est (ut nuper attigi) amplificare modis omnibus Dei gratiam."

[2]Calvin, Ps. 20:1, p. 72: Having the calling of a prophet, David "merito fidelibus dictavit precandi formam, . . . ex doctoris officio ostendens, ad totius Ecclesiae studium et curam spectare. . . ." Melanchthon, CR 13, Ps. 51, col. 1232: "Idem hic dicit David de conversione, et veris cultibus in corde. . . . Vox Evangelii affirmat [homines miseros et

oppressos doloribus] esse templa Dei, et afflictiones eorum, qui ad Deum conversi sunt esse sacrificia, id est, excellentissima opera, . . . et certo expectare auxilium et tandem liberationem. . . . Hos veros cultus inquit David placere Deo, dolores in conversione, fidem, invocationem, spem, etc."

[3]Excepting, of course, the era of the early Church under the persecuting emperors.

[4]That is, as a member of the True Israel and as a believer in the messianic promise of salvation by faith alone.

[5]Melanchthon, CR 13. The commentary found between coll. 1017 and 1224 was written "partim anno 1555, partim 1553 et 1554;" that written in 1552 is found in coll. 1224 to 1244; and the comments dated 1542 "et sequenti" are contained in coll. 1245-1472. Calvin wrote his commentary in 1557.

[6]For an account of the events of those years, see Hajo Holborn, *A History of Modern Germany*, I: *The Reformation* (New York: Alfred A. Knopf, 1961), pp. 215-241; and Karl Brandi, *The Emperor Charles V*, trans. by C. V. Wedgwood (London: Jonathan Cape, 1970), pp. 435ff. and *passim.*

[7]Melanchton, CR 13, col. 1443.

[8]Melanchthon, CR 13, col. 1034: "Interim Epicurei illi, inimici verae Ecclesiae, iactant se paci publicae consulere, et rident stoliditatem recte docentium. . . . Tales multi sunt in aulis regum et pontificum, ut in Anglia Wintoniensis, in Gallia Constabilis, et alibi alii. . . ." Melanchthon was not the first reformer to anathematize Gardiner; after meeting Gardiner at the Colloquy of Ratisbon (1541), Martin Bucer came to see him as "the evil influence behind the scenes, and the bishop who was to blame for the break between Protestantism and England." (Constantin Hopf, *Martin Bucer and the English Reformation* [Oxford: Basil Blackwell, 1946], p. 7.) Although dismissed and imprisoned by Edward VI, Gardiner once again became the bishop of Winchester in 1553 and he served as Bloody Mary's Lord Chancellor until his death in 1555. On Francis I's agreement with the Emperor, see Holborn, *op. cit.,* p. 226.

[9]We assume that this is the event alluded to by Melanchthon when he writes: "Ut nunc cum summa fuerit amicicia inter landgravium et Lycaonem, tamen postea Lycaon oblitus veteris amiciciae et meritorum, conatus est landgravio dignitatem, ditionem et vitam eripere." (Melanchthon, CR 13, col. 1085.) "Lycaon" would be, considering Melanchthon's grief, a fitting name for the Emperor who had, just the previous year, specially sought out the Landgrave (whom Melanchthon sometimes called "the Macedonian") and informally greeted the latter in great amity; but, as it turned out, only to lull Philip's suspicions. See Holborn, *op. cit.,* pp. 277-278; and Brandi, *op. cit.,* p. 542.

[10]*Histoire ecclésiastique des églises réformées au royaume de France,* ed. by G. Baum, Ed. Cunitz & R. Reuss, I (Paris: Fischbacher, 1883), p. 15.

[11]*Ibid.,* p. 61.

[12]Melanchthon, CR 13, coll. 1443-1444.

[13]Melanchthon, CR 13, coll. 1443-1444, 1140-1141; Calvin, Ps. 35:1, p. 130: "Neque enim mirum aut novum videri debet, si nos carpant ac mordeant homines maligni, qui ne Davidi quidem pepercerunt." Melanchthon's comment that there is always a faithful remnant attests to the perception of the reformers and even, from a hostile perspective, of their foes: for example, Luther's (spurious) "Here I stand" and Charles V's reply that " . . . it is certain that a single friar errs in his opinion which is against all of Christendom. . . ." (Quoted in Eugene F. Rice, Jr., *The Foundations of Early Modern Europe, 1460-1559* [New York: W.W. Norton and Co., 1971], pp. 164-165.) Moreover, Flacius' *Magdeburg Centuriae* chronicled the vicissitudes of the Christian Church, increasingly corrupted by papal teachings, although evangelical truth always had its witnesses, as was most recently seen in Luther's restitution of the Gospel (cf. Holborn, *op. cit.,* p. 235).

[14]Melanchthon, CR 13, col. 1024.

[15]Melanchthon, CR 13, coll. 1142-1143.

[16]See note 18, below.

[17]We do not think it far-fetched to infer that Calvin has in mind here the *parlements.* Melanchthon, CR 13, Pss. 119 and 111, coll. 1198-1199 and 1310, writes of the false wisdom of princes who oppose the faithful who know that the fear of God must be followed by His mercy.

[18]Calvin, Ps. 58:2, p. 220: "David ergo bona conscientia fretus, libere prodit in medium, et futiles calumnias quibus eum gravabant apud simplices, refutat, idque proprio eorum judicio, ac si diceret, Ego vos testes habeo meae innocentiae, vos tamen fictis criminibus improbe me vexatis: quomodo vos non pudet innoxium ita gratis opprimere? . . . Coetum ergo

illum compellat David, quem sub specie legitimi consilii vocabat Saul ad insontem opprimendum. Forte vero contemptim vocat filios hominum, detrahens quod titulo tenus concesserat: quia potius latronum turba erant quam judicum conventus. . . . Nos vero discamus, Davidis exemplo, quamvis totus mundus surdus sit, in bonam conscientiam recumbere, atque ita provocare ad Dei tribunal." Also *ibid.*, Ps. 119:22, p. 443: "Simul tamen discamus, nihil magis esse perversum quam pendere ab hominum judiciis." Melanchthon speaks in much the same vein in CR 13, Ps. 7, col. 1030.

[19]Melanchthon, CR 13, Ps. 43, col. 1088: " . . . impios hostes, qui non tantum corpus Davidis e medio tollere conantur, sed insuper causam et doctrinam eius damnant. Ac nobis hoc tempore facilis est accommodatio. Defensores impiae doctrinae . . . genus doctrinae cupiunt extinguere." Calvin, Ps. 27:12, p. 101: "Quare siquando impii in nos non tantum minaciter . . . surgant, sed etiam mendaciis infament, . . . veniat nobis in memoriam Davidis exemplum, qui utroque modo impetitus fuit. Imo succurrat Christum . . . non minus injuriae a linguis mendacibus, quam a gladiis passum esse."

[20]Melanchthon, CR 13, Ps. 59, col. 1143, and especially: " . . . etiam Deo proponis iusticiam cuasae, quia non est petendum, ut causas iniustas Deus adiuvet, et ipse promisit se iustis causis. . . ." Calvin does not exhort against unworthily seeking God's aid, but he does maintain the sequence of public assertion followed by prayer to God: Ps. 58:7, p. 221: "Sed hic ordo notandus est, quod prius de hostium suorum malitia conquestus est David, et bonam conscientiam in medium produxit, quam Deum advocet causae suae patronum aut judicem."

[21]D. P. Walker, *The Decline of Hell* (Chicago: University of Chicago Press, 1964), p. 48.

[22]Melanchthon, CR 13, Ps. 59, col. 1144; Calvin, Ps. 69:5, pp. 254-255: "Quare discamus hoc exemplo, non modo ad incommoda, molestias, mortem denique placide ferendam nos parare, sed etiam ad ignominias et probra. . . . [H]oc verum probitatis est examen, constanter manere in justitiae colendae studio, quamvis tam iniquum praemium a mundo reportemus." Cf. *ibid.*, Ps. 35:1, p. 130, where Calvin says that the only recourse for David and all faithful who are cruelly oppressed is prayerfully to entrust their lives and reputations to God's protection.

[23]Calvin, Ps. 58:7, p. 221: "Porro hoc votum concipere non potuit, nisi invicta fortitudine instructus, ut formidabiles hostium apparatus, Dei arbitrio subjiceret: imo ita precando, totam eorum potentiam sub Dei pedibus prosternit. Ergo haec circumstantia notanda est, ne languescant preces nostrae, quamvis aptatae jam sagittae mortiferos ictus minentur;" *ibid.*, Ps. 109:28, p. 414: "Discamus ergo exemplo Davidis, . . . . Deum a parte nostra statuere, qui instar fumi discutiat omnes eorum conatus. . . . [C]ontra Dei benedictionem [hostes] non praevalebunt." Cf. Melanchthon, CR 13, Ps. 57, col. 1134; and Ps. 119, col. 1198: " . . . sed David credens verbo Dei, scit se posse servari. Sic totius Ecclesiae exemplum intueamur."

[24]See above, note 23.

[25]Pss. 26:3 and 69:5 (KJV, v. 4).

[26]Calvin, Ps. 26:3, p. 96: " . . . nempe quia Dei bonitatem qua sollicite suos conservat, ob oculos sibi proposuit, ne ad perversas artes declinans illius patrocinio se privaret: fidemque ejus sequutus, animam suam in patientia possederit: . . . Atque hoc inter Dei filios et profanos homines notabile discrimen est: quod illi meliorem exitum a Domino sperantes, ab ejus verbo pendent . . . : hi vero posteriores, quamvis bonas causas sustineant, quia tamen ignota est illis Dei providentia, . . . illicita consilia captant, confugiunt ad fraudes: denique nihil aliud habent propositum, quam malum malo vincere. Unde etiam miseri et tristes, interdum etiam tragici exitus. . . ."

[27]See above, note 22.

[28]Calvin, Ps. 56:9 (KJV, v. 8), p. 216: "Fugam suam dicit numeratum esse Deo . . . . Nec de una tantum fuga loquitur, sed mutatio est numeri. . . . Itaque lachrymas suas in utre Dei recondi postulat. . . . Mox vero se adeptum esse pronunciat quod optavit. . . . Quod si piorum lachrymis Deus tantum honoris defert, certe multo minus sinet effluere sanguinem, quin singulas ejus guttas numeret."

[29]Melanchthon, CR 13, Ps. 57, coll. 1135-1136.

[30]Melanchthon, CR 13, Ps. 54, coll. 1125-1127.

[31]*Loc. cit.*

[32]For a full description and analysis of the terms of the Golden Bull, see Holborn, *op. cit.*, pp. 27-29.

[33]We are indebted for our knowledge of the Lutheran doctrine of resistance to a paper read at the Annual Meeting of the American Historical Association, Boston, December 30, 1970: Richard Benert, "Lutheran Contributions to Sixteenth-Century Resistance Theory."

[34]G. L. Pinette, "Freedom in Huguenot Doctrine," *Archiv für Reformationsgeschichte*, 50 (1959), pp. 201-203. (The two preceding quotations were translated in Pinette's article.)

[35]While we believe that David plays an apologetic as well as an exhortatory role in Melanchthon and Calvin, we admit that the use of David as an apologetical tool is perhaps clearer in Calvin's commentary, only because he recalls the purpose of the *Institutes of the Christian Religion* in its preface.

[36]In his exposition of Ps. 58, Melanchthon mentions the enemies of the Gospel, both in David's time and in his own. He asks the question: "Why, when the truth is so clear, do they not believe; why do they defend errors and try to crush the voice of the Gospel?" (CR 13, Ps. 58, col. 1137.)

[37]Another version of the following section has been accepted by *The Sixteenth Century Journal,* and is now in press.

[38]There are two modern biographies of Beza: H. M. Baird, *Theodore Beza* (New York: C. Putnam's Sons, 1899) and P. F. Geisendorf, *Théodore de Bèze* (Geneva: Jullien, 1967). J. E. Neale, *The Age of Catherine de Medici* (New York: Harper Torchbook, 1962), E. W. Monter, *Calvin's Geneva* (New York: Wiley, 1967), R. M. Kingdon, *Geneva and the Consolidation of the French Protestant Movement,* hereafter cited as Kingdon, *Consolidation,* (Geneva: Droz, 1967) and Théodore de Bèze, *Du Droit des magistrats,* ed., R. M. Kingdon, hereafter cited as Kingdon, ed., *Droit,* (Geneva: Droz, 1970), with its Introduction by Kingdon, offer excellent summaries of Beza's role in the civil wars in France.

[39]See Geisendorf, *op. cit.,* Ch. 7, pp. 191-225, and 360-5 for a full account of Beza's war-time activities; cf. also Monter, *op. cit.,* pp. 210-11, and Kingdon, ed., *Droit,* pp. XII-XIII.

[40]R. M. Kingdon, "The First Expression of Theodore Beza's Political Ideas," *Archiv für Reformationsgeschichte,* hereafter cited as *ARG,* 46 (1955), p. 99.

[41]*De haereticis a civili Magistratu puniendis Libellus, adversus Martini Belli farraginem, & novorum Academicorum sectam. Theodore Beza auctore. Oliva Roberti Stephani. MDLIIII.* The French 1560 translation is titled, *Traitté de l'authorité du magistrat en la punition des hérétiques* (s. l. [Geneva], Conrad Badius). For these editions, see F. Gardy and A. Dufour, *Bibliographie des oeuvres théologiques, littéraires, historiques et juridiques de Théodore de Bèze,* hereafter cited as Gardy, *Bibliographie,* (Geneva: Droz, 1960), nos. 80-1. *De haereticis* was intended primarily as a refutation of Castellio's attack on the Genevans for having executed Servetus. See also R. M. Kingdon, "Les Idées politiques de Bèze d'après son *Traitté de l'authorité du magistrat en la punition des hérétiques,*" *Bibliothèque d'Humanisme et Renaissance,* hereafter cited as *BHR,* 22 (1960), pp. 566-9.

[42]Kingdon, ed., *Droit,* p. VIII. The critical passage is reproduced in Appendix I of this work.

[43]Cf. Kingdon, "First Expression," *ARG,* 46 (1955), pp. 89-93.

[44]Kingdon, ed., *Droit,* p. XIII.

[45]*Ibid.,* pp. VIII-IX.

[46]*Ibid.,* pp. IX-X. (On Beza's 1559 French edition, see Gardy, *Bibliographie,* no. 98.)

[47]Kingdon, ed., *Droit,* pp. X-XII. The critical passage is reproduced in Appendix II. (Cf. Gardy, *Bibliographie,* no. 103.)

[48]Kingdon, ed., *Droit,* p. XII. See also R. E. Giesey, "When and Why Hotman Wrote the *Francogallia,*" *BHR,* 29 (1967), p. 582n, where he says that Beza's authorship of the *Droit* was not known until the late 18th century.

[49]Hotman's tract was published in Geneva in 1573. However, the work was not prompted entirely by the massacre (though its publication date was timely), as a large part of it was composed before and during the summer of 1572. See Giesey, "When and Why," *BHR,* 29 (1967), pp. 581-611. Giesey has since incorporated his findings in a *variorum* edition by himself and J. H. M. Salmon of Hotman's *Francogallia* (Cambridge, Eng.: Cambridge University Press, 1972).

[50]See Kingdon, ed., *Droit,* pp. XIII-XXXII for further details. Beza's tract was written in June and July of 1573. There was a mutual influence between Hotman and Beza; see, e.g., note 59, below.

[51]The full French title is: *Du Droit des magistrats sur leurs suiets, Traitté très-nécessaire en ce temps, pour advertir de leur devoir, tant des magistrats que les suiets: publié par ceux de Magdeburg l'an MDL: & maintenant revue et augmenté de plusieurs raisons et exemples.* See Gardy, *Bibliographie,* nos. 299-302 for the French editions. The *Droit* is disguised as an expansion of the *Admonition* of Magdeburg (1550) against Charles V's *Interim* (1548). Although the Genevan Council banned its publication in Geneva throughout the 1570's, the identification of Beza's tract with the *Admonition* fooled them, and an edition appeared in Geneva in 1574, published by Jacob Stoer. There were eight other French editions of this work by itself between 1574 and 1581, but they were not from Geneva. In addition, the *Droit*

was published four times (along with the *Francogallia*) in Simon Goulart's *Mémoires de l'estat de France sous Charles neufiesme*, but they did not bear a Genevan imprint. No French edition of the *Droit* was published after 1581, for, after 1580, Henry III adopted a *politique* position, and the situation of the Huguenots was completely changed. However, a Latin version, *De jure magistratuum* (the work was most probably written in Latin), issued from the presses in 1580, 1590 and in the 17th century. It was joined with the *Vindiciae contra tyrannos* and Machiavelli's *Il Principe*, indicating that these combined editions were directed at an intellectual, international audience and that they were not the work of the Genevans. Cf. Gardy, *Bibliographie*, nos. 303-4; and Kingdon, ed., *Droit*, pp. XXVIII-XXXIV.

[52]*Ibid.*, p. 6.

[53]*Ibid.*, pp. 13-14. In order to avoid the confusing of Huguenots with Anabaptists, Beza (*ibid.*, p. 8) says: "Et quand je parle ainsi, je prie que personne pour cela n'estime que je favorise aucunement à ces enragez Anabaptistes ou à autres seditieux et mutins, lesquels au contraire je croi estre dignes de la haine de tout le reste des hommes, et de tres grieves peines pour leurs demerites." To contrast the Huguenots with the Anabaptists, he continues (*ibid.*, p. 11): "Je louë doncques la patience chrestienne comme tresrecommandable entre toutes autres vertus. . . . Je deteste les seditions et toute confusion. . . . [M]ais je nie que pour tout cela il ne soit licite aux peuples oppressez d'une tyrannie toute manifeste d'user de justes remedes conjoints avec la repentance et les prieres. . . ."

[54]Such is the implication of what he says; cf. *ibid.*, p. 66. On Beza's involvement in the drafting of the edict, see J. H. Franklin, *Constitutionalism and Resistance in the Sixteenth Century: Three Treatises by Hotman, Beza, and Mornay* (New York: Pegasus, 1969), p. 39.

[55]Kingdon, ed., *droit*, p. 44.

[56]*Ibid.*, pp. 39-44.

[57]*Ibid.*, pp. 18 and 53ff. (quotation is on p. 53). We have chosen to translate "la plus saine partie" as "the healthier part" rather than as "the more sober part"; we think this catches more completely the political *and* spiritual connotations of the phrase for Beza.

[58]We have deliberately made explicit what we deem to have been implicitly intended by Beza; this, to be able to show the more clearly the relationships between the *Droit* and Beza's uses of David in his commentaries on the Psalms. On the topic of the elective principle as it was historically applied to the succession to the French throne, see R. E. Giesey, "The Juristic Basis of Dynastic Right to the French Throne," *Transactions of the American Philosophical Society*, 51 (New Series), Part 5 (1961), p. 30 and *passim*.

[59]One of the examples which Beza gives of contractual obligations is the fictitious oath of the Aragonese nobility (cf. Kingdon, ed., *Droit*, p. 38). Hotman also gives the oath in its Spanish form (cf. Giesey, ed., & Salmon, trans., Hotman's *Francogallia*, pp. 306-9). This is further proof of the close collaboration of Hotman and Beza. See also R. E. Giesey, "The Monarchomach Triumvirs: Hotman, Beza and Mornay," *BHR*, 32 (1970), p. 44n; and *idem, If Not, Not: The Oath of the Aragonese and the Legendary Laws of Sobrarbe* (Princeton, N. J.: Princeton University Press, 1968), pp. 21-3 and 162.

[60]Four editions were published in Geneva, three elsewhere; five were in Latin, one in French and one in English: *Psalmorum Davidis et aliorum prophetarum, libri quinque: Argumentis & Latina Paraphrasi illustrati, ac vario Carminum genere latinè expressi: Theodoro Beza Vezelio* (Geneva: [E. Vignon], 1579 [Gardy, *Bibliographie*, no. 229; and P. Chaix, A. Dufour, & G. Moeckli, *Les Livres imprimés à Genève de 1550 à 1600*, hereafter cited as Chaix, *Livres*, (Geneva: Droz, 1966), p. 94]); *idem* (Geneva: [G. Cartier], 1580 [Gardy, *Bibliographie*, no. 231; and Chaix, *Livres*, pp. 96-7]); *idem* (Antwerp: N. Barius, 1580 [Gardy, *Bibliographie*, no. 232]); *idem* (London: T. Vautrollerius, 1580 [Gardy, *Bibliographie*, no. 233; *Short Title Catalogue, 1475-1640*, no. 2032]); *idem* (Geneva: [G. Cartier], 1581 [Gardy, *Bibliographie*, no. 234; Chaix, *Livres*, p. 100; and P. Pidoux, *Le Psautier huguenot*, Vol. II, hereafter cited as Pidoux, *Psautier*, (Basel: Baerenreiter, 1962), p. 170, "b"]).
The French edition which we have used here is titled: *Les Pseaumes de David et les Cantiques de la Bible, avec les argumens et la Paraphrase de Théodore de Besze. Le tout traduit de nouveau de latin en Françoise. Ionte aussi la Rime Françoise des Pseaumes* (s. l. [Geneva]: J. Berjon, 1581 [Chaix, *Livres*, p. 100; Pidoux, *Psautier*, p. 170, "c"; and O. Douen, *Clément Marot et le Psautier huguenot*, Vol. II, hereafter cited as Douen, *Marot*, (Paris: 1879), no. 193]); in addition, there was an English translation by Anthony Gilby of the London 1580 Latin edition: *The Psalmes of David, Truely Opened and explained by Paraphrasis, according to the right sense of every psalm. With large and ample Arguments before every psalme, declaring the true use thereof. . . . Set foorth in Latin by Theodore Beza. And faithfully translated into English, by Anthonie Gilbie* (London: J. Harison & H. Middleton, 1580 [*STC, 1475-1640*, no. 2033]).

After 1581, there is a second edition of this same translation published in London by R. Yardley and P. Short (1590 [*STC, 1475-1640*, no. 2035]). Gilby (cf. *The Dictionary of National Biography*, Vol. VII, pp. 1218-19) was a fierce Puritan who justified civil rebellion. He had been in Geneva, and he also translated Calvin's Commentary on the Book of Daniel (1570).

More importantly, there are two Latin editions and one French edition of the Psalter with Beza's commentaries which were published in Geneva between 1593 and 1597. The Latin editions are titled: *Sacratiss. Psalmorum Davidis, libri V. Duplice poëtica metaphrasi, altera alteri è regione opposita, vario genere carminum Latinae expressi. Th. Beza Vezelio et Ge. Buchanano Scoto Autoribus* (Geneva: F. Le Preux, 1593 [Gardy, *Bibliographie*, no. 236]); and *idem* (Geneva: F. Le Preux, 1594 [Gardy, *Bibliographie*, no. 237]). The second French edition (Geneva: Matthieu Berjon, 1597) is, according to Douen, *Marot*, no. 193, identical to the 1581 French edition, except for the title page; cf. also Chaix, *Livres*, p. 149. See note 72, below.

The 1579 Latin edition contains a dedicatory epistle to Henry Hastings, third Earl of Huntington (1535-1595). Descended on his mother's side from Edward IV's brother, George Duke of Clarence, Hastings claimed, after Elizabeth, the succession to the throne (in opposition to the claims of Lady Catherine Grey and Mary Queen of Scots). He had strong Puritan leanings and was a Huguenot sympathizer; in 1569 he petitioned Elizabeth to obtain permission to sell his estates and join the Huguenots with ten thousand men. Between 1568 and 1572 he acted as an overseer of Mary Queen of Scots. In 1573 he sat on Norfolk's trial for high treason; and he became a Knight of the Garter in 1579. (Cf. *DNB*, Vol. IX, pp. 126-8.)

While Beza certainly intended his commentaries to be applicable to the situation in France (since he requested that they be translated into French and be published for the "Eglises" [see notes 61 and 70, below]), his dedication of the work to Hastings was, because of the latter's religious and political leanings, appropriate. We suggest that Beza may have thought his political comments to be of exhortative and polemical use to Hastings, given his pretensions to the English crown and Queen Mary's rival claim. Although she was executed in 1587, Hastings may have arranged for the republication of the English translation in 1590, again to augment his claim *vis-à-vis* that of James VI of Scotland. This is a matter that should be investigated by Tudor-Stuart historians. (We note, however, that the English translation of the Psalter with Beza's arguments is dedicated by Gilby to Lady Katherine, Hastings' wife.)

[61] The *Registre du Conseil de Genève*, 1579, fol. 50v, 16 March, indicates that approval for publication was given in the following form: "Sp. Theodore de Besze a requis luy permettre d'imprimer les Pseaumes qu'il a traduictz [from previous French versions of Marot's and his Psalms (cf. Pidoux, *Psautier, passim*)] en vers latins avec paraphrase, et s'il échet cy après d'imprimer et traduire lesd. paraphrases en françois, de lui accorder de mesmes avec privilege. A esté arresté qu'on le luy oultroie six ans." (Quoted in Gardy, *Bibliographie*, no. 229.) While the *Registre* does not mention the *argumenta*, they are perhaps subsumed under the word "*paraphrases*," or the Council may not have wished to go on record as having approved the commentaries which contained the political message.

The only other comments we have found on the 1579 edition are in Beza's dedicatory epistle to Hastings (where he dated his epistle 16 May 1579) and in a letter to R. Gwalter (dated 7 November 1579), wherein he characterized the 1579 edition as a "travail que j'espère aussi utile aux Eglises qu'il me fut agréable. Ce fut mon unique consolation au milieu de tant de tracas." (Excerpt from the letter quoted in Geisendorf, *op. cit.*, p. 333.)

[62] We understand Beza's emphasis on Saul's massacre of the innocent priests, at the prompting of Doeg (I Samuel 22), and his application of that story to events in France, as a reference to the St. Bartholomew's Eve Massacre. From his flattering comments on David's private morality, we infer that Beza meant to contrast David with Henry III and his *mignons*. In addition, Beza's use of David not only fits well with the activities of the Protestant chiefs prior to 1572 but also comports with the leadership role assumed by Henry of Navarre after he fled the Valois court in February 1576. Finally, Beza's silence on the role of the Estates and his interpretation of Psalm 109 as a prayer exhorting God to intervene directly and also, one would suppose, to call certain persons to perform acts of resistance, cause us to see a link between Mornay's *Vindiciae contra tyrannos* (probably composed in 1574-1575) and the commentaries. (We shall point out these allusions in the discussion that is to follow.)

On Henry III's character and *mignons*, see N. M. Sutherland, *The French Secretaries of State in the Age of Catherine de Medici*, hereafter cited as Sutherland, *Secretaries*, (London: University of London Press, 1962), pp. 189-90, 230-2, and *passim*; and also A. L. Martin, *Henry III and the Jesuit Politicians* (Geneva: Droz, 1973), pp. 75-6. On Henry of Navarre's assumption of the leadership position left vacant by the murder of Coligny, see Sutherland, *Secretaries*, p. 201. See Kingdon, ed., *Droit*, p. XLI, for a discussion of Beza's bare mention of the "extraordinary calling" in the *Droit* (*ibid.*, p. 16) and its fuller treatment in Question II of the *Vindiciae*; on the latter, cf. Franklin, *op. cit.*, pp. 39, 42-3 and 146-58.

[63]Pidoux, *Psautier*, does not indicate any of the editions of the French Psalms before 1579 as containing these commentaries.  It would seem reasonable that, had Beza written the commentaries before late 1578, they would have been published in some form.

[64]This is attested to by the fact that the *Vindiciae*, while written earlier, was not published until 1579.  Cf. Franklin, *op. cit.*, p. 39; and Giesey, "Monarchomach Triumvirs," *BHR*, 32 (1970), p. 42.

[65]Sutherland, *Secretaries*, p. 210.  The Huguenots had cause to remain suspicious of Henry III even after the Peace of Monsieur.  He was Catherine's favorite son, and she continued to play a paramount role in the governance of the kingdom.  Besides, Henry had himself been implicated in the St. Bartholomew's Eve Massacre.  Even before that event, he had been lieutenant general, had led the royal army in battle against the Huguenots, and had besieged La Rochelle and other Huguenot strongholds.  He disliked Coligny, and had sided with the Guise against him.  After he became king in 1574, Henry vowed to live and die a Roman Catholic and to resume the sieges of Huguenot cities.  His extravagant religious devotions probably did nothing at this point to convince the Huguenots and Beza of his desire to compromise with Protestantism.  See N. M. Sutherland, *The Massacre of St. Bartholomew and the European Conflict, 1559-1572*, hereafter cited as Sutherland, *Massacre*, (London: Macmillan, 1973), Ch. XVII, *passim;* and Martin, *op. cit.*, pp. 46-7, 52-3, 58-9, and 224.

[66]This ignoring of the Estates and emphasis on the inferior magistrates is similar to the approach found in the *Vindiciae*, which suggests that there may have been an influence of the latter (perhaps *via* manuscript or word of mouth) on Beza's commentaries.  Cf. Kingdon, ed., *Droit*, p. XLI.

[67]See above, pp. 98-99.

[68]*Ibid.*, p. XXXIII; cf. Martin, *op. cit.*, pp. 82-3 and 170,  concerning Henry III's subsequent renewal of the treaty.  The standard work on the Treaty of Soleure is: H. Fazy, *Genève, le parti huguenot et le traité de Soleure* (Geneva: Mémoires de l'Institut national genevois, XV, 1883).

[69]Kingdon, ed., *Droit*, p. XXXIII and Appendix III.

[70]That Beza intended his commentaries to be read in France is implicit in his use of the plural "Eglises" and in his desire to see them translated into French.  See the quotations from the *Registre* and from Beza's letter, note 61, above.

[71]For one thing, with Navarre's likely succession to the childless Henry III, Beza and other resistance theorists would not want to press their resistance theory any further, lest it tend to support resistance to the future Huguenot king.  Secondly, after 1580, Roman Catholics began to employ a radical form of resistance theory which justified tyrannicide; such a theory, in the hands of Catholic polemicists, could only work to the detriment of Huguenot hopes regarding the future accession of Navarre as king.  Cf. Kingdon, ed., *Droit*, pp. XLII-XLIII and Appendix V.

[72]See note 60, above, for bibliographic references to these editions.  Pidoux, *Psautier*, p. 170, is somewhat misleading, in that he leads one to think that the editions he cites in sections "d" and "e" all contain Beza's commentaries.  However, we have checked Douen, *Marot*, nos. 216, 221, 222, 227, 237, 269 and 296 (to which Pidoux refers), and Douen's descriptions of them indicate that they contain Marot's and Beza's French translations of the Psalms and the Canticles, but not Beza's *argumens.*
On Henry III's assumption of a *politique* attitude after 1580, see Kingdon, ed., *Droit*, p. XXXII.  It is, on the surface, odd that the inflammatory comments on political resistance would be republished in French in 1597 (as well as in Latin in 1593 and 1594), especially since Navarre had become king and the Huguenot political doctrines had been taken over in an even more radical form by the Catholics (see note 71, above).  However, Henry IV only became king of all the French after his conversion to Catholicism in 1593: this act could well have encouraged the Genevans to remind Henry of the Huguenots' expectations of him and of his duty.  When, by 1597, Henry had not yet proclaimed an edict of toleration for the Huguenots, it is logical that the Genevans would have desired to impart this message still more forcefully, by publishing Beza's inflammatory remarks more publically, i.e., in French.  Geisendorf, *op. cit.*, p. 415, remarks that the Huguenots "au printemps 1597, recommencent à s'agiter."  While he adds that Beza recommended patience, it is not improbable that he and/or the printer Matthieu Berjon saw the reissuing of Beza's commentaries as a useful tactic to elicit the desired response from the king.

[73]Beza, *Les Pseaumes de David*, Ps. 70, p. 332:  "Ce Pseaume est une prière de laquelle il est vray semblable que David usoit ordinairement pendant qu'il estoit chassé du païs, et que mesmes il l'a depuis aussi baillé comme un formulaire pour l'usage de l'Eglise, d'autant que l'Eglise ou pour le moins la plupart des vrais membres d'icelle n'ont iamais faute d'ennemis qui ressemblent à ceux qui ont persecuté David, commes ils sont ici descrits expressément."  Also, *ibid.*, Ps. 11, p. 36:  "Le Prophete monstre en ce Pseaume que les fideles sont en ce monde ainsi que l'oiseau sur la branche

estant constraint de voleter par ci par là à cause des embusches des chasseurs. . . .  Il dit donc que l'issue monstre
à la parfin que toutes choses . . . sont administrées par la providence de Dieu, lequel n'abandonne non plus ceux qui
ont esperance en luy, comme il ne laisse impunis ceux qui ne le veulent craindre ni recognaitre."

[74] *Ibid.*, Ps. 143, p. 719:  "C'est donc ce que David s'est proposé en ce Pseaume:  quand se voyant banni . . . comme
s'il eust esté un seditieux et coulpable de lese-maiesté, qui est la cause aussi que tant en ce Pseaume qu'ailleurs
s'appuyant sur la bonne conscience, il prend bien ceste hardiesse d'appeler à Dieu des faux iugemens qui estoyent
donnez contre luy. . . .  Il nous monstre par son exemple comme il faut . . . que . . . nous nous maintenions en
nostre bon droit quant aux hommes et à leurs calomnies devant le tribunal d'iceluy mesmes."    Beza's argument to Psalm 7
(*ibid.*, pp. 19-20) follows these same lines, and, in commenting on the similarity of David's sufferings to those of the
Calvinists (*ibid.*, Ps. 54, p. 256), he says:  "Nous avons donc à apprendre de là que quand il est question de porter
la croix, ce n'est pas matiere pour en discourir tout à l'aise. . . ."

[75] Neale, *op. cit.*, pp. 60-77, summarizes the vicissitudes of these leaders until the massacre of St. Bartholomew's Eve.
A much more complete study of this period may be found in Sutherland, *Massacre*.  Coligny and Condé were in court
in 1561; Navarre became co-regent with Catherine de' Medici for the ten-year old Charles IX on 6 December 1560.
In early 1562 Navarre was seduced by the "Triumvirate" (Guise, Montmorency and Marshal Saint-André; but also
Lorraine and others), and he joined them, apparently on 28 February 1562.  Thus, he became known as Julian the
Apostate to the Huguenots.  Coligny withdrew from court in February 1562 and did not return except briefly (from
November 1563 to January 1564) until September 1571.  From then until his murder in August 1572, he enjoyed great
influence in court.  Cf. *ibid.*, Chs. I and X.

[76] Beza, *Les Pseaumes de David*, Ps. 26, pp. 95-6:  "Or, au contraire, David tesmoigne en ce Pseaume, que combien qu'il
eust toutes les difficultez susdites à supporter en la court de Saul, que . . . il persistera en sa charge, et qu'il veut tant
plus soigneusement frequenter les sainctes assemblees auxquelles cependant il n'y avoit une seule tache d'idolatrie."

[77] *Ibid.*, Ps. 31, p. 114:  ". . . ce Pseaume ait esté composé. . . lors qu'apres [David] s'estre veu si avancé en la court de
Saul, qu'il tenoit comme le premier rang apres iceluy, tout à coup il s'est trouvé reduit au dernier point de toute misere,
tant par la haine [du Roy] . . . , que par une envie que luy portoyent certains courtisans qui estoyent autant de
soufflets à l'entour de Saul pour l'induire à ruiner David."  Beza would seem to intend to refer to Coligny's experiences
at court.  See note 75, above, on his departure from and eventual return to court in September 1571.

[78] Beza had already done this in *Du Droit des magistrats*.  Cf. Kingdon, ed., *Droit*, pp. 22 and 56-7.  Beza admitted that
David had taken up arms with his men, but he did not suggest in *Droit* that it was for the purpose of deposing the
king; rather, his resistance was for the protection of himself and of his followers.  In his commentaries on the Psalms,
Beza manages to make David justify the deposition of the king; see below, pp. 107-9.

[79] *Histoire ecclésiastique*, Vol. I, p. 169:  "Vous ne trouverés aussi estrange, s'il vous plaist, si, après avoir fait mon devoir
à votre service, je m'estudie à chercher mon salut. . . .  Que si j'y avois esté [au pré aux Clercs], je ne penserois
pour cela avoir rien fait contre Dieu, ny contre vostre Majesté, pour autant que je me suis enquis diligemment, et ay
trouvé qu'on n'y avoit rien chanté que les Pseaumes de David et prié Dieu en ce temps dangereux d'appaiser son ire
contre nous, et nous donner une bonne paix. . . ."  We make no judgment on the veracity of this and similar episodes,
for the whole purpose of the *Histoire ecclésiastique* was to describe, from the Calvinist point of view, the mounting
persecution which obliged and justified the Huguenot revolt after 1562.  Cf. Sutherland, *Massacre*, Ch. I.

[80] Beza, *Les Pseaumes de David*, Ps. 26, pp. 95-6.  After the difficulty of living among tyrants, Beza writes:  " . . . tellement
qu'on s'est quelquesfois voulu faire à croire qu'il se faloit en tels cas accommoder au temps, comme on parle.  C'est
la cause pourquoy les uns se retirent de leurs charges, ayans plus d'esgard à eux qu'au public. . . .  Comme aussi ceste
mesme humeur se void en ce temps en ces transportez Anabaptistes."

[81] *Ibid.*, Ps. 31, pp. 113-4:  "Et nous sçavons comme en ces changemens si soudains il advient par fois à ceux qui se sont
monstrez des plus vertueux, de faire de terribles conclusions et en fin mesmes se laisser aller du tout."

[82] Cf. Kingdon, *Consolidation*, p. 200.

[83] See the comment on the purpose of the *Histoire ecclésiastique* in note 79, above.  Of course, the anonymous *Histoire*
only takes the reader up to 1563; however, its publication in 1580 indicates that the reader would complete the scenario
in his own mind through the massacre of St. Bartholomew's Eve, and even beyond.  In a very real sense, moreover, the
propagandistic character of the *Droit* and the *Histoire* is, *mutatis mutandis*, similar to the commentaries on the Psalms.

[84]Beza, *Les Pseaumes de David,* Ps. 52, p. 240: "Or ce Pseaume est bien d'aussi grand usage qu'il fut onques, puis qu'il n'y a iamais faute ni de Rois et Princes qui persecutent par toutes sortes de cruautez principalement les fideles pasteurs des Eglises, ni encores moins de flatteurs qui enflambent la rage des Princes . . . contre les enfans de Dieu: et n'en faut rechercher les enseignes plus loin que en ce que tout le monde sçait avoir esté aussi malheureusement entreprins, que barbarement executé au Royaume de France depuis quelques annees en ça sur une infinité de povres brebis de Jesus Christ. Le Seigneur l'a veu et le redemandera."

[85]The commentaries are identical in all the editions listed in note 60, above.

[86]As we noted on p. 98, above, two Catholic tracts had blamed Admiral Coligny (and Beza) for the massacre; cf. Kingdon, ed., *Droit,* pp. XXI-XXII. On the responsibility for the massacre and its meaning in the context of French and European politics from 1559 to 1572, see Sutherland, *Massacre,* Chs. XVII, XVIII, and *passim.*

[87]Cf. Neale, *op. cit.,* pp. 86-90.

[88]Kingdon, *Consolidation,* pp. 199-202, in discussing the hardening of Beza and the Huguenots after St. Bartholomew, mentions this as one of the results.

[89]Beza, *Les Pseaumes de David,* Ps. 72, p. 342: " . . . il traitte expressément de tous les points du devoir d'un vray Roy, afin qu'il puisse gouverner non seulement en toute honnesteté, mais principalement en vraye saincteté, ceux qu'il a pleu au grand Roy des Rois luy donner en charge. Il monstre donc qu'il est requis sur tout pour faire que les Rois puissent s'acquitter de leur devoir, que Dieu lui-mesmes leur donne l'esprit de sagesse: comme de fait quand il plaist à Dieu d'en susciter de tels, on les doit bien recognoistre pour un don de Dieu des plus singuliers, tellement qu'il s'en est trouvé mesme bien peu de tels en la maison de David." Also, *ibid.,* Ps. 16, pp. 47-8: "David . . . recognoist . . . que le Royaume . . . luy avoit esté donné de Dieu par sa pure grace, sans qu'il y eust chose en luy qui l'en rendist digne, et que aussi il ne se peut bien acquiter du gouvernement d'icelui, sinon par la mesme grace de Dieu . . . , que une bonne et seure defense des gens de bien."

[90]Beza does not allude in the commentaries on the Psalms to the decrees of partial toleration; he did do so in *Du Droit des magistrats* (see the reference to *Droit,* note 54, above). But there, the purpose was to demonstrate that the king had broken his royal word, not to mitigate his attack upon the crown.

[91]Beza, *Les Pseaumes de David,* Ps. 72, p. 342: " . . . quand il plaist à Dieu d'en susciter de tels, on les doit bien recognoistre pour un don de Dieu des plus singuliers. . . . Il adiouste aussi en peu de propos comme un denombrement fort propre . . . des biens qui reviennent aux peuples auxquels Dieu donne de tels magistrats, afin qu'ils recognoissent un tel bien de leur part, et qu'ils sçachent que c'est pour eux-mesmes qu'ils prient, quand ils prient pour leurs Seigneurs et Magistrats."

[92]*Ibid.,* Ps. 46, p. 207: "[Par ces victoires] la gloire de Dieu est grandement avancée. . . ." Also, *ibid.,* Ps. 59, p. 275: " . . . il est expedient bien souvent que Dieu n'extermine pas tout à coup mais peu à peu les ennemies de son Eglise, afin que ses iugemens en soyent mieux remarquez: qui est un point de grand usage, principalement pour retenir en bride nostre impatience."

[93]These magistrates naturally must be Henry of Navarre and his successors.

[94]*Ibid.,* Ps. 101, pp. 496-7: " . . . le Iugement selon l'usage de l'Escriture est pris pour la roideur et severité qu'il convient exercer envers les endurcis et obstinez, au contraire d'une certaine lascheté et connivence, laquelle non seulement relasche la fermeté des loix, mais mesme la dissoult et aneantit du tout." Also, *ibid.,* p. 497: "Il promet . . . qu'il ne se rendra pas moins severe à exterminer les mechans, que doux et favorable à conserver et entretenir les siens en paix."

[95]*Ibid.,* pp. 497-8: " . . . il dit . . . quel ordre il donnera au reiglement de sa maison . . . et comment il s'acquittera en public de ceste charge et dignité Royale. Suivant donc cela, commençant au deuxième verset à dresser un bon gouvernement par sa propre personne, et en ce faisant se monstrant tout autre que ceux qui ne font rien moins eux-mesmes que ce qu'ils commandent aux autres. . . ."

[96]*Loc. cit.:* " . . . il promet qu'il ne prendra meschans conseils de soy-mesmes, ni n'ensuivra les meschans exemples: comme on sçait que les princes trouvans quelque occasion à propos pour assouvir leurs passions et convoitises, en font volontiers ainsi, soit qu'ils y soyent induits par ceux qui s'approchent . . . pour les induire à tout mal. David donc declare . . . qu'il se gardera . . . de toutes personnes . . . esloignées de la vraye vertu. . . . [A]ux . . . calomniateurs . . . il . . . fera justice capitale. . . . [I]l se servira autant volontiers du conseil des gens de bien et de vertu, les ayant soigneusement recherchez, comme il bannira loin de soy ou deboutera entierement tout cauteleux et rusez."

[97]*Histoire ecclésiastique,* Vol. I, pp. 86-7, 136-7, for example, claims that the Guise were able to persuade Henry II to persecute members of the "true religion" as a way of atoning for his carnal relationship with Diane.

[98]We refer the reader to Martin, *op. cit.,* for a balanced treatment of Henry III as a man and a king. We also recommend F. A. Yates, *The French Academies of the Sixteenth Century* (London: Warburg Institute, 1947), which presents a generous consideration of both Catherine de'Medici and Henry III and their attempts, through the French academic movement, to reconcile the warring aristocratic factions.

[99]"Lignes" or "lignees" (see note 100, below) could mean "lineage" or "offspring"; it would seem that Beza does not refer to the Estates, but to the ten tribes of Israel: see his previous use of "lignees" in Kingdon, ed., *Droit,* p. 59n, where he expressly distinguished between the Estates of Israel and the tribes.

[100]Beza, *Les Pseaumes de David,* Ps. 133, p. 681 (our italics). In his comment on Psalm 75 (*ibid.,* p. 364), Beza writes: " . . . du Royaume auquel il avoit esté eslue en ce temps-là par les voix de toutes les lignees d'un commun consentement."

[101]It was urgently necessary that Beza make this point. After the Peace of Monsieur in 1576, the Catholic League (led by the Guise family) opposed the treaty's tolerant terms and began to put forward the teachings of Hotman's *Francogallia;* using Hotman's arguments about the ancient Frankish kingdom, the Leaguers drew a parallel between their own situation and the seclusion of the last Merovingian king in a monastary and succession of Pepin and the Carolingians to the throne. (This was a particularly pointed parallel, as the Guise of Lorraine claimed to be descended from the Carolingians.) Moreover, Beza's silence on the Estates and his statements on election by the "sons of Israel-*gens de bien*" can be seen as a calculated reaction to the League's domination of the Estates-General at Blois in 1576 (and to the prospect of the repetition of the same situation in future gatherings of the Estates). Cf. Giesey, ed., & Salmon, trans., Hotman's *Francogallia,* pp. 92-3.

[102]Psalm 109, King James Version.

[103]Beza, *Les Pseaumes de David,* Ps. 109, pp. 559-60 (our italics): " . . . on sçait assez de quelle haine il a esté poursuivi si longuement, et de quelle cruauté Saul et les siens l'ont persecuté: et que neantmoins il n'a iamais esté transporté quant à luy d'aucune haine contre Saul. . . . Il s'est donc proposé en ceste indignation saincte, qui l'a conduit en tout ce Pseaume, en tout et par tout la seule gloire de Dieu, et le restablissement du regne dont il avoit pleu à Dieu luy donner la promesse sur laquelle il s'appuyoit. . . . Sçachant donc tous ceux qui apres un Doeg et un Iudas se bandent ainsi contre l'Eglise d'une mesme cruauté, et nommément ceux qui poursuivans les haines particulieres et quereles maudites de leurs maisons ne cessent . . . d'enflamber les Rois qu'ils tiennent comme ensorcelez par leur faux donner à entendre, . . . à l'encontre de tant d'innocens, . . . que tels di-ie sçachent, encores que l'Eglise auiourd'huy n'employe pas *expressément* ce Pseaume . . . à l'encontre d'eux, que neantmoins ni eux ni les leurs peut estre n'en auront pas meilleur marché que ce qui en est representé en ce Pseaume, *voire dés ceste vie mesme:* si Dieu ne leur fait la grace de se recognoistre et de se deporter de telle meschanceté, comme il seroit bien plus à desirer. Tant y a que ce qu'on en peut voir dés ce temps mesme estre advenu desia à plusieurs, monstre bien assez ce qu'en doivent attendre tous ceux qui se prendront ainsi malicieusement aux innocens."

[104]Beza labels each of the psalms by category, e.g., "action de grace," "prophetie," "doctrine," "priere." Psalm 109 is labeled as a prayer; thus, we further understand it as a prayer beseeching God to intervene (albeit through human agents) directly in human affairs. In this way, as we suggested above (note 62), the fulfillment of this prayer can be seen as being an "extraordinary calling," and thus related to the exposition of this concept in the *Vindiciae contra tyrannos.*

# Epilogue

Our study has shown us that, in the Psalm commentaries of Luther, Melanchthon, Calvin and Beza, David acquired a vibrant, personal faith and, thus, religious autonomy and viability. Explaining the contents of the Psalms "time-historically" for David's time, these Protestant commentators chose a hermeneutic method closer to Nicolaus of Lyra's than to Augustine's or Lefèvre d'Etaples' hermeneutics.

Hopefully, the Protestants did do justice to David: hopefully, they did impose upon him beliefs and sentiments which bore at least some resemblance to those he himself had long before embraced and expressed. Yet, even with this acquisition of fullness as a man living under the Old Covenant, there was an unfortunate, attendant result: the implementation of David to accentuate the differences between Christians and even to justify open warfare.[1]

We would like to suggest, moreover, that there is another story that remains to be investigated and told, in addition to a fuller examination of the images of David in the commentaries of other Protestants. This other study would entail an exploration into the use of David as a catalyst for religious reconciliation and reunion during the sixteenth century, particularly as it was manifested in the Neoplatonic-Hermetic movements in Italy and France.[2]

Recent studies by D. P. Walker and Frances A. Yates have offered some insights into what might be termed the sixteenth-century irenic uses of David and the Psalms on the part of liberal, or at least *politique* Catholics. It is now clear that David came to occupy in the Renaissance a place among the so-called Ancient Theologians belonging to the Hermetic tradition. The identification of David with such real or supposed ancients as Hermes Trismegistus, Orpheus, Zoroaster, Pythagoras and Plato, led to a new emphasis not only on David but also on the Psalms themselves; David and the Psalms were now seen as spokesmen for the pristine, ancient theology from which derived the Platonic, Judaic, and Christian philosophies and theologies. This new emphasis put the Psalms in much the same category as, for example, the Orphic Hymns which were used by and after the Florentine Neoplatonist Marsilio Ficino (1433-1499) as prayers and chants in magical healing operations.[3]

The implementation of this Hermetic approach to David and the Psalms is particularly notable among the members of the French academic movement of the sixteenth century. Frances Yates' brilliant studies on this movement and on Giordano Bruno[4] have demonstrated that the French court, guided by Catherine de' Medici and Henry III, employed poets, humanists and philosophers in an attempt to find a healing hellebore that would calm the religious "troubles" of the last quarter of the sixteenth century. One of the elements of this magical hellebore was the Book of Psalms, put to measured verse, which, when sung to musical accompaniment, would move the stony hearts of men consumed by the fires of religious disputes. Just as Amphion's music had supposedly moved rocks to form the symmetrical walls of ancient Thebes, the religious Hermeticists hoped to use the Psalms and the Orphic Hymns in order to bring about the reign of religious harmony where, before, there had only been disharmony.

We hope soon to begin research into the irenic uses of David and the Psalms, especially as they were developed in sixteenth-century France. This investigation will entail once again turning to the Church

Fathers[5] for enlightenment on the patristic legacy on the Psalms and on musical prosody, which is important for the concepts of David and for the putative musical effects of the Psalms suggested by French academicians such as Jean-Antoine de Baïf. This study will also investigate the Renaissance Neoplatonic sources of the French academicians' concepts of David.[6]

We believe that this, our next study, will shed further light on the sixteenth-century concepts of David and that it will complement the present study which has focused on the polemic uses of David in the sixteenth century. It will also, by building upon the foundations so ably laid down by Miss Yates, contribute to a more complete understanding of the irenic and *politique* policy of Catherine de' Medici and, later, of Henry III, from the Colloquy of Poissy in 1561 to the hectic mission of Giordano Bruno to England in the mid-1580s.[7]

## NOTES

[1]This use of David, which we discussed in the last chapter, paralleled, among the Calvinists, the use of the Psalms as war songs and morale builders. The singing of psalms mightily contributed to the identity and unity of the Calvinists, in good times and bad. Catholic mobs, led by the clergy, oftentimes attacked small Huguenot congregations—who were identified by their Psalm singing; and soon-to-be-executed Huguenots sang appropriate psalms, to the great discomfiture of their Catholic executors. Catholic ecclesiastical authorities finally said that such singing "was in derision and to the great scandal of the Christian religion." (Cf. W. Stanford Reid, "The Battle Hymns of the Lord: Calvinist Psalmody of the Sixteenth Century," in Carl S. Meyer, ed., *Sixteenth Century Essays and Studies,* Vol. II [St. Louis, Missouri: The Foundation for Reformation Research, 1971] , pp. 36-54.)

[2]See note 6, below, for a list of writers and commentators who should be studied.

[3]D. P. Walker, *The Ancient Theology: Studies in Christian Platonism from the Fifteenth to the Eighteenth Century* (Ithaca, New York: Cornell University Press, 1972), *sub nomm.* "David" and "Psalms".

[4]Frances A. Yates, *The French Academies;* and *ibid., Giordano Bruno and the Hermetic Tradition* (Chicago, Illinois: University of Chicago Press, 1964). The French academic movement comprised members of the Pléiade and the Palace Academy of Henry III. For a literary background, see H. Weber, *La Création poétique au XVIè siècle en France de Maurice Scève à Agrippa d'Aubigné,* 2 Vols. (Paris: 1955).

[5]Yates and Walker have suggested that the following Church Fathers should be studied for their comments on the musical effects of the Psalms: Clement of Alexandria, John Chrysostom, Ambrose, and Augustine.

[6]We will do research on the Psalm commentaries by such syncretic philosophers as Giovanni Pico della Mirandola and Agostino Steuco, as well as those by Sancti Pagnini, Felix da Prato, Jan van den Campen, and François Vatable (the latter four having been explicitly mentioned by Baïf as sources for his ideas on the musical effects and original meanings of the Psalms). On Pico della Mirandola's Psalm commentary, see Eugenio Garin, "Il Commento ai Salmi di G. Pico della Mirandola," *Giornale critico della filosofia italiana,* 18 (1937), pp. 165-172 (reprinted in E. Garin, *La cultura filosofica del Rinascimento italiano* [Florence: Sansoni, 1961], pp. 241-253.

[7]On Bruno's mission to England (intended to effect a religious and political reunion between France and England) and its relation to the religious policy of the French court, see Frances A. Yates, "The Religious Policy of Giordano Bruno," *Journal of the Warburg and Courtauld Institutes,* 3, iii-iv (1940), pp. 181-207; and Lawrence S. Lerner and Edward A. Gosselin, "Was Giordano Bruno a Scientist?: A Scientist's View," *American Journal of Physics,* 41, no. 1 (January 1973), pp. 30-35.

# Selected Bibliography

Part I of this bibliography contains the primary sources which we have used either directly, in the writing of this book, or indirectly, as affording checks by which to ascertain the verisimilitude of our changing portraits of David for each of the periods which we have discussed.

Part II contains the secondary literature. We have made no attempt to offer a complete bibliography of the voluminous secondary literature on theology and biblical hermeneutics. Listing only those books which we have cited or those which are of paramount importance for a general background, we refer the reader to the very adequate bibliographies which may be found in the works listed below.

## I. Primary Sources

Augustinus Hipponiensis. *Enarrationes in Psalmos*, in *Corpus Christianorum: Series Latina*, Vols. XXXVIII-XL.

————————. *Enarrationes in Psalmos*, in J.-P. Migne, ed., *Patrologiae Latinae cursus completus omnium s.s. patrum, doctorum, scriptorumque ecclesiasticorum*, Vols. XXXVI-XXXVII.

[Beza, Theodore]. *Du Droit des magistrats sur leurs suiets, Traitté très-nécessaire en ce temps, pour advertir de leur devoir, tant des magistrats que les suiets publié par ceux de Magdeburg l'an M.D.L.: et maintenant revue et augmenté de plusieurs raisons et exemples.* Edited by R. M. Kingdon. Geneva: Droz, 1970.

————————. *De haereticis a civili Magistratu puniendis libellus adversus Martini Belli farraginem et novorum Academicorum sectam.* Geneva: Robertus Stephanus, 1554.

[————————]. *De iure magistratuum in subditos, et officio subditorum erga magistratus, Tractatus brevis et perspicuus his turbulentis temporibus, utrique ordini apprime necessarius. E Gallico in Latinum conversus.* S. l.: Johannes Mareschallus Lugdunensis, 1576.

————————. *Les Pseaumes de David et les Cantiques de la Bible, avec les argumens et la paraphrase de Théodore de Bèze.* Geneva: Jacques Berjon, 1581.

————————. *Traitté de l'authorité du Magistrat en la punition des hérétiques, & du moyen d'y procéder, fait en Latin par Théodore de Besze, contre l'opinion de certains Académiques, qui par leurs escrits soustiennent l'impunité de ceux qui sèment des erreurs, & les veulent exempter de la suiection des loix. Nouvellement traduit de Latin en François par Nicolas Colladon.* Geneva: Conrad Badius, 1560.

Calvin, John. *Joannis Calvini, magni theologi, commentarii in librum Psalmorum. In Psalmorum commentariis, praeter multos locos qui Calvini manu ipsius exemplari emendati bona fide hic etiam repraesentatur, Hebraeus quoque contextus è regione Latinae interpretationis additur.* Amsterdam: Johannes Jacobi Schipper, 1667.

Felinus, Aretius [Martin Bucer]. *Sacrorum Psalmorum libri quinque, ad ebraicam veritatem genuina versione in Latinum traducti: primum appensis bona fide sententiis, deinde pari diligentia adnumeratis verbis, tum familiari explanatione elucidati.* Basel: Johannes Heruagius, 1547.

*Histoire ecclésiastique des églises réformées au royaume de France, en laquelle est descrite au vraye la renaissance & accroisement d'icelles depuis l'an M.D.XXI. iusques en l'année M.D.LXIII., leur reiglement ou discipline, synodes, persécutions tant générales que particulières, noms, et labeurs de ceux qui ont heureusement travaillé, villes & lieux où elles ont esté dressées, avec le discours des premiers troubles ou guerres civiles, desquelles la vraye cause est aussi declarée.* Edited by G. Baum, Ed. Cunitz, and R. Reuss. Paris: Fischbacher, 1883-1889. 3 Vols.

Lefèvre d'Etaples (Faber Stapulensis). *Quincuplex Psalterium.* Paris: s.t. [Henry Estienne], 1509.

Luther, Martin. *D. Martin Luthers Werke: Kritische Gesamtausgabe.* Weimar: 1833 ff.

——————————. *Luther's Works (Selected Psalms).* Edited by Jaroslav Pelikan. Vols. XII, XIII, XIV. St. Louis, Mo.: Concordia Publishing House, 1955, 1956, 1958.

Melanchthon, Philip. *Commentarii in Psalmos,* in *Corpus Reformatorum.* Vol. XIII. New York: Johnson Reprint Corporation, 1963.

Nicolaus de Lyra. *Postilla litteralis et moralis in Vetus et Novum Testamentum.* Venice: Octavianus Scotus, 1488.

——————————. *Postilla litteralis et moralis super totam bibliam.* Rome: Conradus Sweynheym and Arnoldus Pannartz, 1471-1472.

——————————. *Postilla litteralis super psalterium.* Mantua: Paulus Johannis de Putzbach, 1477.

——————————. *Postilla moralis super psalterium,* in *Postilla moralis super totam bibliam.* Cologne: Johannes Kölhof de Lübeck, 1478.

Rice, Eugene F., Jr., ed. *The Prefatory Epistles of Jacques Lefèvre d'Etaples and Other Related Texts.* New York: Columbia University Press, 1972.

Tolomeo da Lucca. *Determinatio compendiosa de iurisdictione imperii.* Edited by Marius Krammer, in *Fontes Iuris Germanici Antiqui in Usum Scholarium ex Monumentis Germaniae Historicis.* Hanover, Germany: Hahn, 1909.

Woolf, Bertram Lee, ed. and trans. *Reformation Writings of Martin Luther.* Vol. II. London: Lutterworth Press, 1956.

## II. Secondary Sources

Aldridge, John W. *The Hermeneutics of Erasmus.* Richmond, Va.: John Knox Press, 1966.

Amann, E. "Lefèvre d'Etaples," *Dictionnaire de Théologie Catholique* (Abbrev.: DTC) 9.1: 132-139.

Bainton, Roland H. *Erasmus of Christendom.* New York: Charles Scribner's Sons, 1969.

——————————. "The Immoralities of the Old Testament Patriarchs according to the Exegesis of the Late Middle Ages and of the Reformation," *The Harvard Theological Review,* 23, no. 1 (1930), 39-49.

——————————. "The Bible and the Reformation," Chapter 1 in *Studies on the Reformation.* London: Hodder and Stoughton, 1964.

Baird, H. M. *Theodore Beza.* New York: G. Putnam's Sons, 1899.

Baumgartner, A. *Calvin hébraïsant et interprète de l'Ancien Testament.* Paris: 1899.

Benert, Richard. "Lutheran Contributions to Sixteenth-Century Resistance Theory." Paper read at the Annual Meeting of the American Historical Association, Boston, 30 December 1970.

Beskow, Per. *Rex Gloriae: The Kingship of Christ in the Early Church.* Translated by E. J. Sharpe. Stockholm & Uppsala: Almquist & Wilksells, 1962.

Bloch, Marc. *Les Rois thaumaturges: études sur le charactère surnaturel attribué à la puissance royale particulièrement en France et Angleterre.* Paris: Librairie Armand Colin, 1961.

Bouyer, Louis, Cong. Orat. *Erasmus and His Times.* Translated by F. X. Murphy, C. SS. R. Westminster, Md.: The Newman Press, 1959.

Brandi, Karl. *The Emperor Charles V.* Translated by C. V. Wedgwood. London: Jonathan Cape Ltd., 1970.

Calès, Jean. "Prophecy," *The Catholic Encyclopedia.* Vol. XII. New York: Robert Appleton Co., 1911.

Caplan, Harry. "The Four Senses of Scriptural Interpretation and the Medieval Theory of Preaching," *Speculum,* 4, no. 2 (July 1929), 282-290.

Chaix, P., Dufour, A., and Moeckli, G. *Les Livres imprimés à Genève de 1550 à 1600.* Geneva: Droz, 1966.

Christiani, L. *L'Eglise à l'époque du Concile de Trente,* in *Histoire de l'Eglise.* Vol. XVII. Paris: Bloud and Gay, 1948.

Congar, Y. M.-J. "Aspects ecclésiologiques de la querelle entre mendiants et séculiers dans la seconde moitié du XIIIè siècle et le début du XIVè siècle," *Archives d'Histoire Doctrinale et Litteraire du Moyen Age,* 36 (1961), 35-151.

Courvoisier, Jacques. "Bucer et l'oeuvre de Calvin," *Revue de Théologie et Philosophie.* Lausanne: 1933.

Daniélou, Jean. *Origen.* Translated by Walter Mitchell. New York: Sheed and Ward, 1955.

Dillenberger, John, ed. *John Calvin: Selections From His Writings.* Garden City, N.Y.: Anchor Book, 1967.

Dörries, H. "Calvin und Lefèvre," *Zeitschrift für Kirchengeschichte.* New Series, 44, 544-581.

Douen, O. *Clément Marot et le Psautier huguenot.* 2 Vols. Paris: 1878/1879.

Ebeling, Gerhard. "Hermeneutik," *Religion in Geschichte und Gegenwart*[3] III. Tübingen: 1959, coll. 242-262.

——————————. *Luther: An Introduction to His Thought.* Translated by R. A. Wilson. London: Collins, 1970.

——————————. "The New Hermeneutics and the Young Luther," *Theology Today,* 21 (1964), 34-36.

*Encyclopaedia Judaica.* Vol. XIII. Article on the Psalms. Jerusalem: Keter Publishing House Ltd., 1971.

Fazy, Henri. *Genève, le parti huguenot et le traité de Soleure.* Geneva: 1883.

Franklin, J. H., ed. and trans. *Constitutionalism and Resistance in the Sixteenth Century: Three Treatises by Hotman, Beza, and Mornay.* New York: Pegasus, 1969.

Gardy, F., and Dufour, A. *Bibliographie des oeuvres théologiques, littéraires, historiques, et juridiques de Théodore de Bèze.* Geneva: Droz, 1960.

Garin, Eugenio. "Il Commento ai Salmi di G. Pico della Mirandola," *Giornale critico della filosofia italiana,* 18 (1937), 165-172 (reprinted in Garin, E. *La cultura filosofica del Rinascimento italiano.* Florence: Sansoni, 1961, 241-253).

Geisendorf, Paul F. *Théodore de Bèze.* Geneva: Jullien, 1967.

Giesey, Ralph E. *If Not, Not: The Oath of the Aragonese and the Legendary Laws of Sobrarbe.* Princeton, N. J.: Princeton University Press, 1968.

——————. "The Juristic Basis of Dynastic Right to the French Throne," *Transactions of the American Philosophical Society.* New Series, 51, Part 5. Philadelphia, Pa.: 1961.

——————. "The Monarchomach Triumvirs: Hotman, Beza and Mornay," *Bibliothèque d'Humanisme et Renaissance,* 32 (1970), 41-56.

——————. "When and Why Hotman Wrote the *Francogallia,*" *Bibliothèque d'Humanisme et Renaissance,* 29 (1967), 581-611.

Giesey, R. E., ed., and Salmon, J. H. M., trans. Hotman's *Francogallia.* Cambridge, England: Cambridge University Press, 1972.

Gilson, Etienne. *The Christian Philosophy of St. Augustine.* New York: Vintage Book, 1967.

——————. *L'Esprit de la philosophie médiévale.* Paris: J. Vrin, 1943.

——————. *Introduction à l'étude de saint Augustin.* 2nd. ed. Paris: J. Vrin, 1943.

Glorieux, P. *Répertoire des maîtres en théologie de Paris au XIIIè siècle, II,* no. 345, in *Etudes de Philosophie Médiévale.* Vol. 18. Paris: 1933.

Gombrich, E. H. "Botticelli's Mythologies: A Study in the Neoplatonic Symbolism of His Circle," *Journal of the Warburg and Courtauld Institutes,* 8 (1945), 7-60.

Gosselin, E. A. "A Listing of the Printed Editions of Nicolaus de Lyra," *Traditio,* 26 (1970), 399-426.

Grant, Robert M. *The Letter and the Spirit.* London: 1957.

Hahn, Fritz. "Faber Stapulensis und Luther," *Zeitschrift für Kirchengeschichte,* 57 (1938), 356-442.

Hailperin, Herman. *Rashi and the Christian Scholars.* Pittsburgh, Pa.: University of Pittsburgh Press, 1963.

Hanson, R. P. C. *Allegory and Event.* London: 1959.

Heller, Henry. "Nicholas of Cusa and Early French Evangelism," *Archiv für Reformationsgeschichte,* 63 (1972), 6-21.

Hendrix, Scott H. *Ecclesia in Via: Ecclesiological Developments in the Medieval Psalms Exegesis and the "Dictata Super Psalterium" (1513-1515) of Martin Luther.* Leiden: E. J. Brill, 1974.

Holborn, Hajo. *The Reformation.* Vol. I of *A History of Modern Germany.* New York: Knopf, 1961.

Hopf, Constantin. *Martin Bucer and the English Reformation.* Oxford: Blackwell's, 1946.

Hovland, C. W. "*Anfechtung* in Luther's Biblical Exegesis," in *Reformation Studies: Essays in Honor of Roland H. Bainton.* Edited by F. H. Littell. Richmond, Va.: John Knox Press, 1962.

*The Jerome Biblical Commentary.* Vol. I. Article on the Psalms. London: Geoffrey Chapman, 1968.

Kantorowicz, Ernst. *The King's Two Bodies.* Princeton, N. J.: Princeton University Press, 1957.

——————————. *Laudes Regiae: A Study in Liturgical Acclamations and Medieval Ruler Worship.* Berkeley, Ca.: University of California Press, 1946.

Kingdon, Robert M. "The First Expression of Theodore Beza's Political Ideas," *Archiv für Reformationsgeschichte,* 46 (1955), 88-99.

——————————. *Geneva and the Coming of the Wars of Religion in France, 1555-1563.* Geneva: Droz, 1964.

——————————. *Geneva and the Consolidation of the French Protestant Movement.* Geneva: Droz, 1967.

——————————. "Les Idées politiques de Bèze d'après son *Traitté de l'authorité du magistrat en la punition des hérétiques,*" *Bibliothèque d'Humanisme et Renaissance,* 22 (1960), 556-559.

Koenigsberger, H. G. "The Organization of Revolutionary Parties in France and the Netherlands during the Sixteenth Century," *Journal of Modern History,* 27, no. 4 (1955), 335-351.

Kristeller, Paul Oskar. "Augustine and the Early Renaissance," in *Studies in Renaissance Thought and Letters.* Rome: Edizioni di Storia et Letteratura, 1956.

Labrosse, H. "Sources de la biographie de Nicholas de Lyre," *Etudes Franciscaines,* 16 (1906), 383-404.

Ladner, Gerbart. "Homo Viator: Medieval Ideas on Order and Alienation," *Speculum,* 42 (1967), 233-259.

Lerner, L. S., and Gosselin, E. A. "Was Giordano Bruno a Scientist?: A Scientist's View," *American Journal of Physics,* 41, no. 1 (1973), 24-38.

Levi, Anthony, S. J. "Humanist Reform in Sixteenth-Century France," *Heythrop Journal,* 6 (1965), 447-464.

Lubac, Henri de. *Exégèse médiévale: les quatre sens de l'Ecriture.* Paris: 1959-1964.

McNeill, John T. *The History and Character of Calvinism.* New York: Oxford University Press, 1967.

Mâle, Emile. *L'Art religieux du XIIIè siècle en France.* Paris: Librairie Armand Colin, 1958.

——————————. *The Gothic Image: Religious Art in France of the Thirteenth Century.* Translated by D. Nussey. New York: Harper Torchbook, 1958.

Manschreck, Clyde L. *Melanchthon: The Quiet Reformer.* New York: Abingdon Press, 1958.

Marrou, H.-I. *St. Augustine and His Influence Through the Ages.* London: Longmans, 1957.

Martin, A. Lynn. *Henry III and the Jesuit Politicians.* Geneva: Droz, 1973.

Mesnard, Pierre. *L'Essor de la philosophie politique.* Paris: J. Vrin, 1951.

Monter, E. W. *Calvin's Geneva.* New York: Wiley, 1967.

Moorman, John. *A History of the Franciscan Order from Its Origins to the Year 1517.* Oxford: Oxford University Press, 1968.

Müller, Johannes. *Martin Bucers Hermeneutik*. Gütersloh: 1965.

Neale, J. E. *The Age of Catherine de Medici*. New York: Harper Torchbook, 1962.

*The New Catholic Encyclopedia*. Vol. XI. Article on the Psalms. New York: McGraw-Hill
Co., 1967.

Oberman, Heiko A. *Forerunners of the Reformation: The Shape of Late Medieval Thought*.
Translated by P. L. Nyhus. New York: Holt, Rinehart and Winston, 1966.

——————————. *The Harvest of Medieval Theology: Gabriel Biel and Late Medieval Nominalism*.
Cambridge, Mass.: Harvard University Press, 1963.

Panofsky, Erwin. *Renaissance and Renascences in Western Art*. New York: Harper Torchbook, 1969.

Pauck, Wilhelm. "Calvin und Bucer," *The Journal of Religion*. Chicago: 1929.

Pelikan, Jaroslav. *Luther the Expositor: Introduction to His Exegetical Writings (Luther's Works,
Companion Volume)*. St. Louis, Mo.: Concordia Publishing House, 1959.

Pidoux, Pierre. *Le Psautier huguenot du XVIè siècle*. 2 Vols. Bâle: Edition Baerenreiter, 1962.

Pinette, G. L. "Freedom in Huguenot Doctrine," *Archiv für Reformationsgeschichte*, 50 (1959), 200-231.

Plassmann, T. "Nicolaus de Lyra," in *The Catholic Encyclopedia*. Vol. XI. New York: Robert
Appleton Co., 1911.

Pontet, Maurice. *L'Exégèse de saint Augustin prédicateur*. Paris: Aubier, [1946].

Preus, James S. *From Shadow to Promise: Old Testament Interpretation from Augustine to the
Young Luther*. Cambridge, Mass.: Harvard University Press, 1969.

Reid, W. Stanford. "The Battle Hymns of the Lord: Calvinist Psalmody of the Sixteenth Century,"
*Sixteenth Century Essays and Studies*. Edited by C. S. Meyer. Vol. II. St. Louis, Mo.:
The Foundation for Reformation Research, 1971, 36-54.

Renaudet, Augustin. *Préréforme et humanisme à Paris pendant les premières guerres d'Italie, 1494-1517*.
Paris: Librairie d'Argence, 1953.

Rice, Eugene F., Jr. *The Foundations of Early Modern Europe, 1460-1559*. New York: W. W. Norton
and Co., 1971.

——————————. "The Humanist Idea of Christian Antiquity: Lefèvre d'Etaples and His Circle,"
*Studies in the Renaissance*, 9 (1962), 126-160.

——————————. "Lefèvre d'Etaples and the Medieval Christian Mystics," in *Florilegium
Historiale: Essays Presented to Wallace K. Ferguson*. Edited by J. G. Rowe and W. H. Stockdale.
Toronto: University of Toronto Press, 1971.

——————————. "The Meaning of 'Evangelical'," in *The Pursuit of Holiness in Late Medieval
and Renaissance Religion: Papers From the University of Michigan Conference*. Edited by Charles
Trinkaus with Heiko A. Oberman. Leiden: E. J. Brill, 1974.

Rupp, E. Gordan. *Patterns of the Reformation*. Philadelphia, Pa.: Fortress Press, 1969.

——————————. *The Righteousness of God: Luther Studies*. London: Hodder and Stoughton,
1963.

Salmon, Dom Pierre. *Les "Tituli Psalmorum" des manuscrits latins*. Paris: Les Editions du Cerf, 1959.

Schelven, A. A. van. "Beza's *De Iure Magistratuum in Subditos,*" *Archiv für Reformationsgeschichte,* 44 (1953), 62-81.

Sevesi, P. "B. Leone dei Valvassori da Perego, O.M. Arcivescovo di Milano," *Studi francescani,* 14-15 (1927-1928).

Seznec, Jean. *The Survival of the Pagan Gods: The Mythological Tradition and Its Place in Renaissance Humanism and Art.* Translated by Barbara Sessions. New York: Harper Torchbook, 1953.

Slavin, Arthur S. *Politics and Profit: A Study of Sir Ralph Sadler, 1507-1547.* Cambridge, England: Cambridge University Press, 1966.

Smalley, Beryl. *The Study of the Bible in the Middle Ages.* Notre Dame, Ind.: University of Notre Dame Press, 1964.

Smits, Luchesius. *Saint Augustin dans l'oeuvre de Jean Calvin.* Translated from the Dutch by Egbert van Laethen. 2 Vols. Assen: Van Gorcum and Comp. N.V., 1957.

Spicq, C. *Esquisse d'une histoire de l'exégèse latine au moyen âge.* Paris: 1944.

Spitz, Lewis W. *The Religious Renaissance of the German Humanists.* Cambridge, Mass.: Harvard University Press, 1963.

Steger, Hugo. *David Rex et Propheta: König David als vorbildliche Verkörperung des Herrschers und Dichters im Mittelalter, nach Bilddarstellungen des achten bis zwölften Jahrhunderts.* Nürnberg: Hans Carl, 1961.

Stegmüller, F. *Repertorium Biblicum Medii Aevi.* 8 Vols. Madrid: 1950-1961.

Stephens, W. P. *The Holy Spirit in the Theology of Martin Bucer.* Cambridge, England: Cambridge University Press, 1970.

Stupperich, Robert. *Melanchthon.* Translated by R. H. Fischer. Philadelphia, Pa: Westminster Press, 1965.

Sutherland, N. M. *The French Secretaries of State in the Age of Catherine de Medici.* London: Athlone Press, 1962.

——————————. *The Massacre of St. Bartholomew and the European Conflict, 1559-1572.* London: Macmillan, 1973.

Wadding, Lucas. *Annales minorum.* Vol. VI. Rome: 1733.

Walker, D. P. *The Ancient Theology: Studies in Christian Platonism from the Fifteenth to the Eighteenth Century.* Ithaca, N. Y.: Cornell University Press, 1972.

——————————. *The Decline of Hell: Seventeenth-Century Theories of Eternal Torment.* Chicago: University of Chicago Press, 1964.

Weber, H. *La Création poétique au XVIè siècle en France de Maurice Scève à Agrippa d'Aubigné.* 2 Vols. Paris: 1955.

Wendel, François. *Calvin: Origin and Development of His Religious Thought.* Translated by Philip Mairet. New York: Harper and Row, 1963.

Wolfson, Harry A. *The Philosophy of the Church Fathers.* Vol. I. Cambridge, Mass.: Harvard University Press, 1964.

Yates, Frances A. *The French Academies of the Sixteenth Century.* London: Warburg Institute, 1947.

——————————. *Giordano Bruno and the Hermetic Tradition.* Chicago: University of Chicago Press, 1964.

——————————. "The Religious Policy of Giordano Bruno," *Journal of the Warburg and Courtauld Institutes,* 3, iii-iv (1940), 181-207.

# Index of Names *

---

*The names "David" and "Jesus Christ" do not appear in this index.  They occur so frequently in the text that to list them here would be to list almost every page in this book.

# Publications of the Center for Medieval and Renaissance Studies, UCLA

## I. UNIVERSITY OF CALIFORNIA PRESS

### Contributions

1. Medieval Secular Literature. Editor—William Matthews (1965, 89 pp.)

2. Galileo Reappraised. Editor—Carlo L. Golino (1966, 110 pp.)

3. The Transformation of the Roman World—Gibbon's Problem after Two Centuries. Editor—Lynn White, jr. (1966, 321 pp., hard cover and paperback)

4. Scientific Methods in Medieval Archaeology. Editor—Rainer Berger (1970, 459 pp.)

5. Violence and Civil Disorder in Italian Cities, 1200-1500. Editor—Lauro Martines (1972, 353 pp.)

6. The Darker Vision of the Renaissance. Editor—Robert Kinsman (1974, 352 pp.)

7. The Copernican Achievement. Editor—Robert S. Westman (1975, 380 pp.)

8. First Images of America: The Impact of the New World on the Old. Editor—Fredi Chiappelli; Co-editors—Michael J. B. Allen and Robert L. Benson (1976, 2 vols., 957 pp.)

### Publications

1. Dissent and Reform in the Early Middle Ages, by Jeffrey Burton Russell (1965, 325 pp.)

2. Leonardo's Legacy: An International Symposium. Editor—C. D. O'Malley (1969, 225 pp.)

3. Guide to Serial Bibliographies in Medieval Studies, by Richard H. Rouse (1969, 150 pp.)

4. The Decline of Medieval Hellenism in Asia Minor and the Process of Islamization from the Eleventh through the Fifteenth Century, by Speros Vryonis, Jr. (1971, 532 pp.)

5. Christian Political Theory and Church Politics in the Mid-Twelfth Century, by Stanley Chodorow (1972, 300 pp.)

6. The Song of Roland: Formulaic Style and Poetic Craft, by Joseph J. Duggan (1973, 226 pp.)

7. Studies in Medieval Philosophy, Science, and Logic: Collected Papers, 1933-1969, by Ernest A. Moody (1975, 453 pp.)

8. Slavery and Serfdom in the Middle Ages, selected essays by Marc Bloch (1975, 276 pp.)

9. Marsilio Ficino: The *Philebus* Commentary, a Critical Edition and Translation, by Michael J. B. Allen (1975, 560 pp.)

10. Marius: On the Elements, a Critical Edition and Translation, by Richard C. Dales (1976, 206 pp.)

In Press:

An Italian Lordship: The Bishopric of Lucca in the Late Middle Ages, by Duane J. Osheim

Viator: Medieval and Renaissance Studies (annually since 1970)
*Viator* is a hard-covered journal which averages 350-450 pages; its primary, but not exclusive, focus is intercultural and interdisciplinary research. *Viator* does not include reviews or current news. Editors—Henrik Birnbaum, Patrick Ford, H. A. Kelly, Richard H. Rouse, Speros Vryonis, Jr. and Lynn White, jr.

## II. UNDENA PUBLICATIONS

**Humana Civilitas**

1. On Pre-Modern Technology and Science: Studies in Honor of Lynn White, jr.
   Editors—Bert S. Hall and Delno C. West, (1976, 233 pp.)

2. The King's Progress to Jerusalem: Some Interpretations of David during the Reformation
   Period and Their Patristic and Medieval Background, by Edward A. Gosselin (1976, 128 pp.)

In Press:

The Politics of an Erasmian Lawyer, Vasco de Quiroga, by Ross Dealy

A Descriptive Catalogue of Persian Medical Manuscripts at the University of California,
Los Angeles, by Lutz Richter-Bernburg

Comitatus (annually since 1970, sponsored by the Center since 1973)
The journal publishes works by graduate students of the University of California in the
field of medieval literature.


## III. INDEPENDENT PUBLISHERS

1. Leonardo da Vinci: Studies for a Nativity and the "Mona Lisa Cartoon" with drawings
   after Leonardo from the Elmer Belt Library of Vinciana, by Carlo Pedretti (1973, 49 pp.)

2. In Honor of the Eightieth Birthday of Dr. Elmer Belt, Physician, Scholar and One Who
   Loves Nature, by William A. Emboden, Jr. (1973, 20 pp., out of print)

In Press:

Proceedings of the Conference on the Applications of the Physical Sciences to Medieval
Ceramics, 1975. Editors—Frank Asaro and Jay D. Frierman

Boccaccio: Secoli di vita (Proceedings of the International Symposium on Boccaccio, 1975).
Editors—Marga Cottino-Jones and Edward F. Tuttle